THE RECLAIMING OF POWER

Harvey Jackins

RATIONAL ISLAND PUBLISHERS
Seattle

THE RECLAIMING OF POWER

 For information, address Rational Island Publishers, P.O. Box 2081, Main Office Station, Seattle, Washington 98111, U.S.A.

Library of Congress Card Number: 83-61106
International Standard Book Number: Cloth Binding: 0-911214-86-0
Paperback: 0-911214-87-9

Manufactured in the United States of America

True Power was our heritage
But Society wove us a cage.
Now, piercing confusion,
Rejecting illusion,
Humanity's coming of age.

Table of Contents

FOREWORD

The developments and ideas in this book are no less exciting than in the book's predecessors. In particular these writings cover the period 1981 to early 1983, an extension of the work covered in **The Benign Reality**. For an overview of the work of the world Community of Co-Counseling, and the considerable array of auxiliary publications, I refer you to the Foreword of that book. The new journals launched since that summary are primarily **Creativity**, a Re-evaluation Counseling journal for artists, and **Transcendence**, a companion journal for the dozens of varieties of religious people who participate in the Co-Counseling Communities.

I personally find it necessary to frequently review the earlier, basic literature of Re-evaluation Counseling, as do other leaders of the movement. The present volume, however, contains several clarifying summaries of theory that will make that reviewing somewhat easier and more insightful.

The basic theme of this volume is simple. *The time has come to reclaim our inherent, individual power.* Realization of the ever-present freedom to choose a fresh viewpoint places this step before us in a practical way.

As always, responsibility for the contents is mine, but I have been helped by the entire Co-Counseling Community.

If this book is your first contact with the ideas of Co-Counseling and you are interested in putting these ideas to *use*, you may write to me at 719 Second Avenue North, Seattle, Washington 98109, USA, for information on whom to contact for classes in your locality.

—Harvey Jackins
June 29, 1983

Typesetting was by Valerie Jaworski. Layout and composition were by Valerie Jaworski and Katie Kauffman. Proofreading was by Gloria Berman. The cover photograph is by courtesy of Guoji Shudian. Back-cover photograph is by Ellie Menzies. Typefaces are Baskerville II in medium, italic, and bold face, and Helios in bold face, set on a Compugraphic Editwriter 7500.

THE RECLAIMING OF POWER

Frontiers

The Reclaiming of Power

The overall reality of the world situation in which we live and function, if we face it clearly, calls urgently for at least some, and eventually, all human beings to not only recover their intelligence but to reclaim their power also. We need some individuals who are already functioning with intelligence and integrity and broad vision to do this quickly. This is becoming a necessity for the human race to continue, for the survival of human beings at all.

POWER IS INHERENT

There are a number of indications that complete power over *as much of the environment as one has understood* is a characteristic potential of any human individual's intelligence. There are many indications of this besides the gains in that direction registered in Co-Counseling.

The mythical or tribal heroines or heroes, the legendary people's champions, were traditionally possessed not only of wisdom and courage, but also power. Beowulf, Hiawatha, Lancelot, Hercules, Perseus, the Monkey King, the many goddesses and gods humans have created, in what we think has been an effort to display the human characteristics that distress had otherwise occluded, are nearly always entities of great or total power. We see the eagerness of people everywhere to find or create powerful symbolic figures, whether they choose fighter pilots or singers, scientists or spiritual leaders, popes or labor organizers.

Appeared in **Present Time** No. 52.

For those of us who systematically participate in Re-evaluation Counseling, the most compelling evidence comes from the actual shifts in the behavior of people, who, with discharge and re-evaluation, move steadily in the direction of greater dignity, greater self-respect, and more assumption of power in the environment.

THE SOURCE OF POWERLESSNESS PATTERNS

The occlusion and "abandonment" of our inherent power seems to have occurred to some small extent through individual accidents or defeats. To an overwhelming extent it is the result of the long-time systematic operation of the oppressive societies. These, in their nature, reserve *apparent* power only for a small number of rulers, slaveowners, nobles, owning-class people, but deny any *real* power to everyone. The ruling-class person, accepting the role of "pseudo-power" and resulting rewards, is as much a captive of the oppressive society's structure and conditioning as any one. The societies systematically bludgeon any aspiration to power or even to protest out of the great majority of the population. It resorts to condemnation, persecution, imprisonment, or even death for those individuals whose hurts leave them with patterns of rigid rebellion instead of rigid cooperation.

At the present time, all the rulers of the most powerful states, without exception, act as if they had *no* power to halt or reverse the drift toward nuclear war, but only the "pseudo-power" to prepare for it or accelerate it.

Currently, the individuals who do speak out against the preparations for nuclear war or the extinction of species or the destruction of the environment or the mass mistreatment of human beings act, almost without exception, as if they have no power to do more than protest, however futilely. They seem totally unable to consider *taking charge* of the situations and actually *eliminating* all the conditions and dangers against which they protest.

A concern often expressed these days is that human beings have "fouled their environment" to the point of no return. Certainly our ground waters, soil, seas, and the marvelous matrix of supporting life deserve better care than we, as a species, have given them. From another viewpoint, a deeper pollution of our existence is the tangle of distress patterns in which all present human beings have been caught and immersed and upon which our societies function. We are polluted with patterns; individual ones, which we have individually acquired through accident or contagion, and great complexes of patterns which are systematically installed on each new human being and which regulate and enforce our relations with each other.

PROGRESS AT MANY LEVELS

A substantial number of people, by now, are inspired by and participate in Re-evaluation Counseling. These have been attempting to free themselves from patterns and regain, discover, and understand their own real natures and the potential of those natures. For many of these, their participation in this process has sometimes *appeared* to be a reluctant one. Many individuals have seemed ready to settle for the skimpiest gains, for the mere scraps of a "more comfortable" existence. The majority of Co-Counselors so far have participated actively and in an organized way only from a few months to a very few years. There has often even seemed a great eagerness to "identify" RC with some other concept or structure with which they were already familiar, whether a religion, psychology, social organization, discussion group, or self-help organization.

A smaller group of consistent Co-Counselors have come to understand that these apparent manifestations of a "downward trend" among Co-Counselors are really just expressions of the remaining patterns themselves which are expressed, not as the will of the individual, but as a kind of pleading invitation for help in contradicting and discharging them.

THE LEADING GROUP

A still smaller, but growing, segment of Co-Counselors have

"caught on" to the deeper implications of the possibility of organized re-emergence. They have become better and better Co-Counselors, have established deeper connections with each other, and have pushed the theory forward. They have become increasingly committed to a goal of *complete* re-emergence for themselves and each other and, eventually, for all humanity.

They see as obvious the necessity for preventing nuclear war by "cutting off at the pass" the accelerating atomic armament race of the "great" powers. They are attaining confidence that the job can be done, that the world can be persuaded to peace and that all other problems can be solved, as a by-product of humankind's re-emergence to rationality and the establishment of rational, non-oppressive societies.

They are aware of the difficulties, conscious of the automatic, vicious nature of the opposition which they face, and the entrenched nature of the structures which they must evade or defeat. They have faced the dangers, know how late it is in the timetable of nuclear holocaust and how heavily individual distress patterns and social conditioning have become stacked against their effort, but are nevertheless of good cheer. They are quite able to live with the necessarily uncertain nature of the future and the lack of any guarantee of success for their efforts. They are ready to help each other brush off or peel off any remaining attitudes that "someone else can do it better" or that "I will support but not lead."

It is among these people that the next steps toward reclaiming of power will probably take place. Their examples and their successes, of course, once evident, will be quickly imitated and followed by much larger numbers of people.

HOW?

How do we practically move to reclaim our complete power as individuals and as a group?

It is a fundamental assumption in Re-evaluation Counseling theory, as developed to date, that all human beings, with very few exceptions, start out with vast potential intelligence (that is, a vast ability to think flexibly, to create fresh, new, accurate, successful responses to new situations). We usually assume that this potential is at least ten times as great as the functioning intelligence of the most successful adult humans who have lived to date.

This is, as yet, an assumption. It has not yet been fully confirmed by the functioning of any re-emerging human being. No one has reached maturity, having acquired a large portion of the knowledge necessary to function well in today's civilization, with all or even most of her or his conjectured vast intelligence still functioning. None of us who have been persistent in the struggle to re-emerge have any illusions that we have attained such a goal or reached a close approximation.

There are, however, innumerable indications that we are moving well in that direction. Many people are amazed by the positive changes they achieve in their first two weeks of counseling. The veteran of ten or twenty years of Co-Counseling is usually thinking of the next gain rather than those of the past but is estimated by those who knew her or knew him previously to be profoundly different, to be more able, more successful, more competent, more confident, more buoyant, more broadly aware and more in charge of the situations in which he or she lives. Those of us who monitor and lead this movement think there are clear signs that progress has not only been accelerating but is showing an *accelerated* acceleration that is likely to bring qualitative break-throughs in the functioning of at least a few individuals within a fairly short period of time.

MANY KINDS OF GAINS

Some of the most obvious gains from counseling show up in the cases where the Co-Counselor has chosen not to expand the theater of his or her operation but rather to improve personal effectiveness in the area in which he or she is already operating. Usually there is vastly improved functioning in the limited area. A substantial number of other Co-Counselors have "broadened out," have included in their goals becoming interested in, to them, new factors in the universe and new areas of human endeavors. These have eagerly expanded their knowledge and participation far beyond what they had previously attempted. Each has become a kind of "renaissance man" or "renaissance woman" but have also improved their relationship with the immediate environment and their mastery and benign domination of it. Some have improved their financial resources greatly, some have acquired greater scholarly knowledge or great workman-like competence in fields in which they were engaged or have added to their activities. Some have specialized in the improvement and enjoyment of their relationship with other humans.

All these shifts and many others can be interpreted as moving the individual human in the direction of the conjectured model of a fully re-emerged person, a human being without residual distress patterns, one who is aware of, takes charge of, enjoys, improves, and cherishes the world and universe about him or about her.

The oppressive society, however, continues to dominate a very large portion of the lives of all human beings, and this includes Re-evaluation Co-Counselors. A good bit of the limitations that are observed still operating on the lives of our most successful Co-Counselors are the particular "adjustments" that they still make that leave their lives less than perfectly, consistently rational. These seem to be responses to the overall dominant power of the society in which we live.

(We have termed these societies "pre-human organisms." They operate below the level of intelligence and change in a Darwinian fashion at best, rather than flexibly altering to the occasion or responding to the intelligence of their members.)

Some individuals still have great power over other individuals. A few individuals and collectives have considerable power over a limited part of the environment. Only society as a whole assumes power over all the environment, over all the members in it. This oppressive society constitutes the barrier which interferes with and limits the upward trend of individual human progress. It also threatens all humanity and even all life with disaster by its unthinking manipulation of atomic weapons.

Against this dead, unable-to-be-reasoned-with inertia and momentum of the less-than-human, less-than-intelligent society stands only the intelligence of humans. How can the power of the individual, which we have presumed exists and conjectured will function in the absence of distress patterns, emerge and make itself felt?

PRESERVE THE POWER OF THE YOUNG

One possible channel for this is the preservation of our young people from invalidations and defeats and assisting them in the prompt discharge of those hurts that do occur. There are already certain young RCers whose confidence and buoyancy is astounding to the rest of us. Someone close to them speaks of the young students from the Palo Alto RC "school" as being "unable to be intimidated."

COMMITMENTS AGAINST POWERLESSNESS

To take clear aim against the operation of oppression is another channel that is moving people in the direction of power. For example, the center of what has come to be called The Woman's Commitment—"I solemnly promise that, from this moment on, I will never again settle for anything less than everything"—is in sharp contradiction to the society's assignment of subsidiary, submissive roles to women. Though the special oppression of sexism is the target, the blows in that direction are certainly going to also weaken the larger obstacles to the total power of human beings which stand behind the sexism. The Young Person's Commitment—"I solemnly promise that, from this moment on, I will never again treat any young person, including myself, with anything less than complete respect"—takes sharp aim against the lack of respect and the relegation to unimportance which is the heart and core of the oppression of young people, but will certainly also weaken the larger forces arrayed against total human power which stand behind that oppression as well.

ACTIVITY EDUCATES

The participation of RCers in wide-world changing activities, both within and against the various structures and bureaucracies of the oppressive societies, has certainly enhanced the realization of their power for many RCers. The discovery that "the prominent officials aren't any smarter than I am and don't know any more than I do" has surprised and lifted the hearts of many a Co-Counselor who dared to venture into dealings or conflict with the dominating individuals of society on the political or economic or legislative scene.

HOW TO MOVE DIRECTLY

There are many other channels through which this "seepage toward power" seems to have been taking place in the last few years, but a central question still seems unanswered. How do I, as an individual, move directly to reclaim my power and use it?

I have conjectured previously that if *even one of us* reclaims her power and moves, that one is enough to guarantee the future of the world. I am confident of this since the example and the offering of a rational program by such a person would call forth people who will follow and support from every level of society. How does one directly reclaim one's power?

Here I cannot yet speak with the confidence of accomplishment. I have not yet modeled the total reclaiming of my power in any persistent way. I have not seen anyone else do it as yet, either. Yet I am deeply confident that it can be done, that it is just a task which needs only persistent attack, given our present level of knowledge, to be accomplished. How, then, do I propose that I, and others, do it?

I begin with firm confidence that my power is left intact, and only occluded, by the distress patterns which have been laid upon me by past hurts, by lack of information, and by misinformation. Therefore I do not need to find some external source of power, nor do I need to develop huge bulging muscles or a stentorian voice or become adept with a machine gun, nor acquire huge wealth. My main task becomes *discharging the patterns of powerlessness* which have been placed upon me by the traumas and insults which I have endured.

Here the theory is clear. If a distress is recognized, and a contradiction to it worked out, and it is contradicted, then discharge will occur and the distress will proceed toward being eliminated. How can I contradict the powerlessness distress?

Certainly I can act powerfully. If I am a woman, this may involve at first being unsubmissive and argumentative. It may mean insisting on my views being considered first instead of accepting the traditional last consideration for a woman's view. If I am a man, it may be that I become very patient and tolerant and undictatorial, acting so confidently that I can eventually persuade others to my own way without ever needing to bluster or threaten or dominate or dictate. My posture will be "kingly." My tone of voice will not be distorted by fear or embarrassment or despair or grief. My facial expression will be serenely confident all the time. The words I say will inspire and empower the people around me instead of reinforcing their own discouragement and feelings of helplessness. My tone of voice will be confident and serene but also "not to be argued with."

It will certainly mean that I plan, that I lay out steps to complete my plan, put them in operation, and see that they are carried through. *To act powerfully* on all occasions is going to contradict and put the pressure on the patterns of powerlessness which are my target. Pursued thoughtfully, this should at least begin their discharge.

Will this be enough? I conjecture that it will be a good start. I estimate, however, that enlisting others in a cooperative endeavor to reclaim our power *as a group* will inevitably become necessary.

Attacking A Major Obstacle

The Counseling-With-Supervision Workshop, October 11th to 17th, 1982, at Appel Farm, New Jersey, was attended by approximately fifty Co-Counselors, most of them experienced and active in Community leadership.

The background of the workshop lies in the development of counseling itself. The concepts of our theory have been clarified repeatedly. The basic relationship has been long- and well-defined as *two or more* persons' intelligences dealing with *one* person's distress. Overall, in spite of confusions, distortions of theory, and repeated mistakes, hundreds of thousands of people have re-emerged decisively by counseling each other. Almost every experienced Co-Counselor has had at least one session that gave him or her a glimpse of what rapid, total re-emergence could be like.

Yet the differences in effectiveness between experienced Co-Counselors with roughly equal experience and roughly equal access to theory remain very large. More important and more significant, the gap between most of the counseling of our best Co-Counselors and the results promised by the present level of our theory, and occasionally reached in a particular session or demonstration, is a wide one.

The goal of the workshop was to locate the reason for the gap between the presently available theory and the counseling effectiveness of our most experienced counselors, and to determine an initial course of action for removing the difficulty and enhancing the effectiveness.

Appeared in **Present Time** No. 50.

We used videotape in the main workshop sessions and many of the smaller group sessions. With two video cameras all members of the workshop had a chance to review recordings of their performances as counselors.

The workshop was decidedly successful. The temptation to be distracted into the usual workshop goal of "getting good counseling for oneself" was, in the main, resisted and attention was kept on improvement of the counseling rather than on immediate success as clients. (A great deal of excellent counseling took place, of course.)

Many auxiliary questions were explored in topic and support groups. As the reports on these are prepared and received, they will be published.

Some general conclusions were reached on the main question before the workshop. Since this has been an area where thinking has been difficult, it is interesting that the entire workshop, audience and speaker, yawned together steadily while the principal summarizing reports were given. The consensus was that we were moving through some distress that we had been unable to think well about before and were making slow, but significant and exciting, progress in an important area.

Conclusions (so far) from the workshop are:

The previously not-clearly-faced and not-clearly-challenged factor in limiting the effectiveness of our best and most experienced counselors is a set of life-long habits (reinforced by distress) of attempting to bring up our own distresses on every possible occasion in the hope of discharging them by having someone listen to us. We have apparently been doing this all our lives, since we were first distressed. This collection of ancient habits seems to be "energized" by the presence, or even the promise, of "slack" or free attention from any person in the situation. Thus, for example, an effective counselor, or even a person who assumes a leadership role, is likely to find his or her counselor bringing up or bemused by the counselor's own distresses much more than happens with the counselor's other clients. It is as if the presence (or promise) of free attention makes the patterned pull to bring up or think about one's own distresses even more irresistible or tempting than usual.

This set of habits, reinforced by distress, is defended by another series of patterns which excuse, rationalize, deny, or occlude this first group of patterned habits. We apparently fear embarrassment or humiliation if we were to admit to acting, when counselor, so contrary to our own theory and commitment.

At the workshop we made a beginning at systematically discharging these until-now-little-challenged habits and patterns. First we asked people to volunteer their "favorite excuse" for thinking about their own distresses instead of about the client, when they were in the role of counselor. The list was long and revealing. Examples follow in the box below.

"If I get to client enough, I'll really be able to help other people. They'll get their turn later, but here's my chance." "I HAVE TO DISCHARGE FIRST TO BE THINKING CLEARLY FOR THEM." **"I have to discharge in order to think clearly in this situation."** "I'll be a client because maybe it will get me some discharge and I need that to counsel well." "I can't wait because there may not be much more time." **"IF I DON'T KEEP MY DISTRESS NEAR THE SURFACE, I'LL NUMB IT OFF."** *"If I lose touch with it, I'll lose it."* **"I've never gotten attention before, so it's my turn, and I might as well take it if I can get it."** "I can't help it." "I'VE EARNED IT." *"If I don't, I won't be able to handle the oppression."* **"I don't want to interfere with the natural process."** **"I didn't know it was happening."** "If I don't do it now, there won't be a chance later." "I'M GETTING CONFUSED." *"This will be helpful to others.* "I'm doing the best I can." "BABIES DO IT, TOO."

"Well, I'm caught between the horns of a dilemma over repressing it or being compulsive about it and both are bad, but the repression is obviously worse." **"I don't care."** "I'M DYING RAPIDLY." "The situation is so bad so there is no way of taking charge." *"I'm not doing my client any good; I might as well discharge myself."* **"They are in better shape than I am anyway, so let them give me a hand."** "I need help and I can't survive without it." "I'VE BEEN GOOD FOR A LONG TIME; IT'S ABOUT MY TURN ANYWAY." *"I've never felt comfortable. Maybe here's a chance."* **"Nobody cares about me. Maybe I can get it this way."** "This person is open from discharge. They'll be able to pay attention." **"Only if I client can I keep thinking."** *"If I don't counsel them well this time, I'll always have another chance."* "IT HAPPENS ACCIDENTALLY. I WAS JUST STANDING WITH MY HANDS IN MY POCKETS AND THE PHENOMENON OVERTOOK ME." "They never counsel me well so I might as well client while they are." "I DIDN'T ASK TO BE HURT THIS WAY." *"I just can't do it any better."* **"It wasn't my fault. It has to be somebody's fault. There is nobody else there. Let the other person help me."** "THEY NEED MY HELPFUL EXPERIENCE. MY LITTLE ANECDOTE WILL GIVE THEM AN INSIGHT." "I have done enough." **"It makes me feel better."** *"If I really got out of my stuff, then I wouldn't have an excuse for not counseling well."*

Then we tried adapting the technique (which has been used in the last few months at a number of workshops) of assisting the client to move his or her attention completely out of distress and take and hold it on reality completely outside of distress and contradictory to it. This allows discharge to take place simply from the contradiction of the distress *by the position* without paying attention to the distress at all. (You will see an example of this in the first demonstration on the RC Video Cassette Magazine, *Taking Charge* No. 1.)

I propose that we begin work to eliminate this block to our most expert counseling of each other by (when client) repeatedly making a verbal commitment that it is possible and desirable to end the habit of paying attention to our own distresses anytime that we are not in a session as clients.

"It is logically possible to refuse to pay attention to my own distress all the time (except, possibly, when I am a client in a session with someone who has agreed to be my counselor). If I make this decision repeatedly, some discharge should occur, and after enough repetitions, the habit of paying attention to my distresses when not an agreed-upon client should be replaced by a new habit of keeping my attention in present time at all times when I am not an agreed-upon client and especially when I have agreed to play the role of counselor. I do so choose and decide."

The client then voices any thoughts which follow this statement and then repeats the statement, again voicing any thoughts that follow.

Any particular client and counselor will undoubtedly want to modify, particularize, or "naturalize" the paragraph in quotes above, but without weakening its import.

It seems hopeful, although we have little experience with using it so far, that this will constitute a dependable way for individuals (and even groups) to discharge and begin to think through this previously-unfocused-upon and probably-very-significant block to our effective counseling and to our helping each other to attain it.

What We Seem To Be Learning

Transcript of the Co-Counseling-
with-Supervision Workshop
Sunday AM Class
—Harvey speaking

I'd like to speculate this morning. Such speculating is, perhaps, the most important part of this workshop. I'd like to try to recapitulate what seems to be emerging and propose a viewpoint from which to examine it.

There is one viewpoint, another viewpoint, that humanity up to now has been blazingly, wonderfully successful. How far we have come since the primevil slime!! "A fire mist and a planet, A crystal and a cell,/A jellyfish and a saurian,/Then caves where the cavemen dwell./Then a sense of law and beauty/And a face turned from the sod./Some call it evolution And others call it—"/whatever you want. (laughter) There is that viewpoint of wonder at how far we've come and it's valid. It's good. There are times to take that viewpoint.

If we take the viewpoint of looking at the possibilities instead of at the accomplishments (I think it's all right to indulge ourselves in that viewpoint occasionally and this may be one of the occasions), then human existence with all its potential may have been, until now, like some insect eggs lying, waiting for hatching. The thirty-two years of RC may be a kind of caterpillar stage in which some of the eggs have hatched and some caterpillars have been crawling around busily.

We've gotten a little more perspective of the situation into which we hatched. We have crawled over to the edge of our tree and have gotten an occasional glimpse of sunlight through the foliage. We've put together a rough kind of picture of what must be out there, in a laborious but careful way. We've done this in the way the astronomers and the astrophysicists put together a detailed picture of the universe by analyzing the rays of light they receive through their telescopes and their spectrascopic slits and prisms and their photomultipliers. Their detailed picture has to be approximately accurate because otherwise the light couldn't show these characteristics. We have put together a picture of the role and future of humans in somewhat the same way.

There are changes in behavior in our group of five hundred dedicated bold leaders, the fifty to sixty thousand dedicated active Co-Counselors, and the half-million people who remember what they learned in a Fundamentals class or at a public lecture and most of the time can remember to say something nice to their children.

We've been crawling like caterpillars, with increasing skill and increasing cooperation, but crawling. We have learned not to fight each other for a particular bit of leaf but to share it agreeably.

There is another stage where the caterpillar becomes a butterfly. Our wings have not yet spread. We are leading a much more satisfactory caterpillar existence, but we're not flying. (The storm of yawns at this workshop may mean the onset of the "cocoon stage," except I don't think our "cocoon stages" are going to be very passive.)

There is probably far more before us than we have been able to envisage. I think this is valid. We are probably, in a sense, just entering into the full meaning of our existence, into our full employment.

A theorum has been proved, that is respected by people in the field, that there is only one universe. They have tried making the assumption that more than one universe is possible and that has led to a contradiction with some observable facts. I can't take you through the steps, but people who think well in these fields respect the conclusion that there is only one universe. It's fun in science fiction to think of parallel universes, and the fantasies we can construct about it can be useful to us. But if this is the only universe, the only possible universe, then everything that has happened is okay in the long view. There is no need for anxiety or foreboding. What has happened has been inevitable. The worst disaster that could befall can not possibly obliterate the fact that we have lived, that we have had our three-and-a-half billion years of existence on this marvelous planet, this beautiful planet of water and clouds and blue sky and slowly but persistently evolving life.

We have been part of the emergence of independence and mobility, of complex central nervous systems, of sexual reproduction (with the marvelous flexibility that confers on our evolution). We've had the potential of thinking and the beginning of thinking. Awareness operated when the armies clashed on the windy plains of Troy and Homer came around to sing about them. We gained awareness that we had central nervous systems that could stop and notice things and wonder about them and notice them again. "Oh Lord, I fear thou'st made the world too beautiful this year. My heart is almost out of me. Let fall no burning leaf, prithee, let no bird call."

If we are caterpillars approaching the time when we become butterflies, then some of these particular tough leaves we are chewing on are probably necessary items for our diet in order that we can make the transformation. It is a possibility that we have, through no fault of our own, gotten deeply entrenched in this habit of seeking to be client on all possible occasions. Whatever survival value that had (and it possibly had some at one time) it does not suit our present situations. Now that we know, now that we have grasped, now that we have been able to repeat to each other many times that seeking attention only works if you take turns, then the old habits that interfere with the effectiveness of our taking turns must be examined with a view to changing them.

However dense we may feel, however much we have to yawn to think about them at all, these probably are basic insights. They may, at first, seem trivial compared to some of our earlier insights, but I think they will turn out to be fairly monumental too. They are not to be dismissed lightly. This sleepy, yawny, difficult, elusive concept that we are coming to here is probably quite fundamental.

Through no fault of ours we fell into the deep habit, reinforced by all the distress of it not working, of trying to be client all the time and this habit has persisted past our insight that *taking turns* will work. It has concealed itself. It has discolored our turns as counselor. It continues to discolor them to the point that our progress from now on requires that we root it out. If we can only root it out with two broken fingers or a sprained arm holding a toothpick at arm's length and picking it out grain by grain, that's the way we are going to do it. (If that's the only way we can.) Right now it feels to me (doesn't it to you?) that to stop being client in a session when you're supposed to be counselor is to "give up show business"? (laughter)

Everything about our counseling up to now has been contaminated with this deep habit of always trying to be client. We have also learned at this workshop that we are deep in defensiveness about this, that we have patterns defending this, rationalizing it, that we tend to feel wounded and shut down at any hint of someone pointing this out. Our chronically trying desperately to be client, even while counselor, is so rationalized and defended because of an apparent fear of humiliation that "seems" to be unbearable.

Now, would I die if a squad of you were suddenly to force me to confront how much I rationalize about my clienting in my clients' sessions? I don't think so. I suspect that it would be just "terrible" feelings like all the other "terrible" feelings we've discharged at other points in our progress; but I did not see any exceptions in this workshop to the conclusion I draw about myself, that we have, as yet, been unable to be eager or enthusiastic when we get to that point.

We have been unable to discharge it directly. Probably the tools we have discovered before are necessary here, the counselor furnishing us a contradiction in a bright, cheerful tone of voice. This is probably about as critical as we can respond to. Our counselors' endless praise and approval will probably lead us to looking critically at ourselves much faster than any "pointing out" that is ever done.

I am not quite sure about this. It seems to me that in some of my most brilliant counseling of a client I often do point out inconsistencies and nonsense. I point them out with a cheerful voice and with a direction against them and I model the direction, but I don't always just rely on praise and approval and confidence that the person will eventually see it themselves. If I would just approve of people enough, would they make the turn against nonsense themselves, would they move if they just got enough approval and support? I can't quite think that's the whole picture even though I think it's true that being listened to attentively is the biggest and most basic tool.

To summarize again for my own use if not for yours; as far as we can see to the bottom of the situation, there seem to be two big patterned anomalies scurrying around in the counseling situation pretending to be part of the normal equipment. One is a deeply ingrained habit of trying to be client on every possible occasion, including when we have agreed to be counselor, particularly when there is the slightest smell of "slack" in the air.

The other anomaly is the bundle of rationalizations, the patterns of defending, excusing, and explaining away the first anomaly, insisting that these habits cannot be contradicted and certainly not by anybody pointing out or criticizing our counseling or insisting that we are not already doing the best that could be done.

I don't know how we're going to get past that one. I guess it's up to me to try it. I don't yet know if I can be brave enough that you can tell me directly that I am clienting in my client's session, if you can point it out and make me face it and have me do anything but shut down.

I was "shut down" Tuesday night to Wednesday morning. I didn't know I was shut down until I discharged a bit in talking to you about it the next morning. I do know that I can climb out of the shut-down and appreciate it because that's what happened here. I came out of the fog and saw, to some good purpose, how dramatizing I had been in Gladys' session the night before.

We seem to have uncovered two downward trend factors in our usual counseling, two factors that are not our fault because they have seemed to be pro-survival; the first seeming to be for our own hope of re-emergence and the second to maintain our self-respect (which we have learned is essential to good functioning). Out of habit we have grasped every chance to be client no matter what, and have not been able to put this aside when we try to be counselor. Out of fear of humiliation we have insisted that there are good reasons why we did it and we have gone on defending it.

Trust Your Own Thinking

There are no "shoulds" in the universe. Contrary to everything that has been beaten into you, there are no shoulds, there are no supposed-to's, there are no requirements in the universe. The only guide that's any good at all to you is your own thinking. If it's hassled up with patterns, it's still the only guide for you.

If I could say one thing to the RC Community as the spaceship is about to lift off, if I could shout only one message back to all of you, it would be:

TRUST YOUR OWN THINKING. TRUST YOUR OWN THINKING. TRUST YOUR OWN THINKING. IT'S GOOD THINKING.

Sure, you have reason to suspect that patterns are still running around in it. So what? It's *your* thinking. Trust your thinking. It's the only thinking that's any good for you. Other people's thinking can be good information for you, but it can't replace your thinking. Your thinking is good. Depend on your own thinking. This is your only guide to what you would like to do, what your best judgment is; not anybody's shoulds, or society's rules, or anything of the sort.

You'll make some mistakes, of course, if you trust your own thinking; but if you make the mistake while trusting *your own* thinking, you'll be alert to the fact that the results aren't working and you'll correct it quickly.

From a talk given October 8, 1981, in Swarthmore, Pennsylvania, USA. Excerpts appear in **Present Time** No. 48.

If you've bought into a "should" or into relying on somebody else's thinking, you've already stopped thinking. You've shut down your own thinking in order to take somebody else's judgment. Then, if you make a mistake (and usually there will be at least a little mistake), you won't notice that things are going wrong. You'll get in deep.

If you trust your own thinking and make a mistake, you'll correct it quickly.

Increasingly, of course, you'll have confidence, as you find out your thinking is brilliant.

Trust your own thinking. Listen to your guide. Run your own life. Trust your own thinking and it will work out fine.

Take A Look At Our Motivations

We have learned to be clear about our goals. We've learned to counsel on goal-setting and to remind each other of what our goals are, and to check on whether we are moving on the goals that we have set. We are getting better and clearer about *what* we are trying to do.

It is also useful to ask ourselves *why* we are trying to do it. What motivations move us to the actions that we are engaged in or are contemplating? Such a question need not throw us into self-doubt and confusion. We can be realistic and frank about our motivations, especially if we examine them in a counseling context.

Most of us who have assumed leadership and responsibility in Re-evaluation Counseling have had, to begin with, to use existing patterns to move us in a direction parallel to rationality. We seek out people for leadership, for example, who are compulsively responsible rather than those who are compulsively irresponsible, since individuals who are not compulsive one way or the other in the area of responsibility are rare. (We have made the point in the past that we must not lose track of the fact that we are "using" the person's patterns and must not allow their functioning to cement them deeper into the distress, but instead counsel them well enough to remove the compulsive component of it.)

We have learned to "ride a pattern into battle" if there is no better steed available. We have used determined despair as a contradiction to lack-of-confidence. We have used fatalism to

Appeared in **Present Time** No. 44.

contradict anxiety patterns ("Fifty years from now it won't make any difference..."). None of us should condemn ourselves or invalidate each other for the fact that we have often moved towards good goals on patterned motivations.

There is a real advantage, however, to revealing and identifying patterned motivations that are operating, to keep them in awareness, to check that they are not distorting our thinking or the programs of the Community, and to plan to discharge them as an integral part of our re-emergence. In beginning liberation work, for example, where the conditioned discouragement and hopelessness of the group as a whole is often heavy, a patterned desire for prominence or applause has enabled some individuals to take leadership and achieve bold accomplishments that would otherwise have been difficult or delayed. This was the best leadership that was available. We have often accomplished a great deal and moved lots of people forward, with leaders operating largely on these motivations. There comes a time, however, if these motivations remain unchecked and undischarged, that they begin to slow down the progress of the whole group and eventually cause disaster.

It would be good, in our sessions and in our thinking, to check on what motivations are operating for us and, as much as possible, make sure that we do not take attitudes or handle projects in any way that would not arise from completely rational motivations. The pattern may still be there, but we can awarely check that it doesn't determine our actions, that feelings connected with it do not substitute for our best logical thinking.

What is a rational motivation? A teenage RCer (who is still active in RC now many years later) gave me one of the best definitions that I have heard when she said, "Once you glimpse the possibility of *having everything right,* how can you ever settle for anything less?"

If, as we counsel and are counseled, discharge and think, struggle and rest, take stock of the situation and plunge into action, we also check on patterned motivations that might be operating to see that we take no action in their grip that does not square fully with our determination to "have everything right," we will do well.

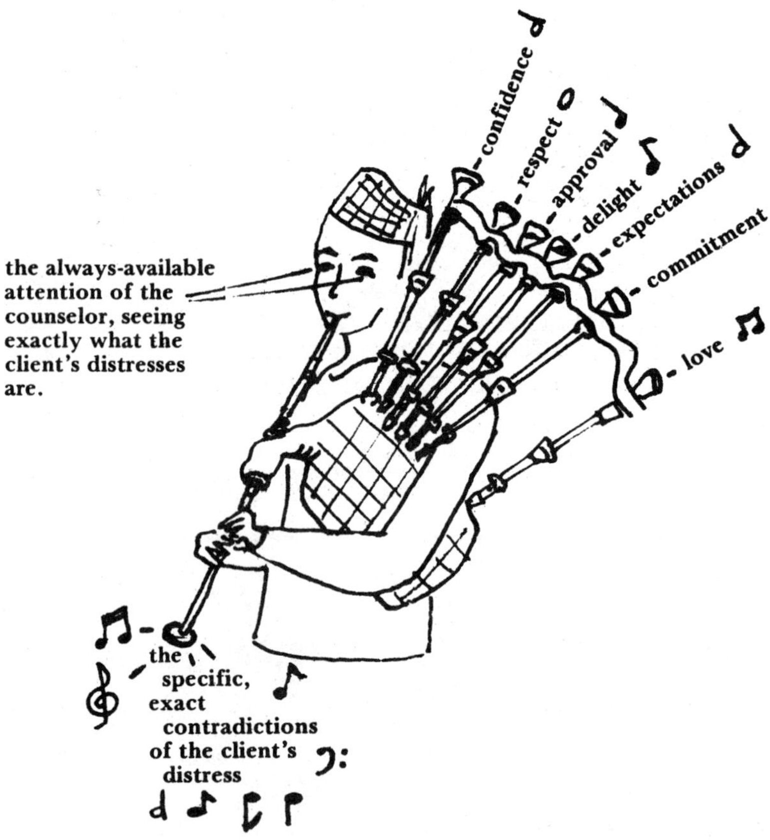
confidence
respect
approval
delight
expectations
commitment
love
the always-available attention of the counselor, seeing exactly what the client's distresses are.
the specific, exact contradictions of the client's distress

The Counselor As Bagpiper

An effective counselor can be compared in some ways to a skillful player of the bagpipes. The bagpipes, as you probably know, are an ancient wind instrument that occurs in many cultures, the best known being the Scottish one. The pipes have several drone pipes, that is, pipes that play one note consistently, steadily, all the time, and on this background, one single pipe with finger holes in it (called the chanter) which plays the melody. Most of the skill of the piper is expressed through the chanter, and anyone who can blow can fill the bag with air and allow the drones to sound, although there may be more fine points to that part than I am aware of. The drone pipes playing steadily all the time are a very important part of bagpipe music.

I would propose that the counselor consider herself or himself as having at least seven drone pipes attached to his or her counseling bagpipe and make sure that these are all working and in tune before attempting to use the chanter. The chanter's melody would be the specific skill, the flexible, individual, fresh approach to contradicting the client's distress and allowing him or her to discharge well.

Any good counselor should have drone attitudes operating toward the client at all times of (1) approval, (2) delight, (3) respect, (4) confidence in, and for, the client, (5) high expectations of the client (this means *relaxed* high expectations and not anxious pressure), (6) commitment to the client, and (7) love to and of the client.

When these attitudes are steady toward the client, then the

Appeared in **Present Time** No. 48.

melody of the chanter, that is the counselor's flexible aware intelligence seeing exactly what the distress is, thinking how to contradict it and then contradicting it effectively, are reinforced by these consistent attitudes and "the sweetest music this side of complete re-emergence" will take place. The client will not only have lots of discharge and a wonderful session, but will make decisive steps towards his or her re-emergence.

Can Old Grievances Be Redressed?

It has been an assumption in most of our cultures for a long, long time, probably even prior to the development of class society, that insults or injuries of one person or group by another should be revenged or redressed. It has been taken for granted that compensation from, or revenge on, the person or persons who hurt us is a necessary part of our recovery from the hurt. Christianity's "turning of the other cheek" principle has been more a "curiosity in a glass case" than the actual behavior of Christians. In all Christian cultures to date people have heartily devoted themselves to revenge, retribution, getting even, and the redressing of their injuries.

Can such redress actually be accomplished? Is there such a thing as achieving a balance of revenge? Can one achieve a rational gain by doing an injury in return for injury? Is it possible to "get even" in any rational way?

I suspect that the whole tradition is simply a long-perpetuated pattern that has been replicated and persisted with in order to serve some of the mechanisms of the oppressive society. I suspect that no one ever "won" in a blood feud or act of revenge or by "getting even." I would guess that actually the revenger was harmed by being embedded more deeply into his or her distress pattern by the act just as the revengee was being harmed by the physical hurt or loss or restimulation that occurred.

If this is so, will it not make sense, not only in real life, but also while clients in our counseling sessions, for us to take a

Appeared in **Present Time** No. 51.

sharp stand against all pulls to dramatize or fantasize revenge, redress, or "getting even"? Would it not make sense to avoid all these familiar dramatizations? It is undoubtedly true that clients have sometimes been able to dramatize such "getting even" in their sessions and get some discharge, particularly when they had not dared to express these feelings before. To "act out" the unfamiliar role inside a distress pattern is well-known as a "first step" toward discharge for a client heavily "bogged down" into one patterned role. However, this is also well-known to be not very useful in any ongoing way. It is much better, as soon as possible, to go directly outside of all distress to the realities of what was going on. From this viewpoint we are likely to get more discharge and more progress as we see how two people were being hurt by one pattern, and how the pattern was perpetuated by the back-and-forth nature of the revenge or the feud.

How can we contradict these patterns? By forgiveness? By understanding? By role-playing an eager willingness to "assume the blame"?

What do you think?

Major Summaries and Policies

Preliminary Report to the 1981 World Conference

The 1981 World Conference of the Re-evaluation Counseling Communities meets in an atmosphere of progress and accomplishment. Most of the goals which we have set ourselves at past world meetings have been achieved or advanced decisively.

The main decision of the 1977 World Conference, to establish functioning supportive cores of Co-Counselors that are looking to each other's re-emergence effectively in every Community, has come to pass. The primary goal of the 1979 World Conference, to decisively raise the level of effectivess of Co-Counseling, has also been accomplished almost everywhere.

NUMBERS AND MATURITY

Our Communities have grown a great deal, mostly through the establishment of new Communities in new geographical locations and populations, but increasingly in the last few months by the expansion of existing Communities. Our leadership resource has increased a great deal numerically and also in maturity. We have at least doubled the number of our leaders who are confident in themselves about what they are doing and the role that they play and who move independently and with influence in an upward trend direction in all areas of their lives and among their constituencies.

Appeared in **Present Time** No. 44.

Our high priority goals for this next period should include decisive numerical growth through an increase in Community membership, division of existing Areas and Regions, and establishment of new Communities in at least as many more geographical locations as we are established in presently.

It is time for an increased rate of growth. We now have in most places such adequate models of Co-Counseling skill and leadership as to allow new people to learn to Co-Counsel, and to be responsible in the wide world, well and quickly. We have enough theory and accumulated experience in print, at least in English, that new RCers will be able to avoid most of the difficulties we earlier RCers worked our way through. (We learned a great deal in the process of making and correcting mistakes, but also used a great deal of time and effort.) This benefit we cheerfully pass on to our new recruits.

INFLUENCE

As we determined to do in 1979, we have extended our influence widely outside the Community membership. We have done this in the face of a rapidly worsening world situation, including economic recession and horrendous inflation. We have expanded our publishing considerably, and we have maintained an increasingly effective network of classes and workshops. We have continued the translation of at least some of our basic literature into a total of fifteen languages. We have, as a group, become much more united, much more mutually supportive, much more confident of what we are doing, and much more aware of the underlying supportiveness of the reality in which we operate.

Our theory is already influencing people far beyond the Community membership. It will continue to do this both under its own name and in a thousand other guises, as RCers offer correct policies and assume leadership in many non-RC situations. It is time for a goal to be set for every Co-Counselor whom we accept into our Communities (which will not be everyone who learns to Co-Counsel) to be, on the one hand a Community builder, taking responsibility that our base, the RC Community, become strengthened and extended, and on the other hand a leader, with a constituency in the wide world. Our RC leaders must become leaders in the wide world also, but many of our wide-world leaders also need to become leaders inside the Community. Any patterned tendency to separate the two aspects of leadership or to emphasize one at the expense of the other can be eliminated, with the two fields instead being viewed as two sides of a common effort.

Our rate of development of leaders seems a marvel to non-RCers who are aware of it, but we cannot be satisfied with either our previous or our present rate of development. Every human being is potentially a fully capable leader, and the lack of leadership that exists almost everywhere in the wide world (including certain situations that are crucial for the survival of all of us) must be filled. Certainly we hope and expect that leadership will spontaneously arise in many situations (as it did with the Solidarity experience in Poland) but we cannot afford to be passive or "spontaneous" on this question. We must expect to develop large numbers of competent leaders very rapidly.

THEORETICAL ADVANCES

Our theory has moved forward powerfully in these last years. Recognition of the basically benign nature of reality gives us firm support for the most courageous initiatives. Understanding the never-absent *freedom to choose one's own viewpoint in every situation* is perhaps the most powerful theoretical tool that we have discovered, and practically it leads to the actual regaining of power, which, earlier, we had only been able to glimpse theoretically.

UNDERSTANDING LEADERSHIP FUNCTIONS

Separating the functions of leadership in our Communities from the notions of titles, roles, and authorities is proving to be a major step forward out of past organizational drudgeries and difficulties. Where it has been applied, the analysis and separation of functions (see **Present Time** No. 42, pages 30-39) has found Community members willing and eager to share responsibilities.

SKILL AT PROBLEM SOLVING

We have a powerful assumption which arms us in dealing with practical problems. "There is always at least one elegant solution to any real problem." For example:

—Early problems in getting RC theory into written form were solved by counseling on writing blocks and intensive efforts to write, often carried on together.

—Problems in publishing rapidly enough or in adequate form were solved by recruiting and training a publishing staff, collecting money for advanced typesetting equipment, and arranging a publishing subsidy from International Workshop income.

—Problems in having the written theory distributed and read are in the process of being solved by Community libraries and literature agents, and by support groups and workshops on reading difficulties.

"NATURALIZING" RC

We have one important problem in our outreach to new people and new populations which is not satisfactorily solved as yet. We might call this the "naturalizing" of RC. (I borrow the word from what botanists, agriculturalists, and plant geneticists do in introducing plants into new environments.)

This problem exists primarily at the level of teaching and *practicing* Co-Counseling. In spite of the non-standard English of much of our literature, and the many difficulties of translation, most new friends and new populations "like what they read" of RC theory. It is the unaware trappings which latch on to its use in practice that "put them off."

Black Co-Counselors often say that they hesitate to bring their black friends to visit an RC class or function because the "whiteness" operating there would repel their friends. Industrial workers say something similar about "chintziness" or "middle-classness" driving their new recruits away. I have witnessed a new RCer being reproached by a "veteran" (of at least three months) for "not yet" being a "committed vegetarian," with no intervention by other RCers present. Women RCers have been told that their desire to solve relationship problems with men is "out-of-date."

This accretion of individual and group nonsense onto RC and offering itself as RC (temporarily) is probably inevitable and will continue to occur. We have considerable experience at "peeling it off." What I think we need to be concerned about here is the acceptance of this phenomenon as an excuse for not "naturalizing" RC to the individuals we know well or the groups to which we belong.

Industrial worker RCers: The mannerisms with which RC is taught sometimes, and to which you object, are simply the ways in which these particular teachers and individuals have found themselves able to communicate RC, coming out of their individual and cultural patterns. *You* know (or will if you think about it and discuss it) how RC should be presented to industrial workers. Please take the initiative and do it that way.

Third World RCers: The above holds for you too. *You* know (or will if you think about it and discuss it) how RC should be represented to other Third Worlders. Please take the initiative and do it that way.

All others who hesitate to take RC to your own groups or to bring people from your groups to RC: Doesn't the above make sense for you, too?

SOME CULTURAL PATTERNS INTRUDE REPEATEDLY

Some of the conditioning of the oppressive society, completely contradictory to our policy and theory, intrudes into our Communities repeatedly, and apparently will continue to repeat with each wave of new arrivals as they are assimilated. These often take the form of "demands" for the "modification" of RC to fit the intruding distress. Some such repeating patterned demands or "ideas" are:

1) The RC Communities must regress from individual leadership and working consensus to committee leadership and parliamentary majority decisions, and go back to the pseudo-"democracy" of the Western oppressive societies.

2) Our no-socializing principle must be either abandoned or "witch-hunt"-enforced, instead of continuing to be a valuable summary of experience and a guideline principle for everyone.

3) "Our" particular oppression is worse and more important than any other group's oppression, and must have precedence in attention, resources, counseling, and finances over every other group's needs.

4) Liberation policies originating in groups outside RC must be accepted as policy inside RC. (Currently, much energy needed for productive Gay liberation activities in RC is being channeled instead to a "campaign" to establish that RC publications must identify an individual, *in print,* as Gay, if that individual requests it. This is usually presented as "the individual must have the right of disclosure," which he or she certainly has, and is an entirely different matter.)

5) The best way to keep leaders "honest" and "on their toes" is to criticize them, attack them, expect and demand one-way counseling from them, and compete with them. (Never

willingly help them with the work, never remember that they, too, are struggling humans, never take responsibility for their being effectively counseled.)

These are only examples. Actually we deal with such intrusions better and more relaxedly all the time. They still tend to catch us by surprise and restimulate us occasionally, however.

"CAPTURE THE COMMUNITY" ATTEMPTS

We are not so skilled in containing "take-over" attacks, however, particularly when they are disguised as "criticisms" of or attacks on, an individual leader. If the attack is cleverly restimulative enough, naive individuals are often pulled to debate the "merits" of the attack or "seek information" rather than recognizing the real nature of the attack and refusing to cooperate in spreading the restimulation.

The current campaign (at least one such arises before every World Conference) had temporarily nearly dis-assembled two Area Communities before it reached the stage of the "poisoned letter" mailings around the International Community.

It is not intelligent to not promptly deal with this sort of thing or to leave it up to the leader who is attacked. Such naivete may be understandable, but not very pro-survival for the Communities, and cannot be excused as "restimulation" since the attacks are calculated to have precisely that effect.

In an earlier time when political "witch-hunting" was the restimulative basis chosen for a "take-over RC" campaign, leaders and individual RCers grew a great deal from meeting the challenge head-on and decisively.

Probably the current attacks will soon seem an amusing memory, as past attacks seem now, but individual RCers need to deal with them more promptly.

WE ARE IN *FINE* SHAPE

Overall, our Communities, our Co-Counseling, our theory, our leaders, our outreach, and our re-emergence are in *fine* shape. We have every reason to be proud of ourselves and confident of the future.

The achievements of our journals continue to amaze and astound people who are aware of them and continue to be major channels for the emergence of fine, decisive, and powerful thinking. Their publication continues as fast as the finances and the writing permit. One new journal, *Forever and Ever,* has been launched in the last year, and an artists' journal and a journal on religion are in preparation. The improvement in *Present Time, Sisters, Working for a Living, Wide World Changing,* etc., etc., is a source of great satisfaction to all who read them or have participated in preparing them. *The Benign Reality*, just published, is a major theoretical work.

We are dealing with all issues with much more confidence, are relating to wide-world movements in a more effective manner, and are learning from every problem and every difficulty that we encounter.

A HIGH PRIORITY ISSUE

One issue, I think, must take precedence in our thinking and must receive concentrated attention in this current period regardless of how little we feel ready to deal with it. This is the issue of nuclear weapons. Many of our Co-Counselors and their friends are vigorous social activists for such issues as the protection of the environment, for eliminating toxic agents from food, and for exposing the dangers of nuclear power. The issue which our fears have kept us from facing in any decisive manner as yet is that nuclear *power* as a danger is relatively unimportant compared to the enormous danger of nuclear *weapons.*

It is plain at this point that we *will* solve all other problems, given our present state of emergence, if we are permitted enough time to do so. Nuclear weapons threaten to deny us that time. The missiles in the silos and the patterns which move towards their proliferation and their use *are* dangerous. It is *possible* that the entire world will be sterilized of all life down to the level of bacteria, and that the upward trend would have to resume again from that level. Panic will not help us. In fact, the fear is what has kept us numbed and powerless and ineffective in this area, but I don't think we can wait for our Co-Counselors to spontaneously feel "ready" to deal with this issue. I place before the World Conference and the entire International Community the priority of counseling away every distress that has kept us from promptly, decisively, and effectively eliminating nuclear weapons.

This involves finding ways to contradict the pervasive, numbed powerlessness and terror enough to discharge it.

At least one workable approach has been explored already. The client is asked to finish a sentence in a calm, reassuring voice, "It won't happen because ________________." (The counselor repeatedly models the tone of voice.) So far, discharge has come quite easily and the sentence is finished with an ever-changing series of answers that move steadily towards more confidence, more power, and more initiative.

In 1981, in spite of the perils of nuclear armaments, in spite of the intense hardships being caused everywhere in the world by a collapsing society, the world is still in basic good shape. Reality is benign, and we are living in the most exciting, challenging, and enjoyable time that humanity has ever experienced.

Early and Basic Concepts

The Key Concepts and Insights of Re-evaluation Counseling To Date—Part I

In later classes at this Conference, I will be dealing with the advanced or newer concepts of theory which are so valuable to us in offering the possibility of accelerated re-emergence. First, however, I remind you that all our experience indicates that we must wage at least three struggles at the same time, that every RC meeting needs to contain at least three elements. One is the review of the theory which we supposedly already know, but which continually becomes occluded by restimulation and patterned fall-out. Two is keeping up-to-date with the emerging theory (and our theory is continually emerging). Three is actual participation in the re-emergence process. Even at our crowded leaders' meeting this morning we managed to get in some very good demonstrations of just two or three minutes apiece where people actually moved or began to move decisively with clear directions as to how to continue.

This morning I am going to list and comment on the basic RC concepts which we have absorbed and integrated partially but the forgetting of which seems to be behind almost every serious difficulty that our Community experiences.

This will be, I suspect, an incomplete list. I spent some time putting it together and then spent some more time going over it with the International Reference Committee. The list seems to lengthen the more we think about it.

The first insight is not limited to RC. We share it in common with all sciences and with all useful philosophies. This is the assumption or realization, however you come to it, that **AN**

A report to the World Conference, 1981. Appeared in **Present Time** No. 45.

OBJECTIVE UNIVERSE EXISTS. We assume that it would exist or does exist independently of our observation of it, at least on the macroscopic level, at least on the level of large bodies and more-than-nuclear distances. There is some question whether our observation of it does not become an integral part of it on very, very small distances and on sub-atomic relationships, but on the level of relationships with which we ordinarily deal, our assumption is that the universe exists independently of our thinking about it.

Now, to the particular insights of RC. The first is that **THE DISTRESS EXPERIENCE IS THE SOURCE OF AND THE EXPLANATION FOR HUMAN IRRATIONALITY**. Most of us have integrated this, but we sometimes don't act as if we had. We still blame and reproach people. This is the key insight into the (up-until-now, and outside of RC) unsolved problem of human irrationality that threatens every other phase of human existence.

THE RECORDED DISTRESS EXPERIENCE IS THE SOLE SOURCE OF HUMAN IRRATIONALITY. The only thing wrong with people is the result of mistreatment. (I am not saying *deliberate* mistreatment, because most of it is not.)

The second is that the process which we call discharge, the complex process or set of processes dependably characterized by tears, trembling, yawning, many kinds of laughter, live, righteous storming, interested, non-repetitive talk (or in some cases, thinking enhanced by the expectation of eventual talk, which is the case with "rapid review"), this set of processes that we familiarly refer to as **"DISCHARGE" IS THE RECOVERY PROCESS FROM IRRATIONALITY, FROM DISTRESS**. Our great respect for discharge is justified. We act in many counseling circumstances as if discharge were our goal. We even tell students in Fundamentals classes that "all you are after is discharge," which is not quite true and has to be corrected in later classes by reminding the students that the real goal is re-emergence, not discharge. Because discharge has been so inhibited and the inhibitions on it are a principal obstacle to re-emergence, we often treat discharge as if it were the principal goal of our Co-Counseling activity.

Third is the concept, the understanding, that **RE-EVALUATION OCCURS SPONTANEOUSLY FOLLOWING DISCHARGE**. All the notions that still circulate in the society and in the educational systems—that a counselor or teacher must replace the "bad" ideas with "good" ideas—are false. Only a person's own thinking is good enough to guide that person and *that* thinking takes place spontaneously following discharge. This does not mean that we don't share experiences and information. It doesn't mean that we don't find inspiration in each other's ideas, but it does mean that the person's *own* thinking is the crux of the matter and that thinking occurs spontaneously. Our assistance to each other is not in "helping each other think" even though we use that phrase carelessly sometimes. Our assistance to each other is in helping each other discharge so that we *can* each think for ourselves.

Four: **ANY DISTRESS CAN BE COMPLETELY DISCHARGED**. This real possibility of the *complete* discharge of any distress is little realized and less practiced in our Communities until now. This was demonstrated many times in the early days of RC, in Seattle, when we followed one-way clients for a long time and made it a practice with many of them to clean up distress completely. It has only been done once in the Community to my knowledge. A year ago Ann Starr, with a combination of great determination, effort, and some good luck, cleaned up an incident in the full view of a big teachers' and leaders' workshop. The possibility of the complete discharge of distress is very important even though it has been neglected in the familiar "half-hour each way" sessions which dominated Co-Counseling in the early years of the Communities.

Following from this and right alongside of it is the complete recoverability of the human capacity which the distress has occluded. **ONE'S OCCLUDED ABILITIES AND CAPACI-**

TIES CAN BE COMPLETELY RECOVERED. This goal is paid lip service to but is not yet fully achieved in our Communities for reasons for which we should not reproach ourselves but which we can and will do something about.

Next is **THE FUNDAMENTAL DIFFERENCE BETWEEN THE PATTERN AND THE PERSON**. They are two separate entities even though one is sitting at the back of the other's head and often manipulating its voice, even though one follows the other around and appears to speak for it. There is a fundamental distinction between the human being and the distress pattern. They are two completely separate kinds of entities. We tend to remember and comfort ourselves with this, and pull ourselves out of confusion with it over and over, but I doubt if it could be restated too much because I doubt if there is any confusion that is more widespread or one that creates more difficulty in the wide-world activities of human beings than just exactly this, confusing the pattern with the person and the person with the pattern. We slip into this confusion often. Whenever we argue with distress, we have slipped into this. Whenever we blame or reproach the person, we have slipped into this. It is not yet so well understood or so well remembered that we do not need to repeat it again and again. The distress pattern is of a completely different character than the human being.

Next is the integral, wholesome goodness of the human being. In this insight we reject thousands of years of cultural mistakes and hundreds and hundreds of religions and theories which assume, for understandable reasons, that the human being is a mixture of good and evil. The comic strip portrays us as having a "bad" conscience and a "good" conscience. We reject this. It is crucial and important that **THE HUMAN BEING, AS A HUMAN BEING, IS INTEGRAL, IS WHOLESOME, IS GOOD**. The patterns may be of infinite variety, including some pseudo-survival varieties, but the human being, as distinct from the pattern, is one-piece, is consistent, is wholesome, is good. The human being, as a human being, distinct from the distress patterns which parasite on it and infest it, is completely "upward trend."

The next important concept is our rejection of any cultural standards of "normality," our refusal to accept any cultural definitions of what is a fully-functioning person. (If you get A's in school, if you shine your shoes regularly, if you contribute to charity and brush your teeth. . . .) We are not opposed to any temporary goals for improvement, but we refuse to accept any of the present limits which cultures place upon the flowering of human beings. We insist that the boldest and freest definition of a human being is misleading, that the capacity of a human being is limitless and cannot be defined. We haven't any notion of what any real limits for a human being might be. Any goal that we set, once attained, immediately projects a further, loftier goal. **WE REFUSE TO ACCEPT ANY CULTURAL DEFINITION OF NORMALITY OR GOODNESS THAT PUTS LIMITS ON THE HUMAN BEING.**

FEELINGS ARE NOT A RELIABLE GUIDE TO ACTION. This seems familiar to most of us by now, doesn't it? We remember it, we tell it to other people, we even act on it ourselves part of the time; but isn't it hard to remember all the time? Isn't this a continual struggle that we wage, to not act on our feelings, no matter how righteous they sometimes seem?

ONLY LOGIC IS A RELIABLE GUIDE TO ACTION. If we have good feelings, fine, enjoy them, but do not act on them. If we have terrible feelings, contradict them and discharge them, but do not act on them. Act on logic and logic alone. (Or the best approximation of logic that we can make in sometimes confusing conditions.)

If I am not clear on any of these, please interrupt me. All I am trying to do here is clearly state these key insights or concepts, but if I don't do that, interrupt me. Yes?

Q: What is logic?

I can give you first a circular definition; (group laughter) it is the way the human mind works in the absence of distress. It has also been defined in workable, useful ways by logicians starting with Aristotle. Aristotle and his successors and, more recently, Goedel and Church and a number of other people, have been able to get outside the confusion and distress and state the rules of logic very concisely and very accurately. One of these rules is that a statement cannot be true and untrue at the same time in the same situation. Another is that if statement A means that statement B is true, and statement B means that statement C is true, then statement A means that statement C is true. Others are a little more complicated. Actually, in the work of the last fifty years, if you can handle the symbols (I am not good at it), the essence of logic has been reduced to a very small number of propositions. These are dependable tools. If my counseling goes well enough, I should like to someday start a new career as a mathematical logician. In the meantime, I urge all our logicians and our mathematicians to start applying what they know, or should know, to RC.

PATTERNS ARE ADDICTIVE IN THEIR ACTIONS. PATTERNS TEND TO FORCE THEIR VICTIM THROUGH A RE-ENACTMENT OF THE ORIGINAL HURT THAT CAUSED THE PATTERN. It is an important insight that a pattern tends to force its victim through a repetition, as far as possible, of the original hurt. What are called addictions in ordinary usage are the *effects* of patterns. Patterns are addictive in the sense that yielding to the compelling feelings embodied in patterns is the necessary and sufficient explanation of addiction. Understanding this opens the way to effectively freeing people from addictions.

(Asked to repeat)

Patterns are addictive in their effect. A pattern tends always to force its victim through as close a repetition as possible of the original hurt experience. What are ordinarily called addictions, i.e., addictions to poisonous chemical substances, operate on exactly this basis. Patterns are addictive in themselves. Chemical addictions operate only through patterns. With these insights, addictions can be removed and the victim can become free from them by applying what we know about counseling.

(The withdrawal period for an addict coming off a chemical addiction is described in the usual literature as a terrible experience. Such people are locked up in steel cells alone because nobody "can stand to be around them" as they go through withdrawal. This is exactly wrong. Withdawal is just the thawing out from numbness of the feelings of hurt of the original poisoning. The feeling is felt as it thaws out, and discharge accompanies it. The withdrawal procedure can be greatly expedited by giving counseling attention to the person.

D.T.'s, the wild clamoring and the wild shaking traditional to alcoholics sobering up, is exactly discharge taking place. It can be greatly accelerated and expedited and completed by giving counseling attention to the person doing it.)

Complete self-appreciation is possible. It is justified by reality, and attempting it is very productive. **COMPLETE SELF-APPRECIATION IS A REASONABLE AND USEFUL GOAL.** Realizing this was one of the great turning points in the practice of Re-evaluation Counseling. *Complete* self-appreciation, no reservations. How many have done it lately?

This next crucial insight is the content of the first scroll we ever produced. It continues to outsell all the others. What it says is, **"EVERY SINGLE HUMAN BEING AT EVERY MOMENT OF THE PAST, IF THE ENTIRE SITUATION IS TAKEN INTO ACCOUNT, HAS ALWAYS DONE THE VERY BEST HE OR SHE COULD DO AND SO DESERVES NEITHER BLAME OR REPROACH FROM ANYONE, INCLUDING SELF. THIS, IN PARTICULAR, IS TRUE OF YOU."** It is still just as fresh as it ever was, isn't it? It is one of our key insights, often forgotten temporarily but returned to, over and over.

OUR PAST IS DETERMINED. OUR FUTURE IS FREE CHOICE. Just incidentally, this resolves one of the great philosophical dilemmas that had persisted for thousands of years—the controversy between determinism and free will. It resolves when you run the line of present time between the past and the future. The two halves of the dilemma fall open and there is no longer any contradiction.

The insight arose out of our practical work, and it has great practical significance. As counselors, we can clearly, without hesitation, throw all our influence to contradict the client's regrets and self-reproaches about the past or his or her powerlessness or apathy about the future.

There have been partial insights into this many times. Omar said, "Come, my beloved, lift the cup which clears alike of past regrets and future fears." He rejected the past regrets at least, even though his recommended booze is not the solution. In another verse he said, "Oh, but my computations, people say, reduced the year to better reckoning. Nay, t'was only striking from the calendar unborn tomorrow and dead yesterday." He had partial insights. Other inspirationists have said, "Choose. Your life is before you. Think not on the barren past. Go bravely into the future." Only out of the practical work of counseling clients day after day, however, did the two parts finally come together in this very important insight. The past is determined. Waste no regrets. Waste no remorse. You cannot bring father back to life by wishing you had told him to take the train instead of the plane. You can only say your goodbye to him and shed your tears thoroughly. But, on the other hand, "I never could" doesn't mean "I can't." The future is free.

This next insight is fundamental, but it has only quite recently been stated clearly. **ANY DISTRESS DISCHARGES WHEN IT IS CONTRADICTED SUFFICIENTLY.**

How can you be a successful counselor and always help your client achieve discharge? We can now state a three-step rule for successful counseling. Applying it may stretch you a little bit occasionally, but it is a dependable rule. Step one, pay enough attention to the client to see what his or her distresses are. This includes, of course, asking them questions and listening to them, as well as observing them. Step two is to think, to think how those distresses can be contradicted. Step three is to contradict them sufficiently. If you do these three things, discharge will always come.

The most common mistake that we make in our counseling is that we contradict the distress a little bit and if we don't get discharge, we conclude we are on the wrong track. We stop short. We fail to put our confidence into the situation. The words *enough* or *sufficiently* are important here. Incidentally, sufficient contradiction is not best achieved by giving your client orders on how to act and then sitting back idle. The person free to contradict the distress the most is, of course, the counselor. This implies no lazy counseling.

It is important to remind each other of the next important concept. **THERE IS NO RATIONAL CONFLICT OF INTERESTS BETWEEN HUMAN BEINGS.** Contrary to almost everything you have been told, contrary to the appearances of much of what you see going on in this society, this insight breaks through to reality. There is no rational conflict of interest between any human beings.

There is an ancient cartoon: Two donkeys are tied together midway between two piles of hay. The donkeys are straining, choking each other, each trying to reach their pile of hay. The cartooned solution is that the donkeys agree, join together to go eat one pile of hay first and then go together to eat the other. There is an ancient story: While still alive, a man is taken to visit Hell and then Heaven as a special dispensation to guide him on his behavior. When he comes to Hell, he hears behind closed doors great wailing and reproaching and gnashing of teeth. When the doors open, the condemned souls are sitting at tables where a great feast is spread. It is lovely food, but the condemned souls are starving. Out of their hands grow long spoons and forks, so long that they cannot reach their mouths with them, and they are starving in the midst of plenty, unable to reach the food, in despair, suffering terribly. The visitor is then taken to Heaven, to an identical building. Happy sounds are coming from the closed doors. There are murmurs of laughter, of joy. When the doors open, the blessed souls are sitting at tables spread with a succulent feast. Out of their arms also grow spoons and forks too long to reach their mouths, but the blessed souls are contentedly feeding each other.

There is no rational conflict of interest between human beings. This is a very important touchstone to refer to since most of people's effort, most of people's energy, most of people's time is enlisted by the irrational, oppressive society in irrational conflicts.

A great part of the effort of wide-world liberation forces gets turned to mass mailings, to billboards, to thundering from pulpits, to leafletting, to mass meetings. These are not generally effective. **FOR IMPORTANT IDEAS, ONE-TO-ONE COMMUNICATION IS NECESSARY.**

It is always possible for any individual to take the initiative in any situation. Because of the early conditioning to be helpless and powerless, this has been a difficult concept to comprehend. Sometimes the initiative might simply be to yell for help although one has been conditioned not to do that. This idea is very close to the freedom to choose one's viewpoint, which is one of our more recent insights, but this one has been with us some time. It is part of the Postulates. **IN ANY SITUATION, IT IS ALWAYS POSSIBLE FOR AN INDIVIDUAL TO TAKE THE INITIATIVE AND TO TAKE CHARGE OF THE SITUATION BY DOING SO.**

The next concept is that **COMPLETE RESPONSIBILITY IS THE NATURAL ATTITUDE OF EACH HUMAN BEING.** The almost universal helpless, irresponsible, hopeless, dragged out, bewildered attitudes are all conditioning, all stuck on by hurts. The attitude of complete responsibility was the inherent one. Occasionally we are getting back to it in practice.

LOVE IS THE WAY PEOPLE NATURALLY FEEL ABOUT EACH OTHER. Our loving attitude to others is waiting there to be uncovered as the distress is removed. It is not something to be beaten into a child with punishment. It is not something to be attained by the restimulation of sexual feelings, although glimpses of it are occasionally caught that way. It is the way people *naturally* feel about each other.

GOALS CAN BE AWARELY CHOSEN AT ALL LEVELS OF RESPONSIBILITY AND FUTURE TIME. There is a goals chart in the back of our fundamentals manual. We drew it up about twenty-eight years ago. Every once in a while, a teacher focuses attention on the importance of this, and a bunch of students begin to clarify whole areas of their lives. Usually, it is treated very routinely; but if you ever want to think about goals, this will help you. The concept in this goals chart is revolutionary. It breaks through all kinds of confusion.

Every so often, I get a request from some wide-world organization asking if they may reproduce the chart in their organization because it is exactly what they have been looking for. They find it tremendously exciting that one can deliberately set goals.

ONE CAN SET ONE'S OWN GOALS. IT IS POSSIBLE. ONE DOES NOT HAVE TO HAVE GOALS SET FOR ONE BY ANYONE ELSE. This is itself a revolutionary concept. One can set goals for all of the different concentric spheres of one's responsibility. One can set goals for oneself. One can set goals to achieve in relation to one's close intimate loved ones, for one's extended family, for one's various groups, for one's city, county, state, nation, province, for one's continent, for one's species, for the world of living things and for the universe as a whole. Not only *can* one set goals at all these levels, but setting them at *all* levels greatly reinforces the power of the goals. Every level of goals becomes more workable if integrated with all other levels.

One can also set goals at all levels of time. In fact, one *needs* to set goals for all levels of time. One needs to plan at least what one will accomplish today, this week, this month, this year, and in ten years. One needs a clear picture of what one wants to do before one climbs the ladder to the space ship to colonize the next planet. (I used to say before one dies, but not any more.) To set these goals for all these times and at all these levels and integrate them makes immediate goals much more easily achieveable. Our practical experience is that if a person sets only an immediate goal, she or he will mill around indefinitely and discharge on that goal without achieving it, but that if a farther goal is set, he or she will discharge while achieving the immediate one and will tackle the next one, just like that.

It is possible to set goals in at least two dimensions of time and responsibility.

AN UPWARD TREND EXISTS IN THE UNIVERSE COUNTER TO THE ENTROPY TREND, but compatible with it. Our position in the universe is on the rising point, the advanced point of the upward trend. The upward trend exists everywhere. I have been thinking lately about the great adventure stories that have thrilled generations of people. Almost always the climax of the story is at a point when the hero or heroine has done his or her best, has been confused and bewildered, but has struggled onward. Then the upward trend appears from out of its occlusion. The upward trend appears and buoys up the hero or heroine's efforts, and triumph takes place. No wonder these stories thrilled us. The writer intuitively reached for this great insight.

Leadership functions must be performed if a group is to function well. An operating leaderless group is a contradiction. A leaderless, collapsing group is, of course, common. At least one person must think about the group as a whole rather than just her or his role in it. This is the key leadership function. **THE LEADERSHIP FUNCTIONS MUST BE FILLED FOR ANY GROUP TO OPERATE WELL.**

We have these beautiful big printed sheets out on a table in the foyer which you can take home and use to have your whole Area analyze its needed leadership functions and fill them all. We are getting past *one* person leadership. When we said "*at least* one person must think about the group as a whole" and we put key responsibility on the Area Reference Person, it sometimes came to be distorted in practice to mean *only one person* was encouraged to think of the group as a whole. We are learning to organize with charts to push ahead the realization that every person in a group can share the general leadership function of thinking about the group as a whole and can handle the specific leadership tasks by a division of responsibility.

IT IS POSSIBLE FOR A RATIONAL GROUP DISCUSSION TO TAKE PLACE. It astounds some of our wide-world friends when they first run into the simple concepts of an RC topic group or discussion group. They are simple concepts, but they work well if you take them into the wide world. You'll find in the magazines, in **Present Time** and in **Sisters** especially, many stories of how these concepts of group operation are having astounding results in the wide world. "No person speaks twice before everyone speaks once." "No one speaks four times before everyone speaks twice." "Discussions shall involve issues but not personalities." "Everyone shall be listened to with respect." "A summary of the important things said in a sub-group shall be prepared for the larger group, oral and/or written." Just these simple guidelines have unleashed a tremendous flood of excellent thinking of which we have been able to capture just a portion in our journals. As we prepare more written reports at workshops, we will have to support the journals better so they can publish more frequently.

INDIVIDUAL THINKING IS GREATLY ENHANCED BY ATTENTIVE, NON-RESPONSIVE LISTENING. One of the brightest jewels in our crown of innovations is the Think and Listen Group. (They have often been misrepresented by calling groups by this name which take turns speaking on a common or assigned topic; Think and

Listens are not the same at all.) The opportunity to be listened to with great respect and have *no* response tremendously enhances a person's thinking. To have such an experience gives one a clear view of how much our thinking and our speaking are usually inhibited by fear of the response of the person listening. When we set up a real Think and Listen Group, and our thinking is protected by this crystal chalice of non-intervention, our minds flower and brilliant thoughts come forth. We have not used this as much as we deserve to.

(Question about choice of topics.)

There is no assignment of topic. That is right. We have another kind of discussion group where we all take turns being listened to as we think about a particular topic, but that is not what we have meant by a Think and Listen Group.

The last concept I will try to deal with this morning is: **IT IS POSSIBLE TO DELIBERATELY CREATE OASES OF SAFETY FOR THINKING, FOR DISCHARGE, AND FOR RE-EVALUATION.** This has often not been said as clearly as it might have been, but this is what we have intuitively done. In our sessions we have certain agreements that are supposed to be followed. This is true also in our topic groups, in our Think and Listens, in our classes, in our Communities, in our workshops. When these agreements are followed, it becomes possible to achieve things because of the safety that we cannot achieve under other circumstances. Violation of these agreements makes progress difficult and leads to some disappointing situations. Awarely facing and keeping these agreements enhance our functioning greatly.

What is so wonderful about a session? The counselor and client are agreed on how each is to behave. If the counselor gives her or his opinion or reproaches the client or allows an upset look on her or his face when the client is trying to get at some sticky material, the safety is destroyed. You know what happens in a workshop when someone is laboriously trying to say something important about their oppression and somebody from the oppressor group's guilt flames and they get up and interrupt and "correct" the speaker. The safety is gone.

Those of you who were at Liberation I and II remember the great turning point in that long afternoon when no whites were allowed to speak until all Third Worlders had spoken as much as they wanted to. That made the difference. The workshop got safer and safer and safer and the Third Worlders thought better and spoke more clearly and our liberation work was splendidly launched. We create atmospheres of safety.

I have tried to think of analogies. The best one I have thought of so far is of those Middle Ages cultures where everybody went around in armor. What do we create in the session, in the support group, in the class, in the workshop, in the Community? We create an environment where it is possible to risk taking off your armor so you can wash your underwear. Is that a meaningful analogy? (General agreement) If you have to wear your armor, it is pretty hard to wash your underwear. In a good session, a good workshop, a good support group, where the rules are not forgotten for anybody, we can flourish.

Every once in a while at a teachers' and leaders' workshop, everything falls together and people take huge strides forward. There are other times when people are not that responsible. Sometimes we still accomplish something, but we accomplish it on bruised, scraped knees and with gritted teeth. Bringing this concept up into awareness, that our RC environments, wherever we can set them up, are basically oases of safety and the more deliberately and carefully we can create them, the cleaner our underwear will be. Also, we'll be able to get by with lighter-weight armor for the times in between because we will be so confident. Our oases can grow bigger. Everyone can take the safety of a workshop home and extend it to their family and their neighborhood.

Insights About Oppression

The Key Concepts and Insights of Re-evaluation Counseling To Date—Part II

OPPRESSION EXISTS UNIVERSALLY IN PRESENT SOCIETIES. EVERY PERSON IN OUR SOCIETIES IS LOCKED INTO BOTH OPPRESSED AND OPPRESSOR ROLES. I sometimes get the impression that we have gotten used to this concept very quickly. Then I hear discussions that completely ignore it and get way off track as a result. Out in the wide world this is still almost unknown and unfaced—this realization that everyone in our societies has been forced into operating within both oppressor and oppressed roles.

OPPRESSION ONLY OPERATES, AND CAN ONLY OPERATE, THROUGH DISTRESS PATTERNS. This, again, is one of the most powerful insights about oppression. It has been useful to us but is desperately needed by oppression fighters and liberation movements in the wide world. This is useful, in part, because otherwise the disheartening appearance of human beings, who we assume are good and wholesome, acting in such oppressive, unwholesome ways tends to destroy our morale and blight our spirit over and over again. No person would ever agree to or submit to being oppressed unless a pattern of oppression had first been installed, in the first place by adultism in our early childhood. Adultism, and the installation of patterns of oppression through adultism, is the foundation that allows other oppressions to be installed.

Only the distress patterns left by adultism allow other oppressions to be accepted. Only the installation of oppressed patterns makes it possible to force a person to continue to function

A report to the World Conference, 1981. Appeared in **Present Time** No. 46.

as oppressed. **NO ONE WOULD AGREE TO OR SUBMIT TO BEING OPPRESSED FOR MORE THAN AN INSTANT EXCEPT FOR THE INSTALLATION OF DISTRESS PATTERNS.** A victim of oppressive forces might bide his or her time and keep a submissive facial expression while the gun is pointed at him or her, but the oppressor would be overthrown very quickly if the distress patterns of being oppressed were not internalized to enforce the person. More than that, no person would agree to function as an oppressor for an instant if the patterns of oppression had not first been installed (by that person being oppressed) and the person then manipulated into the oppressor role in the pattern.

THE OPPRESSOR, THE PERSON WHO FUNCTIONS AS AN OPPRESSOR, HAS ALWAYS FIRST BEEN OPPRESSED AND THEN MANIPULATED INTO THE OTHER END OF THE OPPRESSION PATTERN. The great breakthrough insight here came from England at an Arundale workshop. Those of you who were there remember when the first "born to rule" caucus met. (You were in it, C—, remember?) About six people were hanging onto each other and shaking wildly as several of their number reported on what it was like to be ruling class in England. I remember one describing the extra oppression of preparation for being "presented to the Queen." Others told of how they were taken from their parents at an early age and sent to special schools called public schools (as far as I can tell because they are so private) and there systematically tortured and degraded in the most inhumane ways. They were then manipulated in later years into the other end of the pattern, forced to give the same vicious treatment to the younger boys in preparation for their "ruling" role.

This realization, this principle, is met with indignation by victims of oppression at first. "You're trying to tell me that those were innocent humans, those people who tortured and shot and gouged out my family's eyes? You are going to tell me that Hitler was a human being?" Yes. It is of great support to us to realize that the most viciously functioning person in the world was a human being underneath the distress and functioned so viciously only because of the distress. This empowers us and emboldens us to seek allies much more widely, to keep up our own morale and our strength. We have a scroll saying that "If a distress pattern attacks you (and nothing else ever does), help is always close at hand. This is the human being locked inside the distress pattern, the pattern's victim and your best ally, who can be reached in ways that we are learning to do."

(Asked to repeat)

The person who functions as an oppressor does so always and only because he or she has first been oppressed, and the pattern of oppression thus installed and has then been manipulated into the other end of the pattern in order to function as an oppressor. **IF WE CAN HELP THE PERSON ACTING OUT AN OPPRESSOR ROLE IN A PATTERN TO DISCHARGE THAT PATTERN OR MANIPULATE THE PERSON OUT OF IT, THAT PERSON WILL GLADLY CEASE FUNCTIONING AS AN OPPRESSOR AND WILL BECOME AN ALLY.**

OPPRESSION CAN BE AND IS INTERNALIZED. The realization that oppression is usually internalized, if we can communicate it widely enough, will make a great difference in our work. If we can reach the liberation forces of the world with our understanding of internalized oppression, we will redouble their strength several times. People are eager and willing to understand this.

MOST DAMAGE DONE BY OPPRESSION IS DONE BY ITS INTERNALIZED FORM. To realize this is of importance in eliminating oppression, in discharging oppression patterns. The blows from outside came early, they will still come occasionally, they come viciously sometimes when the struggle is joined; but almost all the damage done by oppression is done by its internalized persistence, by the self-invalidation, self-attack, attacks upon each other by the members of the oppressed group and by the fierce attacks and competition between different oppressed groups that otherwise would be, and can become, each other's supportive allies.

(Asked to repeat)

The blows first come from outside, but day in and day out we wreck ourselves, wreck each other in the internalized continuation of the attacks. A classical example, spotted by sociologists long ago, is the game, The Dozens, played by young U.S. black men in which the object is to remain "cool" and "calm" while insulting each other and degrading each other in the most vicious possible ways. The game continues on and on. Each new generation of young black men is expected to participate in this cruel, cruel invalidation procedure. It has been traced to its origins in the necessity for black mothers under slavery to humiliate their male children into submissiveness in order that they could remain alive. Under slavery, if male black children showed any trace of spirit or rebellion, this so severely frightened the slave owner that they were subject to instant execution. Black mothers deliberately kept their black sons alive by humiliating them and degrading them and forcing them into submissive patterns of behavior in which they were expected to endure without resistance. This did keep them alive. The tactic was successful; but the internalizing of the oppression has carried on generation after generation to this day (with some reinforcement, of course, from new oppression) with the persistence and contagion which we have recognized that patterns can have.

Another realized insight is not yet acted upon widely enough. Our skills here are slow in developing compared to our knowledge. **THE PERSON OUTSIDE A PARTICULAR OPPRESSION CAN BE POWERFULLY EFFECTIVE AGAINST THE INTERNALIZED FORM OF THE OPPRESSION.** Contrary to what *seems* to be the reality (and, of course, is actually our fears), when blacks invalidate each other, compete with each other, pool their discouragement and hopelessness and the white draws back and wouldn't dare say anything about black oppression because the white is "of course not an expert and doesn't want to intrude and make a fool of himself or herself," contrary to that is the reality that an aware white in a black group can be decisively effective in interrupting the internalized oppression simply by seeing the viciousness of it and speaking clearly from the outside. Roberto and Emma were present the morning after the Latino workshop, when the Chicana women were speaking out of their internalized oppression of how ugly they felt and how they longed for long blonde straight hair all the time they were growing up. I felt sincerely indignant because these were beautiful women, all of them without exception, and I spoke from my heart and said, "How can you talk that way? You are the most beautiful women in the world." At first they felt that I was being sarcastic and wanted to fight with me but then they heard that I meant it and heavy discharge took place, just enormous discharge on this material. With each other up to that point they could only be sarcastic. The person outside the oppression can be very effective against the internalized oppression.

We have only begun to do this a little bit. It is nearly an exact analog of the intelligence of the counselor speaking from outside the individual distress pattern. If the counselor is not caught in timid passivity but sees the client's distress as it is going on, and acts to contradict it, what a great lift it gives one, as client. How heavily we discharge! It is almost an exact analog of this, that the person outside the oppression can contradict the internalized oppression effectively.

For some time we men stood around bewildered and timid and fumble-footed while we watched the struggle of women to liberate themselves. Just now we are beginning to find out that we don't have to stand back, ashamed of our sexism and apologizing for it forever. We can move in and be of great assistance to the emergence of women from the internalized oppression.

The leaders' meetings a year ago saw a spectacular demonstration of this. Charlotte and I will always remember it with great pleasure.

LIBERATION FROM OPPRESSION REQUIRES A THREE-POINT PROGRAM: ONE, A CLEAR LIBERATION POLICY: TWO, UNITY OF THE GROUP AROUND THAT POLICY, AND THREE, THE WINNING OF ALLIES. The first steps are best tackled together in that the members of the oppressed group should participate in the working out of the policy. (Not necessarily without a first draft being written by someone else. We have found that one can write a first draft of a liberation policy with considerable ease from outside the oppression compared to doing it from inside, but then the group itself should review and revise that first draft so that they participate in working out that policy.) This will help to organize the group. To participate in working out the policy can help to achieve unity. You will achieve the policy and the unity at the same time.

The third step is the winning of allies. This has been known intuitively (outside of RC) in a very few quarters, but almost all liberation movements have neglected it, almost entirely. Almost all the liberation activities of the 60's floundered and wasted their resources for lack of that third action, the winning of allies.

PEOPLE NEED SEPARATE DISCUSSIONS WITHIN EACH PARTICULAR LIBERATION GROUP BEFORE THEY CAN HOPE TO COMMUNICATE WELL TO, OR UNITE WITH, THE OTHER GROUPS. This principle revealed itself at Liberation I and II Workshops. Whenever it has been applied, it has been very powerful. Where it has not been applied, such as in the drift into having an oppressed group and its allies in the same mixed support group or workshop, we have inevitably developed difficulties that take time and trouble to sort out. Each group *must* caucus separately first in spite of their fears of segregation and their eager desire for unity. They must have a time to get themselves together in the safety of their similarities, their commonalities, or their homogeneity. People having the same backgrounds need to first discuss and agree on what they want the other groups to hear from them. Once that is accomplished, they can come together and listen to each other with respect and achieve the real unity that they would otherwise seek too quickly or too simplistically.

This principle has been forgotten over and over. Working-class support groups, for example, have started enthusiastically and then many times tended to wither because of the considerable differences in backgrounds among the twenty or thirty people that enthusiastically come out at first. They have one or two good meetings and then, unsafety. Individual members complain bitterly about "the things they had to listen to." The underlying unity is obscured by the differences.

Recently, we had the first workshop restricted just to industrial workers, and it was so fine and free. Everyone there knew what everyone else was talking about. Discussions quickly came to agreement. It was delightfully different from past workshops. Yet in the future when we have a workshop where the industrial workers who have been working by themselves come together with the medical workers who have been working by themselves and the clerical workers who have been working by themselves, we have enough experience to say confidently that the different groups will understand each other and come to a fine unity. This principle of the necessity of preliminary separations whenever there are differences—in order to communicate well towards a wider unity later—deserves to be dusted off and proclaimed over and over again.

EACH PARTICULAR OPPRESSION HAS CERTAIN FEATURES IN COMMON WITH ALL OTHER OPPRESSIONS. Every oppression, for example, includes a lack of respect for members of the oppressed group. There are many other such elements which are common to every oppression.

EACH OPPRESSION IS ALSO UNIQUE AND NEEDS TO BE UNDERSTOOD IN ITS UNIQUENESS. RCers need to master the knowledge of these particular characteristics. Some examples would be the "settling for less" conditioning of women by sexist oppression or the denial of education and information to U.S. blacks by white racism. It is desirable for an RCer to become an expert on the oppression of every group of which she or he is not a member (in order to be of decisive assistance against the internalized oppression of members of the group) and to become an expert on combatting the internalized oppression of her or his own group.

SOME PARTICULAR OPPRESSIONS PLAY KEY ROLES IN THE OVERALL STRUCTURE OF THE OPPRESSIVE SOCIETY AND IN RELATIONSHIP TO THE OTHER OPPRESSIONS.

The oppression of the working classes, which is, in its foundations and at its core, economic exploitation, is the fundamental oppression in this society. Taking the value they produce from the working persons who produce it by the persons who "own" is what the whole society is "all about." **ALL OTHER OPPRESSIONS WERE DEVELOPED AS MEANS OF ENFORCING CLASS OPPRESSION, AS MEANS OF DIVIDING THE ECONOMICALLY-OPPRESSED AGAINST EACH OTHER SO AS TO SECURE THEIR SUBMISSION TO AND COMPLIANCE WITH THEIR ECONOMIC EXPLOITATION.** This began in the first slave societies and continues to the present day. Working people are divided on lines of gender, on lines of age, on lines of race, physical ability, size, presence or absence of physical handicap, sexual preference, religion, nationality, culture, and language and are turned to oppressing each other and thus discouraged from uniting against the economic exploitation.

The oppression of young people by adults is the "training ground" for all other oppressions. If adults did not install powerlessness patterns early in the life of each young person, if the young person's submission was not enforced during this early time of physical smallness, insufficient information, dependence on others, and naive expectations of good treatment from surrounding humans, then later oppressions would be difficult or impossible to install. **THE PATTERNS LAID IN BY THE ADULTIST MISTREATMENT OF YOUNG PEOPLE ARE USED AS A FOUNDATION FOR THE INSTALLATION OF ALL THE OTHER PATTERNS OF OPPRESSION.**

OPPRESSION OF JEWS (ANTI-SEMITISM) IN THE WESTERN AND ARAB COUNTRIES PLAYS THE ROLE OF A "PRECEDENT-SETTER" OR AN "ENTERING WEDGE," FOR THE USE OF VIOLENCE AGAINST ALL OPPRESSED GROUPS IN TIMES OF SOCIAL CRISIS. The oppression of Chinese in Southeast Asia and of East Indians in the countries of East Africa is very similar.

Classically, Jews have been a visible, distinct minority population in the countries of their exile with a highly developed culture and skills of survival. They, or their leaders, have been required to function as a tool of the ruling groups of the majority population as a condition of the Jews as a whole being tolerated. At the same time a continual low-level, "unofficial" campaign of anti-Jewish propaganda is kept evident among the oppressed majority population. In times of threatened revolt by the oppressed people of the majority population, this is replaced with violent *official* anti-Jewish propaganda. Pogroms, massacres, and expulsions are organized to turn the resentments of the oppressed majority population, which was on the point of rising against the oppressors, against the Jews (or Chinese or East Indians), using them as scapegoats. This tactic has been used over and over and over again in the last two thousand years. When the oppressors have diverted the revolutionary fervor of the oppressed into such shameful activity, it leaves the people who threatened rebellion ashamed of themselves and discouraged, and the Jews dispersed and plundered.

Later the Jews either are forced to be re-instated in the country of the violence, or in the place to which they've emigrated, back into the role of visible agents of the oppressors.

This scapegoating imposed upon Jews (and upon East Indians and Chinese in the other sections of the world) has been possible in the past in part because, until recently, there was no homeland nation with power to support the Jewish populations in other countries and the homeland nations of the Chinese and East Indians were, until recently, under colonial domination and so almost powerless to protect their emigres on the world scene.

Ending one oppression requires ending *all oppressions.* **ELIMINATING ANY ONE OPPRESSION, THOROUGHLY, COMPLETELY, REQUIRES ELIMINATING ALL OPPRESSIONS.** No one is free as long as there is one person oppressed. This appeals to our intuition when we have our heads out of our distress, but it is also very practical. Any example of oppression going on with another group of people drags down and fetters our own struggle repeatedly. The white male working-class movement has continually floundered and weakened itself, in every practical sense, by going along with sexism, by going along with racism.

In the feudal society of the southern United States between the post-Civil War Reconstruction period and the Second World War, the enmities assiduously cultivated between the white sharecroppers and the black sharecroppers, the serfs of this feudal economy, kept both groups viciously and perpetually oppressed. Neither group could move out of the bondage as long as they tolerated the bondage of the others.

The Empowerment of the Individual

The Key Concepts and Insights of Re-evaluation Counseling To Date—Part III

ANY PHENOMENON CAN BE UNDERSTOOD BETTER IF IT IS EXAMINED FROM A VARIETY OF VIEWPOINTS. This has been recognized, at least partially, in a number of places besides RC. Start with the trivial example that it is better to walk around a house that is white on your side before you say confidently that "the house is white." Another side may very well be painted red. In the development of science, of mathematics, of literature and art, it happens over and over again that the knowledge about a certain subject is pronounced "complete." Then someone looks at the subject from an entirely new viewpoint and there is great excitement in the field as tremendous quantities of knowledge proceed to develop from the new viewpoint.

This leads us close to another insight I will discuss later (the freedom to choose one's viewpoint), but just to recognize this much, that any phenomenon will be understood better if it is looked at from a variety of viewpoints, should arm us against any conclusion that any subject is closed, that everything is already known about anything.

Looking back, we have looked at Re-evaluation Counseling from many different viewpoints as it has progressed and evolved. An early view and still a beginning view for many people who come into counseling is that RC is something that will make one feel better. It has certainly motivated many of us to have our first session or kept us going until we had our first good session. Later, when we tackle a chronic, we discover a

A report to the World Conference, 1981. Appeared in **Present Time** No. 46.

new viewpoint and think of counseling as a way to help us think better and function better but not necessarily to feel better immediately.

Some people with no real knowledge of RC go into print with the viewpoint that RC is an "interesting, simplistic attempt at therapy." RC has been called "do-it-yourself psychiatry," and some people that we welcome in RC and who, because of their experiences, can help us expose and combat the mental health oppression system, will have to start with this viewpoint. Coming from where they come from, they have to think of it that way at the start.

We have moved through a number of viewpoints. The important viewpoint of the last couple of years is that **RC THEORY AND PRACTICE IS THE UNCOVERING AND REVEALING OF REALITY.** RC acts to strip the pseudo-reality from reality, rolls back the false reality which has occluded reality for almost all of us almost all our lives. The pseudo-reality has accumulated from the falsehoods, the invalidations, the pain, the unwarranted assumptions which have been presented to us as reality, assumptions that we are helpless, that whites are smarter than Third Worlders, that women's place is behind the kitchen stove, that working people are dumb, and so on. There are also much more subtle ones, such as the great foundation of liberal philosophy that "it is all hopeless but we must still do our best." *(Group laughter)* Viewed from one viewpoint, Re-evaluation Counseling is the stripping off of the false reality which has been imposed by patterns, oppression, and mis-information and the revealing of the actual nature of the reality in which we function.

The attitude of powerlessness is almost universal. Even our RCers who have been raised to be "owning class" or to "rule" have a very limited concept of power. It may seem to those of us "raised poor" that they feel very powerful in their patterns compared to the way we feel in the patterns we wear, but their's is a very limited concept of power. **THE ATTITUDE OF**

POWERLESSNESS CONDITIONED ON ALL HUMANS IS A FRAUD, IMPOSED BY DISTRESS AND CONCEALING AN ACTUALITY OF TOTAL POWER FOR ANY INDIVIDUAL OR RATIONAL GROUP. We are familiar, by now, with the slogan, "Powerlessness is a fraud."

(Audience questions: Concealing an actuality of what?)

Of total power for any individual or rational group. I think it is necessary to put the "rational" in front of the group. We assume the individual person is rational but I don't think it is safe to assume it about any existing group.

OUR POWER CAN BE RECLAIMED. We have not yet been able to break through to too much performance with this one. We are still pretty much pointing at it as a goal but we are coming closer. Just the insight, just grasping the concept of total power immediately strengthened a whole number of other work fronts. Commitments began to work much better with the concept of the reality of reclaimable total power in the background. Our work against oppression got stronger. It is as if reaching for power "put lead in the pencil" of a lot of our previously discovered concepts. To actually reach for power itself leads to a much more effective scorning of fear. To reach power has not been well demonstrated, as yet. I have been trying to *sound* powerful before workshops and to get other people to at least *sound* powerful.

Help is coming from another direction, however, from the concept that I will talk about in a minute. The freedom always to choose our own viewpoint appears to put the absolute recovery of power right at our fingertips. So far we must be realistic and not pretentious. We have *not yet* implemented the complete recovery of power.

This next concept was on the cover of a *Present Time*. **IF ANY ONE INDIVIDUAL RECLAIMS HER OR HIS POWER AND MOVES, THAT ONE INDIVIDUAL CAN GUAR-**

ANTEE THE FUTURE OF THE WORLD. One such example will undoubtedly bring everyone else out of the timid bushes to fall in behind them, ready to take charge of things.

It is always good if we can find a little gleam of light in the culture, a little crack in the pseudo-reality toward these concepts of reality that we are uncovering. The fact that even one individual acting out of confidence in her power will draw the necessary forces to her automatically is exemplified for me, at least a little bit, by a scene in a Charlie Chaplin movie (I think *Modern Times*). Unemployed Charlie, good-hearted, earnest, stands bewildered in a street filled with unemployed people. A truck comes by with a red cloth fastened to a stick protruding from the back, warning of a long load. The truck hits a bump and the stick with the red cloth falls off. Charlie notices it, rushes out onto the street, grabs the stick with the red cloth on it and runs after the truck to return it, but they don't hear him and the truck goes off. The little tramp puts the stick over his shoulder and walks on disconsolately. The camera shows him walking on and on but a sound begins and gets louder and finally you recognize it as the tramp of feet and the camera swings past Charlie and thousands of people are marching behind him *(group laughter)*, following him and his flag.

These other concepts about reality lead to the big one. **REALITY IS BENIGN.** In these efforts toward uncovering reality that we call RC we have drilled test wells through the grubby pseudo-reality in a number of places. RC began with one little piece of pseudo-reality being challenged. My first client was, fortunately, balanced just right between deep distress, classified as hopeless by professionals, and an eagerness to discharge, so that, in spite of my misguided efforts (misguided by the pseudo-reality that I, too, had bought into that if people are crying the most helpful thing you can do for them is to stop them) no matter how many times I stopped him and he agreed to stop, if I took any initiative he started crying again. As you know, my pattern wore out and I finally let him cry. That certainly was a great break. I could have started with someone not so ready to emerge. The next thirty-five clients I worked with who were deeply distressed didn't respond like that at all! *(Group laughter)*

The first little gleam of light came there. From underneath the pseudo-reality, that said that to assist someone who is crying is to stop them from crying, came the gleam of reality that if a person is crying it is good for them to let them cry. That was all we had for a long time. It was at least six months before the crack widened a little bit and we realized that one could not only permit the person to cry until they stopped but one could even bring their attention back to the subject they were crying about and they would then cry much more effectively with much greater results. As we began to drill test holes deep into this pseudo-reality, we had other glimpses of reality here and there. The deeper we went the better the results.

How responsible is a person? Questioning went on session after session. How much responsibility can I take? The concept of responsibility broadened and deepened. I can take responsibility for myself. For my family? Yes, that fits cultural conditioning. What about responsibility for people I don't know? Oh, woe. Each step of additional responsibility that people moved to worked better until we came to the concept of *total* responsibility.

In the essay "Who's in Charge?" we reached the concept that if one doesn't assume responsibility for the farthest atom in the farthest star in the farthest galaxy, one has put oneself inside inhibiting limits. Once the concept was projected, people tried it in their thinking and, lo and behold, total responsibility turned out not to be a chore but a great liberation idea. We had drilled a hole all through the pseudo-reality and there was sunshine and fresh air on the other side.

(Would you explain what you mean by total responsibility for the farthest atom? I don't understand.)

I mean that one must not shut that atom out from one's awareness or concern. If one knows about something, that something is taken into account in one's thinking. It doesn't mean that we pretend that we can reach instantaneously to the other side of the star and manipulate that atom or anything like that, but it means that we assume responsibility for including that knowledge in our thinking, that we do not put up a barrier and say, "I will not think beyond this point because I can only handle this much."

During the Vietnam War a man came in for an interview, looked at me and said, "Well, I don't know about your outfit." He said, "I saw you marching in that peace parade, and I don't know if I want to get mixed up in anything like that." I questioned him, "Is it not all right to take some responsibility for foreign policy?" He said, "The President knows what he is doing. I have enough to think about just to take care of my family." He became a client, and worked on other matters. He "looked after his family" and left it up to the President to decide what was going on in Vietnam. Later, he came to me with his tragedy. His son had been drafted and sent to Vietnam and killed. The supposedly pro-survival limiting of responsibility had revealed itself as the crudest non-survival.

We drilled holes in the pseudo-reality in other areas. How can you motivate children to learn? There were some "enlightened" theories from wide-world attempts in this field that you praise them for "good" results. You criticize them not too unkindly when they don't shape their letters right but you praise them if they get them facing the right way. You encourage them to do art as long as it is "reasonable" and "really means something," but you encourage them not to waste their time with "scrawls" you don't like. That got challenged. People thought a little beyond that. Praise everything they do. Don't pay much attention to it, just praise it with glassy eyes. That was a little better. Thinking crept on. Finally, we drilled all the way and the concept arose that if you just make the information available children will themselves decide what they want to learn, how they want to learn it and what is exciting for them. Everything fell into place, reality recognized at last, although not yet widely practiced.

Wherever we drilled a test hole in the pseudo-reality by challenging it and wherever we dared punch the hole deep enough, sunshine, fresh air, bright colors, flowers, good sense drifted through. There was apparently something different on the other side. It was much better than the globby guck we were used to living with.

ANY OF THE NON-BENIGN APPEARANCES OF THE PSEUDO-REALITY THAT HIDES REALITY, INCLUDING THE MOST THREATENING, THE MOST HORRIFYING, *CAN* BE FACED CLEARLY, *CAN* BE CONTRADICTED, *CAN* BE DISCHARGED ON, AND *CAN* BE ELIMINATED. We do not have to wall off from our attention or thinking any of the negative concepts or the negative appearances of the pseudo-reality even though we have been trained or conditioned to avoid them.

I think this is quite important. Consider death. We have already done some work towards challenging this. The phenomenon of death can be faced clearly and the fears of death can be discharged. Of course we have always had examples from the wide world of people whose professions place them up against death repeatedly and who necessarily discharge to the point where they can look death in the eye with contempt.

For a long time in RC this was difficult until we got some concepts out in the open to support us. It was difficult for people to work on death, difficult to face the death of a loved one. People were too horrified as they tried to think about the possibility of their own death, and at best escaped to pretense. "I am not going to die," I had an early client tell me. I said, "Why do you think so?" and he said, "The proof is all around you; I haven't died yet." *(Group laughter)*

Consider the Nazi holocaust, the genocidal holocaust of the Gay people, the gypsies, the Jews, the militant trade unionists. Too horrible to be thought about? No. In practice we have found that this horror can be contradicted, that discharge can be obtained, and that it can be thorough.

What holds us back from doing a better job there? The lack of bold, effective counseling. All the way along on these clear, theoretical concepts we are up against a practical limitation which all of you know too well and frequently allow yourselves to be discouraged about. "Where am I going to get effective counseling?" Where are the confident enough words from outside? I rehearsed this discouragement at you a little bit at the beginning of the Conference. "Where can I get someone who is more confident that I am when I get restimulated by the latest of the long line of attacks made on me all my life?"

Consider the threat of nuclear holocaust. We have begun to work on it. I am very pleased with the way the three or four demonstrations we had the other night were beginning to reveal the variety of results that can come from one basic approach to contradicting this fear. Do I agree that we should put this by in order to emphasize the murders of the Atlanta children? No, I do not. I can understand this urge to deal with a restimulative but "smaller" issue instead, but I think it is an expression of our feelings that we are too powerless. I think the murders of the Atlanta children will be dealt with also if we throw our full weight against this numb horror of the overhanging nuclear holocaust. If we discharge on that, we will eliminate the fear that keeps us from taking care of these other issues.

Any particular clump of pseudo-reality, including the most threatening, such as terror of nuclear holocaust, can be faced, can be contradicted, can be discharged, and can be eliminated.

(Asked to repeat)

We do not need to avoid facing the most threatening clumps

of the pseudo-reality by turning instead to ones we can face more easily, either as a priority or as a comfort or avoidance of the severe ones. We have the resources at this point. (We did not have them in the past or we would have come to this point earlier.) We have the resources, both in insights and in the advanced emergence of large numbers of people, so that we can now face the most threatening aspects of the patterns well. If we do this, we can then relate to the more localized, not-quite-as-intimidating aspects and deal with those at the same time with even greater power.

Question: I am a little confused by the concept of attacking the "larger" issues in order to think more clearly about the "smaller" issues. This occurred to me when you were talking about the comparison between nuclear holocaust and the Atlanta murders. It seems to me that there are times when people have to respond first to what is the primary life-threatening factor to them in order to think clearly about survival in the short term. If I am a citizen of Upper Volta and my primary need is getting enough food to live on, it seems difficult to ask me to contemplate nuclear holocaust when I may starve unless I search for food. It seems to me that there are primary and perhaps secondary levels of intensity or of concern about life-threatening issues. Clearly for me in that position, starvation is much more primary than is nuclear holocaust, although it is also clear that if nuclear holocaust happened, it would be all-embracing. It seems to me it is important theoretically to make some kind of distinctions in our lives between dealing with those issues which are most life-threatening for us immediately and in the longer term. It may require us to counsel or discharge our distress on what is immediately life threatening for us just in order to survive, before we can concentrate on other issues. I would like you to try and incorporate that kind of thinking in your proposals. I believe you are right in your conceptualization of the importance of preventing nuclear holocaust, but I think we should discuss this other factor, too. This comes up for me over and over and over again. It is hard to decide what to emphasize because some people simply cannot relate to the holocaust concept, not because of their numbing fear but because it is not an immediate or primary life-threatening factor.

Yes. This is one of the places where we really have to think our way through. In a way we have come against this difficulty before in goal-setting. I talked about this the first morning, about the patterns about goals with which our early Co-Counselors had to contend. The imbalance of goals came in many categories but tended to fall in two familiar ones. There was the person I mentioned who couldn't be bothered with our policy in

Viet Nam because he had to look after his family and that was very short-sighted; but also there was the wide-world-changer, the revolutionary, the social change artist who never washed his underwear nor looked after the feeding of his family. Back in the 30's, I met a radical Montana farmer who talked like I was thinking, but when I asked other farmers what they knew about him, they were full of contempt. They said, "He talks about changing the world. Hell, he didn't even get his crop in this year." It was plain that the imbalance of goals, the imbalance of emphasis, made him ineffective. Although his heart was in a new society, he wasn't going to get anywhere near a new society and no one would follow him because of the imbalance of goals. Our conclusion was that we had to have a program of goals at all levels for our goal-setting to function well.

The conclusion we reached was that we have to deal with everything. We must deal with the threat to the children of Atlanta, we must deal with where our next meal is coming from, and we must prevent nuclear holocaust. We have a whole spectrum of issues that have to be dealt with. Even for the resident of Upper Volta who has starvation staring him or her in the face, the issue of eliminating nuclear weapons must be faced when there is slack to do so.

We have slack. We are sitting here in a comfortable auditorium with an opportunity to think, an opportunity to work out policy that can mean a lot to all the people of the world, that can perhaps be crucial. We must not allow one concern to reject the others. Maybe I am saying it better here. We must not allow our concern for the Atlanta murders and our need to do something about those to, in effect, reject thinking about nuclear holocaust and discharging our fears of that. Is that better?

Question: This brings up "When does the counselor know best?" Obviously most of our work is client-centered and client-led. Often, I think, a counselor can better see the road ahead and at times it is very useful for the counselor to direct the client's attention. Sometimes it is useful for the counselor to insist that the client move ahead. At other times I think not, because if the client can't feel that issue or can't deal with it yet, the rightness of the fact that that is the next issue doesn't really help the clients move from where they are. I think this is true not only in what order we discharge our distresses, but also in what issue we put our attention on. The fact is that nuclear holocaust is the central issue for us all. The question is, is each person in a position where they can focus on it? And if they are not, is it correct to push toward it and try to work on it or more important for them to discharge where they are? I don't have an opinion. On that subject particularly, I am not sure; but I think that is the question. I think it is a serious question because I think that question affects our one-point program as we see ourselves becoming a little more activist.

Two points further on I am dealing with just exactly the question you raised and I thank you. For now, I would just remind you that we are meeting here not as clients but as the thinking leadership of a world-wide community. I think that in that context we will come out okay.

Recent Discoveries

The Key Concepts and Insights of Re-evaluation Counseling To Date—Part IV

Now to the advanced concepts relating to counseling itself. **DISCHARGE AND THINKING CAN AND SHOULD TAKE PLACE SIMULTANEOUSLY.** If we fully grasp this, this can revolutionize the practical work of our counseling. It shows up spontaneously and very clearly in the exchange of commitments, but once looked at, we remember earlier examples from other techniques that we tried that worked only under special conditions.

Probably the best example is the use of the repetition of a phrase. A while ago when I had reports on almost every session that took place in the world (that is some time ago), I would have estimated that ninety percent of all counseling consisted of the counselor urging the client to repeat a phrase, "Again!" "Again!" We had a little joke about the persons who became so rigidly enamored of RC that if you said "Hello" to them, they shouted, "Again!" The phrase repetition worked; it worked and it worked. Trainloads of distress were discharged with the counselor sitting there saying, "Again!" It worked. We can be glad; but it is plain now that we achieved all of those results by the use of a bludgeon when a scalpel would have produced even better results. We got the client's attention, they handed us the phrase that made their chin tremble and we said "Again" and they began crying and we let them cry until they ran out of contradiction, blew their nose, and then we said, "Again." That was enough, thank goodness. They thought of what it was we were asking them to say. That was enough contradiction. They cried again and as they cried, they shut down. They ran out of contradiction, they reached for a kleenex, they woke up, they

A report to the World Conference, 1981. Appeared in **Present Time** No. 46.

saw that we were there. We shouted, "Again!" and got their attention out a little bit, they remembered the phrase and its contradiction, they cried. It worked. We got a lot of distress out.

Then, remember the technique we called "Present and Future Reality"? Many of you never saw a demonstration of this. When it worked, it was spectacular. We asked the client to talk only, with no hesitation or ambivalence, about what the future was going to be like from now on because she was going to see to it that it was that way. When it got going, the client discharged and discharged as she talked very excitedly and very elatedly sketched powerful use of her resources, told how everything was going to be different. It was thrilling to listen to the client, but she would also be discharging a storm all the while. Frequently, in about two-thirds of the times that it worked, at the end of the time the client turned and said, "That was great, but shouldn't I have discharged?" She hadn't even noticed that the floor was wet with tears in a big ring around her, or that she had been shaking, laughing, and yawning, because her attention was so completely on her thinking. It was thrilling to see.

We published a description of it, and Co-Counselors were not ready for it and shabby, pretentious distortions of the process were "demonstrated" and passed around until we got word out to withdraw it temporarily; the "market" was not ready for it.

The possibilities became clear with the exchange of commitments. Those of you who have seen two people exchange their commitments well have noticed that as the roles of client and counselor shift back and forth, the counseling gets sharper and sharper. Generally, the person who is counselor is shaking too (but speaking clearly) while the one in the client role cries, shakes, and laughs with an occasional yawn. As soon as the roles switch, however, the new counselor keeps shaking (and crying a little bit perhaps) but pays very keen attention. As the roles shift back and forth, the relationship obviously works better and better the more they do it, because they are thinking better and are getting more attention from each other.

When I start a couple of people out on commitments, they almost always work well with me because I am a good counselor, I pay attention, I do the right things; but when they shift over and start exchanging commitments with each other and the process begins to operate well, they discharge better with each other than when they were working with me. They simply surpass my effectiveness. I see this happen over and over again. This seems to be because we have developed a situation where thinking and discharge can take place simultaneously and *this allows us to realize that they always should.* Maybe they always do somewhat but some of our practices have not enhanced this but have interfered with it.

Consider a familiar example, repeating a phrase to and by your client. Incidentally, good counselors know that it isn't usually clients who repeat the phrase. You always act like you expect them to repeat it because that makes them think of it, but you know very well it is mostly the counselor that repeats the phrase. I worked on one phrase for three or four months of long sessions with one client and he never said it once, but, oh, did I repeat it a lot. The discharge was solid. The next time you feel like settling down to repeating a phrase, instead ask your client to keep talking in that direction, keep thinking aloud in the direction that the phrase opened. If he or she can do it, if she or he can break out of the bad habits that we have put on each other of stopping thinking while discharging, you will see the difference. Thinking and discharging can and should take place at the same time.

(How do you recommend we work as counselor at whatever distress listening to repeating phrases puts on us?)

By having your client do what I have just said. A client is never boring when their thinking is sparkling. They are fascinating. Most of us were able to stay fascinated with clients while they were repeating a phrase by paying attention to the changes that were taking place in them.

(Asked to repeat)

Instead of asking your client to repeat phrases, have them talk, have them verbalize thoughts in the new direction.

(No, I mean the situation where I, as counselor, have to take the job of saying the phrase.)

I say you don't have to. Instead, have them talk fresh thoughts, go a step beyond repeating the phrase.

There will be times when they cannot think out loud while discharging, and there is nothing wrong with going back to repeating the phrase. Pick up your bludgeon and keep going. This other, though, is a whole new level of effectiveness. It opens up if we can master expecting each other to keep talking in a new direction against the pattern while we keep discharging.

This next concept is quite important. This is the first time I have spoken of it. It is a clarification of something that we have been unclear about all through our history. I will say it carefully. Passive counseling (by which I mean *only* listening) may be a necessary stage in a counselor learning not to make patterned interventions into the counseling relationship, but this is only a learning stage. **ACTIVELY THINKING, AND INTERVENING, WITHIN THE CORRECT ROLE OF THE COUNSELOR, IS NECESSARY FOR THE COUNSELOR OR THE COUNSELING TO BE FULLY EFFECTIVE.** We have this confusion between the dogma that we lay on beginning Co-Counselors and that we repeat to each other that our job is to just listen and pay attention, and the fact that, in practice, we do many other things. If you watch me demonstrate before a workshop, you will see me taking many other active initiatives.

We correctly say that when you are in trouble, when you don't know what to do, go back to just listening and most of the time if you really listen, the client will find a way to get to the discharge. All this has been correct. But it is time to clarify here that it is not the fundamental role of the counselor to be passive.

The actual relationship between the client and the counselor includes two fully active, fully thinking, fully participating people. The roles of the client and the counselor are different. This is clear even in one of the most advanced forms of counseling, the exchange of commitments. The roles shift back and forth rapidly, but they are clearly defined. It is always very clear who is counselor and who is client, even though both are discharging.

We will continue to lay emphasis in the early stages of learning to counsel on the counselor "shutting up" and listening and paying attention, because almost all of us come to learn counseling with very bad habits of "shooting our faces off," offering opinions, intervening thoughtlessly, taking the client's role away from our client by "remembering" an experience like the one she or he is telling about and interrupting the client's narrative with our own. (All of these can be viewed as unaware [and disruptive] attempts to force some clienting for oneself.) When we start out to be a counselor, we're so conditioned and so desperate that we continually interrupt and intervene and make comments and pass judgments, and do other unworkable things. So, in the early stages of learning to counsel, it has been correct to be fiercely insistent that the counselor only listen, and be interested, and pay as much attention as she or he can at that point.

In later practice, however, we must move more and more toward an active role for a counselor as we become more experienced and better counselors. I preach to workshops, "Don't be a lazy counselor; don't just sit there and give directions to clients and let them handle it." I remind Co-Counselors that the counselor repeats the phrase (if that's what you're doing) much more than the client. I try to demonstrate before workshops the very complex array of things one can do with a client. I give support from the expression on my face, from the tone of my voice, by the way I'm holding the person, by my cheek against his or hers, by the bit of poetry I remember to quote that will contradict the distress. I do a great array of things, actively. We need to say clearly that the passive role of the counselor is a learning stage—a powerful, effective one to be reverted to in many situations, especially when we have not yet paid enough attention to the client to know accurately what the distress is.

We had a fine demonstration of that this morning, with M— in the leaders' meeting. In the rush to demonstrate something fast in front of the short meeting, I tried seven or eight active approaches, and none of them worked. I dropped back and just listened, and soon she said, "My shame," in a vibrating voice, and I said, "Tell us about your shame," and full-scale discharge began immediately. So, when we're uncertain, we drop back to just listening, but when counseling is in full drive, when we're thinking, when we're paying attention, when we're successfully fulfilling our roles, then the counselor is very active, thinking hard, intervening, calculating, adding new contradictions to the distress, finding a new viewpoint that will catch the distress pattern by surprise with a sneak attack, taking all kinds of inventive initiatives.

These are the full roles of Co-Counseling: a very active, thinking-all-the-time-as-well-as-discharging client, a very active thinking-all-the-time and actively-intervening-against-the-distress, skillful counselor. Does that makes sense? *(Audience: Yes.)* Actually doing it is another stage, but if we can define it, it should be easier to do it.

THE WORD FROM OUTSIDE THE PATTERN, OR OUTSIDE THE OPPRESSION, CAN HAVE GREAT, ALMOST UNLIMITED EFFECTIVENESS IN CON-

TRADICTING DISTRESS. Much of the counseling practice I observe involves considerable counseling passivity and a failure on the counselor's part to use his or her power to contradict the distress.

(I've used the sketch at workshops of a long lever arm, with a weight representing a load of distress sitting on one end of the lever. The client stands underneath the weight, pushing up against it with no leverage. The fulcrum or balance point of the lever is very near to that weight. The carefree, untrammeled counselor stands at the other end of the lever, with great leverage for dealing with and contradicting the weight of the client's distress.)

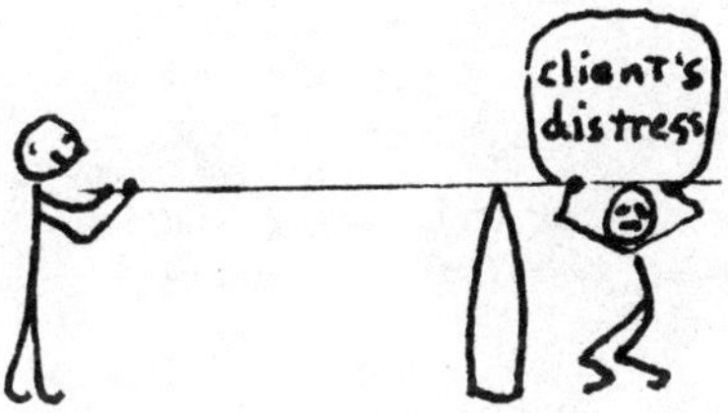

The client is always a perfect client. We have advanced this statement in recent times, and I think it's been helpful. It has interrupted the sneaky practice of blaming the client for poor counseling. As counselors, we had best assume that if the client could do any better, he or she would be doing it, but that our intervention from the freedom of the counselor's role always has many more possibilities and opportunities than we have used at any time.

I do not think I can prove it, but I think it is true that there is no human being in distress of any kind, no matter how deeply distressed—catatonic or worse—who could not be taken into full-scale discharge very quickly by a counselor who was really able to think about and act to contradict the distress. I say "quickly" rather than "immediately," because perhaps it takes a little time for the word to get through the distress to the client. They say that the photons that reach us from the sun left the surface of the sun eight minutes before, but they've been on their way out from the center of the sun for several million years. Perhaps it takes a little time for the word from outside to get through the brushpile of distress to the client; but I conjecture that the most severely distressed person could be very quickly brought to discharge by a counselor who was fully in touch with her or his power, freedom, initiative, ability to choose a fresh viewpoint, and acting on them. I think we're coming closer to this state of affairs all the time. Questions on that?

Voice: Yes. Are you suggesting that if the word from the outside doesn't seem to be working, that one would persist—say for days or weeks, if it doesn't work within a few tries?

I think one can never know ahead of time whether the contradiction of the distress is not accurate enough, or not intense enough, or if more time is needed for it to soak in. One could make one's best guess, and then, perhaps, hedge one's bets by finding some new ways to communicate the word from outside that you thought should work, and also try a few other shots from slightly different directions.

The next formulation is long, but I'll say it in a shorter form afterwards. Any intelligence always has freedom to operate from a different viewpoint than any previously adopted, or than is suggested by others, or than is attempted to be enforced on the person by any force outside the person's intelligence. Viewpoint always remains the free choice of the individual. This always-present freedom to choose one's viewpoint places the reclaiming of power within reach of any individual in any situation.

Let me say it in fewer words. **WE ALWAYS HAVE FREEDOM TO CHOOSE OUR VIEWPOINT.** This freedom cannot be denied to us, no matter how much the pseudo-reality tries to insist that it can. Thought control never worked, even with huge secret police forces. It never worked. "Die Gedanken sind frei." Thinking is free. You may tie me up, blindfold me and gag me, encompass me with irons and sink me in the depths of the deepest sea, but as long as I'm thinking, you cannot tell me what to think. In particular, you cannot take away my freedom to choose my own viewpoint.

A quick inspiration from the first faculty workshop has become a small classic. It's been repeated many times. Suppose you're on a jet plane. You're sitting near the emergency exit. It fails. The pressure in the cabin blows you out at 41,000 feet. Will you despair? You may, if you wish, but what good will that do? You still have freedom to choose a different viewpoint. You can unzip your jacket, spread it for a pair of wings, look for the nearest body of water, steer toward it, enjoy the unusual view you have of the world during the next five minutes, and calculate the best angle of approach to the surface of that water. It may not work *(laughter)*, but what have you lost? If you choose despair, what have you gained? At the very least, you'll have a much more interesting five minutes. *(Laughter)*

There's always freedom to choose one's viewpoint. This needs to be explored and applied. I think most of us have grasped it as a powerful support for our actions in the wide world, a comforting philosophy to always be there. Remember the tale of Peter Rabbit? "Peter gave himself up for lost, and shed great tears, but his cries were overheard by some friendly sparrows who flew to him and begged him to exert himself." Remember that? Peter gave himself up for lost, but the friendly sparrows came in with the word from outside and offered him a different viewpoint. As you remember, he then managed to escape from the gooseberry net.

Beyond its philosophical support, this is a powerful counseling tool. I've had a few chances to apply it, and hopefully, we can get time to do some demonstrations. I would like to try it with one or two people who feel "pinned down" or "stuck" and unable to move from some uncomfortable position, to show what can be done. So far, for me (as a counselor) at least, it takes a lot of work. It isn't light; but insistence on a change of viewpoint for the client by the counselor eventually seems to heave the great bulk of distress up out of the mud.

ANY CLIENT'S FEAR CAN BE SCORNED EFFECTIVELY BY THE COUNSELOR, AND THIS WILL

LEAD TO ITS DISCHARGE BY THE CLIENT. "Scorning fear" has become a slogan. By this we mean not respecting fear, treating fear with contempt, with amused derision. About two years ago, we faced the fact that some of our most experienced counselors tended to be going round and round on some not very important grief, and not progressing rapidly. We recognized that people, in a way, did not know how to discharge fear, or, more correctly, were not receiving enough encouragement and support against their fear to leap this boundary between tears and shaking. We used the slogan "Scorning Fear" to highlight the proposed solution.

I have great good news for us, in case you didn't already know it. Most of our experienced counselors are now shaking freely, and enjoying it at least as much as they used to enjoy their crying. Patterned distortions crept in, as usual, however, and I found in many places fear being "scorned" by the counselor sitting back and saying, "Scorn your fear, client," *(laughter)* and then complaining that the technique didn't really work *(laughter)*. The reality of the matter is that the client has been scorning the fear all along just as much as she or he could figure out a way to do it, and the real improvement necessary is for the counselor to scorn the client's fear. If we don't keep that clear, we will get into distortions such as the counselor reproaching the client for having fear, or something like that. Workable practice consists of the counselor taking an unafraid attitude toward the client's fear.

Question: Will you give us a demonstration of this sometime in the workshop?

HJ: How about right now? What are you scared of, L—?

L—: Standing up and asking this question. (Laughter from group) I'm scared right now of talking to you.

HJ: That's an interesting fear.

L—: Yes (laughter).

HJ: You will probably meet your death from it, but keep on. I can see the headlines now: "Innocent Conference Attendee has heart attack on floor of Conference." *(Much laughter from L— and group.)* "Careless treatment by leader charged." *(More laughter)*

L—: I'm glad I raised this question (laughter, shudder).

HJ: What are you afraid will happen?

L—: I'm afraid that I will say something really stupid.

HJ: I think you can count on that. *(Much laughter from group and L—.)* (To audience) Light pleasant sarcasm is not the only way to contradict the fear. Once the shakes get going, you'd better get your arms around him and let him feel that there's some unafraid support there and do many other things, but humor is not a bad way to get started. (To client) That's a very interesting fear you have there. What else might happen?

L—: I might be massively rejected by this entire group for asking questions.

HJ: Care to look around and see the expressions on their faces about your interruption of their valuable time?

L—: They seem delighted (laughter).

HJ: I don't get that impression *(much laughter from group and client).*

HJ: Okay to put a check on it?

L—: Yes.

HJ: Fear is scorned *by the counselor.* Incidentally, as in most counseling, tone of voice, facial expression, and the communication of relaxed confidence is very important.

To get started, we're going to have to be a little daring. When the client says, "I'm afraid of death," we can say in a relaxed way, "That's interesting. Do you think you'll ever die?" and if the client says mumble, mumble, we can happily say, "Well, you probably will," and the tension will get contradicted and the client will begin discharging. You may choke on it a little the first time *(demonstrates to group laughter),* but if you try, somebody's going to discharge a little *(group laughter),* some small slack will come in, and we'll be able to begin modeling for each other.

The basic fact here is that in order to get restimulated by our client's fear, we have to identify our fear with the client's fear. This takes a lot of work. You have to make a great effort to restimulate your fear by the client's fear. You think it's automatic, but that isn't so. It takes a lot of effort. Anybody here who has a fear of death? *(Laughter)* Okay. Whose death? Yours?

Client: Yes.

HJ: (To audience) Now, I'd actually have to go through a lot of work to think, "Oh, me too. I'm afraid of death. We are both afraid of death. We are in the same boat. Tell frightened me about it." *(Laughter)* That takes a lot of work. You want to remain rational. When she says "my death," you say, "*Your* death doesn't frighten me." *(Much laughter from group)*

Question: I got confused because you're joking about the fear, and I can't see how that will bring trembling.

HJ: Did you tremble when we joked about it?

Q—: A little bit.

HJ: Okay. What were we working on?

Q—: Concentration camps.

HJ: Oh, it was somebody else's experience. You're saying that you want to get to discharging about your own fear of death and your own fear of the war? I don't want to take the time for another demonstration, but I assure you that my lighthearted approach *will* bring discharge, though not necessarily instant approval, from you. You saw what happened when I told L— that I wasn't afraid of her dying.

It takes persistence. You know how music tapes usually have a "leader" on them? Discharges of trembling and tears often have a "leader" of laughter that comes first, because all of us have been made embarrassed about our discharge, so always be happy to help your clients get started laughing, even though it is other discharge that they are after. Be happy if they laugh because the other discharges will follow right behind. I didn't pursue it with L— because I need to finish my talk.

R—: I have found as a counselor that if the client says one thing, such as "I am so alone," and then I say, "You're not alone," often the client does not discharge. (Much group laughter) Is that not contradicting the pattern?

HJ: To use "opposite" words to contradict a pattern seems an obvious thing to do, but it works in general only with the most eager or with the most shut-down clients. The reason why it doesn't work most of the time is that the client has been trying to do this for years, and the whole area has become calloused. "I am no good," "I am good," "I am no good" goes the internal argument with the pattern. This has been going on for years, and the entire area is numb. All the pattern's defenses are over here resisting this approach. If you ask the person to say, "I am good," the pattern's voice will say, "Aw, to heck with that, I'm no good and I know it," but if you ask, "Would you say, 'Once upon a time I had a small, good intention, even though I couldn't carry it out'?", the pattern isn't set for that, the slight contradiction slips in, and the client begins to discharge.

Question: It seems to me that the contradiction has to be elicited from the client him/herself. If you provide the contradiction, it doesn't necessarily provide discharge, but when you echo what the client says, like you just did, the client comes back with a contradiction him/herself. For example, "I am not alone." The client says, "I am not alone," and you say, "You probably are," and the client laughs, because the client can then think of a list of contradictions.

HJ: Yes, but the first thing you said isn't quite true. Most of the contradiction will need to be furnished by the counselor. In the elders' caucus last night—can I talk about it, E—?

E—: Yes.

HJ: E— was set to lead the group against women feeling that they weren't good looking anymore when they got older, and she did a great job of exhorting people to resist those feelings. "What has been your big experience against it? I think we should just take a stand against this!" There wasn't a lot of discharge, so I butted in. It took a little time to do it, but I asked her to admit that she was ugly. *(Laughter)* I didn't look at her like I thought she was ugly, and I had enough of a relationship with her that she knows I don't think she's ugly, but the idea of lightheartedly counting the wrinkles and the crow's feet became very, very funny, and she got more and more beautiful by the minute. The only thing that was threatening her with ugliness was the strain on her face from defensively insisting tha she wasn't ugly. She looks just wonderful this morning. If we get rigid as we try to think of contradicting the client's pattern, we see the client's pattern, and we wonder how to contradict it, and we think, "Ah ha, here it is, a brick wall in plain sight. How does one contradict that brick wall? Ah ha, client, lower your head and butt that wall." *(Laughter)* We wind up blaming the client because the client looks at the contradiction we suggest and says, "Uh uh. No thank you." *(Laughter)* If we insist that they do it, they do it numbly, unawarely. They're mainly occupied with thoughts about how stupidly we're counseling them. We forget that a pattern cannot bear *any* contradiction. If the pattern says, "I'm no good," and you can, instead, offer the suggestion that you had a vague report that they were one millionth of one percent not bad, the pattern will begin to discharge. Once you get discharge started, you can add more contradiction, and keep piling it on, but keep them *believable* contradictions.

This is what's wrong with the heavy-handed contradiction. It isn't believable. A client says, "I'm no good," and you say, "I want you to say, 'I'm the most wonderful person that ever lived,'" he or she will look at you like you're out of your mind. It's impossible for the client to get any belief through the heaviness.

Question: It's not clear how what you said contradicted "ugly."

HJ: The pattern was not, by this time, "feeling ugly." It was "defending against the possibility of being ugly"—a defensive posture. That was the pattern. If, when you look at it, you conclude that the pattern was one of "feeling ugly," you miss the boat. All her dramatizations were a defense against considering the possibility of ugliness, see? So I get her to quit defending. I asked, "How's your ugliness this morning?"—and discharge started. Now, a week or two later, I may drop by and say, "I've always thought you were beautiful," just to remove any lingering invalidation that might have stuck in there. But the point is that you contradict the actual distress.

E—: You did say afterwards that I was good-looking.

HJ: A little bit. *(E— laughs; group laughter.)* Now she laughed much harder at that than if I had passionately insisted that she was beautiful, because my tone of voice indicates that I do not share her tension about her looks. That's the big thing. When I tell J— I don't care if she dies or not, there may be a little wince ("My God, Harvey, I thought you were my buddy"), but the main thing is, somebody in the situation doesn't share her worries about dying. That's why she laughed a little bit, and if we'd kept on with it, there'd be shakes.

"A COMMITMENT" IS A SERIOUS PROMISE TO ACT AT ALL TIMES AGAINST ANY DISTRESS. SUCH A COMMITMENT ACCELERATES RE-EMERGENCE. That's short, but it touches the heart of the meaning of the very powerful commitment. It is a promise to take the direction of one's life away from the patterns, a promise made to be kept, not just used in session, but to be kept all the time. When the commitment first began working, it certainly looked like most of us would re-emerge quickly. It looked like we could finish up re-emergence. What has happened instead is that the forgetting power of the pattern has moved in, and the commitments are not being used consistently. The only remedy for that is to remember to use them consistently.

D—: This is something that I get confused about, or perhaps I have trouble with some of the words used in counseling. Telling someone to act against distress, for some of us who use it as a general way for trying to deal with distress, doesn't seem to discharge the patterns that we have. In other words, I wind up not trying to re-emerge, but just sort of grimly holding to an anti-feelings direction.

HJ: Trying to make more shoes per shift?

D—: Well, I always try to do that.

HJ: It isn't a good contradiction, D—, if that's what it does. Instead, would you promise me, for example, that you will always pat yourself on the back and give yourself a little gift at the end of every day for what a good person you've been?

D—: I'll try (laughter).

HJ: It's all right to be determined. Ride any pattern into battle until you can get rid of it. Take advantage of your determination pattern. Also, though, will you promise me that you will pat yourself on the back in front of a mirror while smiling at yourself, and give yourself a little present everyday from now on?

D—: No. (Laughter) I'll try.

HJ: Okay. I don't think that's a very brilliant contradiction yet, but we'll find one that will work....

TO EXCHANGE COMMITMENTS BETWEEN TWO COUNSELORS IN A SESSION OR SERIES OF SESSIONS IS TO SIMULTANEOUSLY ENHANCE THINKING AND DISCHARGING BY BOTH PARTIES AND CONTINUALLY INCREASE THE SAFETY IN THE RELATIONSHIP. I'm talking now about the exchanged commitment. It's extremely powerful. How can one refrain from doing it all the time? I don't know, but I forget to do it!

W—: For me the idea of thinking and discharging happening simultaneously is clear in terms of an exchanged commitment. Can you say something about the counselor discharging, to shake off some of the numbness, to be there for the client, also in situations where it's not an exchange of commitments?

HJ: Whenever the counselor can discharge and still pay attention to the client, it accelerates the process. In general, it takes considerable safety before this can take place. You have to have a very warm, trusting relationship with the other person, or you have to set up the counseling in some such safety-enhancing form as the exchange of commitment. We can't achieve it by telling people to. We can say, "It's great if you can do it. Never hold back your discharge if you can continue to pay attention to the client at the same time," but I don't think we can do it as a direction. It takes the safety of (a) making close, warm friendships, having a deep relationship with as many Co-Counselors as possible (which I spoke about earlier this morning), and (b) using such forms as the exchange of commitments.

THE GOAL OF IMMORTALITY, TAKEN SERIOUSLY, CONTRADICTS AND PERMITS THE DISCHARGE

OF IMPORTANT DISTRESS FOR EVERY CLIENT. IT WILL CERTAINLY ENHANCE THE POSSIBILITY OF, AND MAY POSSIBLY LEAD TO, IMMORTALITY, TO LIVING INDEFINITELY. See the journal **Forever and Ever** No. 1 for more details. *(Laughter)*

THE EXPLOSIVELY RESTIMULATING CHARACTER OF SEXUALITY DISTRESS IN OUR PRESENT CULTURES MAY BE SAFELY DE-FUSED (THAT IS, THE RESTIMULATING PROPENSITY MAY BE CONTAINED) AND THE DISTRESS DISCHARGED, THROUGH PERSISTENT COUNSELING RESTRICTED TO THE EARLIEST SEXUAL MEMORIES, THE EARLIEST MEMORIES CONNECTED TO SEX IN ANY WAY AT ALL. This is the safe path through one of the stickiest swamps that we have to traverse. It was a great practical discovery when we finally realized it. We can save an enormous amount of time otherwise spent restimulating ourselves and getting away from restimulation. See **The Benign Reality** (pages 185-200) for a more detailed discussion.

Question: I'm curious to know if the work that was done in the Incest Topic Group was done from this approach.

HJ: I'm sure it was, but we won't go into that now.

Voice: It was.

RELATIONSHIP EXPECTATIONS BETWEEN HUMANS NEED TO BE CAREFULLY DEFINED BY EACH PERSON IN THE RELATIONSHIP, WITH EACH ONE'S SEPARATE EXPECTATIONS CLEARLY STATED BY BOTH PARTIES, AND THE SUBSET OF THOSE THAT CAN BE AGREED UPON CLEARLY DEFINED IN ORDER FOR THE RELATIONSHIP TO OPERATE WELL. This was in **Present Time** No. 43—the article by Tim. This is a profound breakthrough. He did the talk two years ago; I only heard it three months ago—I got the paper, read it, and immediately decided I would xerox copies of this article and give it to anyone before I allowed them within twenty feet of me. I may not be quoting this exactly, but what Tim said was that each of us bring his or her own definition of what he or she expects from the relationship to the other person, and assumes, without the slightest shred of evidence, that this is what the other person expects and agrees to. Often the two sets of expectations have very little in common. Carefully spelling out each set and finding out which expectations are in common and agreeing upon those and agreeing not to agree on the others, not to try to fulfill the others, is crucial to a good relationship. I wish I'd known that when I was eleven years old.

Question: Couldn't this lead to rigidity? It takes a long time before you know each other, and you shouldn't start with assumptions of what the other person is like before you're acquainted. In order to have expectations, you need to know what the other person is like.

HJ: Yes, but you've not understood what I've said. This may be because I didn't say it well enough. The unaware assumptions are already there. These are what we're trying to get out in the open where we can look at them. Some of them may be patterned, some of them may be simply lack of information or misinformation, but the assumptions are already there, already turned upon the other person. What Tim is proposing is that they be revealed and communicated clearly, and only those which are agreed to by both parties remain as expectations. See **Present Time** No. 43, the first article in the magazine. It will make a big difference in our relationships.

Comment from audience: I think the key to avoiding that rigidity is understanding this principle so we can take charge from the beginning not to intrude our expectations, but first allow the getting-acquainted to happen, and then as that develops, the other communication can begin.

RATIONAL CLOSE FRIENDSHIPS WITH MANY MEMBERS OF THE OTHER GENDER ARE DESIRABLE AND POSSIBLE OF ATTAINMENT FOR ANY WOMAN OR ANY MAN. Beginning theory on this is in the current **Present Time** (No. 44): "Close Friendships Between Women and Men." I refer you to that article for expansion of this point.

(From the audience) For the benefit of those of us who haven't seen one, I want to see a demonstration on the Framework.

HJ: The next point is about the Framework. **A CLEAR STATEMENT, WRITTEN IN THE FIRST PLACE BY THE COUNSELOR, OF THE REALITY OF THE CLIENT'S LIFE HISTORY, GOALS, AND RELATIONSHIP TO THE TOTAL ENVIRONMENT, WRITTEN FROM A POSITION OF TRIUMPHANT APPRECIATION AND EAGER EXPECTATION (A FRAMEWORK) WILL ENHANCE AND STABILIZE THE RE-EMERGENCE OF THE CLIENT.** See **Present Time** No. 43.

> I'm tempted. Would you like to see the first Framework as it has seasoned? C—, come up. This is the woman around whom the Framework first grew, on a long drive from Albuquerque into the Jemez Mountains. She was driving the car, and I was giving her what seemed to be just directions to start with but which kept growing into this breakthrough phenomenon.
>
> *(Proceeds with demonstration, asking for comments as she proceeds through her Framework. Following the demonstration with C—, a demonstration with S— on her Framework.)*

The next insight is about what we've called the Panel. This is an arrangement for representatives of oppressed groups to speak directly to the general population and to each other on six points: What's been positive about being Wygelian, a member of the group from which you speak? (I say "Wygelian" to mean a member of any oppressed group.) Inside the oppression which you have endured, what's been positive about being a Wygelian? What's been hard about being a Wygelian? Why are you proud of being a Wygelian? What do Wygelians wish other people understood about them? What do Wygelians want other people never to say or do again? What do Wygelians require of others if they're to be effective allies for Wygelians?

THE "PANEL" PRESENTATION GREATLY ENHANCES COMMUNICATION ACROSS OPPRESSION BARRIERS. There's a general principle surfacing here that will enhance our work in this area.

Usually the "Panels" have been a dozen or fewer people. At the Evanston Teachers' and Leaders' Workshop we tried it with eighty-five people. One evening we arranged the eighty-five people in a big circle. Each one was asked to speak about only one oppression, and to speak about these six points. There was some distraction by patterns. One or two tried to "sell" their philosophies to the listening eighty-four. A few obviously felt a great pull to tell the whole story of their lives once they had this captive audience. In spite of these distractions (which I was slow to interrupt), we listened with great interest from 7 until 10:30 the first night, and from 7 until a quarter 'til eleven the second night. (Eighty-five people is a lot of people.) It was one of the most moving and unifying experiences I have ever seen. It appeared as if every one of that group felt close and at ease with every other member of the group when it was done. I am eager to try it with a small non-RC wide-world group of, say, six or so people. I think you can do this with any group (and they'll be delighted to have the experience) and tear down barriers between them wholesale. It's very powerful. This is what we have called the Panel. It was described in **Present Time**. It's also described in **The Benign Reality**. It can be applied in a great variety of flexible forms.

Question: Are you now omitting the statement by each panel member that he or she assumes that the people listening are his or her allies?

No. This is a worthwhile act in itself. We started out expecting people to say, "I'm going to assume you're my allies." Then we found, in a series of workshops, that practically no panel member could say that sincerely. To attempt to say it is fine. Each panel member makes a statement as close to that one as she or he can say with sincerity.

FOR CONSISTENT IMPROVEMENT OF COUNSELING, EACH PERSON'S PERFORMANCE AS COUNSELOR NEEDS TO BE REGULARLY SUBMITTED TO CRITICAL APPRAISAL BY ONE'S PEERS. The Golden Circle marked a great turn-around in ending the tolerance of bad counseling from each other on the part of leaders in many of our Communities. It was awkward, cumbersome, time-consuming, but it led to a flexible, easy tactic which will be useful in every session.

The Golden Circle consists of a group of Co-Counselors choosing one of their number as client and then taking turns counseling that client while the others watch, by

(a) Offering a validation to the client that is so accurately matched to the client's hurt from not being appreciated that it produces discharge, and, in a later round,

(b) Offering a direction to the client that is so accurately and believably counter to the client's distress that it produces discharge.

Success in these two stages requires that the Counselor accurately observe the client and the client's distress, think well about formulating the contradicting validation or direction, and be courageous and effective in offering it.

After each attempt the other members of the group offer their explanations of why a particular attempt worked or didn't work, with the client speaking next-to-last and the teacher or leader of the group speaking last. The group member whose attempt is being evaluated is encouraged to discharge during the evaluation and to counsel on any revelations later.

The Golden Circle crunched through the self-conscious defensiveness about bad counseling which had accumulated. Remember how uncomfortable we were at first to actually submit our counseling to critical evaluation of our peers?

Getting through this protective, defensive embarrassment has made it fairly easy for a counselor now, at the end of any session, particularly a demonstration, to ask, "How was that good counseling and how could it have been improved?" Continual improvement of counseling will result from the discussion if this is done.

Comment: I thought that instead of using the word "improved" you could use the word "different" because it invites a wider variety of creative suggestions.

HJ: Yes, I think that is good. Daniel made this point the first time we tried it. He said, "I cannot say how it could have been improved; I can tell you how I would have done it differently." That's a valid form of comment.

Question: Does the counselor or the client speak last?

HJ: I think the counselor needs to speak last. The client's voice is the compelling one, but the counselor needs to speak in terms of his own learning after hearing all the others. The process works especially for the improvement of the counselor.

Comment: Asking how the counseling could have been different would be a mistake in some Communities I know because the people will offer lots of different criticisms, but not improvements.

HJ: I think that if you use the word "different" you must ask, "How would *you* have done it differently," referring to that specific person. I think that will keep them on their mettle enough that they won't just offer patterned criticism, or, if they do, it will be noticeable.

ANY PERSON'S FUNCTIONING IN ANY JOB WILL IMPROVE IF THE PERSON CAN BE LISTENED TO WITH ATTENTION BY FELLOW WORKERS WHILE SHE OR HE SPEAKS TO (a) HER OR HIS STRONG POINTS IN THE JOB AND (b) NEEDED IMPROVEMENTS, AND THEN HEARS THE OTHERS' COMMENTS ON THE SAME TWO POINTS. Self-estimation is a very powerful process. It is a tool that people will eagerly use in work situations in the wide world. To use your counseling skills during a lunch hour chat, to bring out how each one is a good worker, and how each one does a good job, and how it could be improved, is to unleash great forces for unity, communication, and self-esteem among workers.

TO BLAME ANOTHER HUMAN FOR ONE'S DISTRESSES OR TROUBLES IS TO ACCEPT POWER-

LESSNESS FOR ONESELF. I've talked about this so far only with the International Reference Committee here at this Conference, and we all agree that it needs to be clarified more, but there is agreement that it's important, whenever possible, to decide not to blame. Essentially, I have noticed that, among thousands of clients, the ones who blame and reproach others for their distress, even if their blames and reproaches are restricted to the actual agents of the hurts that were put on them or the ones who actually perpetrated the hurts on them, are in trouble. They sometimes seem to have an easier life, they seem to be comfortable blaming others, they seem to be carefree compared to the rest of us. Yet they pay a very, very heavy price for it in powerlessness. Those, on the other hand, who accidentally, or possibly by merit (it's very difficult to know), decided not to put reproaches or blame on anyone else, not to pass on the hurt, but to accept the responsibility for dealing with it, even though they sometimes mistakenly blame themselves a lot in the process, and sometimes seem to have tougher lives, live longer and everybody likes them better. They're much closer to re-emergence. I don't know what to suggest that you do with this, except perhaps to recommend that you and your Co-Counselors examine any points in your life where you decided your difficulties were someone else's fault, and direct special attention to discharging those, so that you get your full integrity back a little faster. I have no experience to offer on this yet, just the observation that those who go the blaming way "seem" to have it easier but really pay a big price in temporarily lost humanness as a result.

A GOOD THEORY AROUSES MUCH GREATER EXPECTATIONS THAN ITS PRACTICE CURRENTLY SATISFIES, AND THIS IS DESIRABLE FOR THE GROWTH OF BOTH THE THEORY AND THE PRACTICE. The gap between the expectations which our theory arouses, and the achievements which our practice furnishes, has been the excuse for a great deal of expressed disappointment, inactivity, and even hostility from some former or present Co-Counselors. Perhaps this disappointment can be avoided by clear communication in the beginning that this gap exists, that as our practice improves our theory is also going to improve and stay ahead of the practice. Trying to close that gap is what improves the practice of counseling, but this is the responsibility of the person, himself or herself, and it is not the responsibility of the Community or other Co-Counselors to do it for him or her without the person's own efforts. Such disappointment is not realistic.

THERE ARE NO "SHOULD'S" IN THE UNIVERSE—NO OBLIGATIONS. YOU DO NOT "OWE" ANYONE ANYTHING. YOUR OWN FRESH THINKING WILL ALWAYS LEAD YOU TO DO A BETTER JOB FOR YOURSELF AND OTHERS THAN ANY "SHOULD'S" WHICH YOU TRY TO LIVE UP TO. This is very close to your freedom to choose your own viewpoint. People seem able to hear and act upon the insight that "There are no should's in the universe."

Question: Does that exclude parents, in the parenting role?

HJ: No. This is where I first realized this. I had many older parents come to me as professional clients, who spent a great deal of their time with me complaining bitterly about their grown-up children. They said they had educated them, they had fed them, and now they never came around to visit them. "I don't get any support from them." This irritated me, and I became very clear at pointing out to these parents that the obligation between parent and child was strictly one-way, that the child does not owe the parent anything. I was very firm about it, and I got a lot of discharge from them this way. I would say, "But, of course, the parent is obligated to the child. You chose to bring the child into the world. Its care is up to you," and I was very confident about this.

It was many years later, in trying to get out of my feelings of obligation to every dependent client demanding that I give him or her free counseling forever, working step-by-step with my counselor, that I reached a point of saying that "I am not obligated to anyone, except, of course, my children." After a while that wasn't getting discharge, and by analogy with the complete appreciation of oneself, or being totally in charge, I decided to risk saying in a session that I didn't even "owe" my children anything. It took only three repetitions and one burst of tears to realize that, of course, I would do anything for my children that I possibly could, rationally. I didn't need heavy feelings of obligation to make me try to be a good parent, that the obligation assumption was rather getting in the way of my best parenting.

TRUST YOUR OWN THINKING. No one else's thinking about you and your affairs can possibly be accurate enough and well-informed enough about you to be a guide for your decisions. (The only situations in which you should ever trust someone else's thinking about you [temporarily] is in accepting a direction to contradict a chronic pattern; and even here the direction should bring discharge in a reasonable time to continue to be accepted.)

TRUST YOUR OWN THINKING. It will take thoughtful examination of your thinking to distinguish between your thinking and your patterned compulsions or assumptions, but you will always be able to tell the difference if you check.

TRUST YOUR OWN THINKING. You *will* make mistakes if you do anything meaningful at all, but if you are acting on your own thinking, the results will quickly be noticed by you and you will correct the mistake promptly. If you have accepted someone else's thinking as your guide, you have already stopped thinking for yourself and the mistakes will go uncorrected much longer.

TRUST YOUR OWN THINKING. Trust your intuitions. Check on, but respect, your hunches, your "gut feelings."

TRUST YOUR OWN THINKING.

These are at least most of the key concepts and insights which Re-evaluation Counseling has achieved to date.

A Program for Action

The Key Points of Emphasis For the RC Communities in 1982-83

Meetings of Regional Reference People were held this past summer in the Midwest USA, Western States USA, East Coast USA, British Isles, and the Continent of Europe. The current situation in the world and in RC was discussed at length and the following recommendations were agreed upon:

I. DECISIVE IMPROVEMENT IN COUNSELING AT ALL LEVELS

A. Newer Co-Counselors

1. Clarify, refresh, and up-date Fundamentals teaching. Keep the nature of the Co-Counseling relationship clear. (Two or more intelligences dealing with *one* person's distress.)

2. Use summarizing "triad" of "How to counsel."

   a. Pay enough attention to the client to see clearly what the distress is.

   b. Think of all possible ways to contradict that distress.

   c. Contradict that distress sufficiently. When done sufficiently, the client will always discharge.

3. Use summarizing "triad" of "How to become a good counselor."

   a. Be counseled well. Discharge your distress.

   b. Integrate the theory until it becomes "second nature." Read, re-read, and re-read the literature.

   c. *Decide* to be completely for the *client. Decide* to leave all your patterns out of your client's session. *Act* on that *permanently*.

Appeared in **Present Time** No. 49.

4. Make plain from the beginning the requirements for Community membership.

5. Offer and model decisive counseling. Expect and require rapid advance into competence and leadership.

6. Use each Fundamentals class as the start of a new, rapidly-spreading, leadership-producing International Community.

B. Experienced Co-Counselors

1. Estimate (How has this been good counseling and how could it have been improved?) all sessions, in groups when possible. Work to eliminate *all counselors' patterns* from sessions.

2. Guarding against dependencies, extend the Co-Counseling commitment beyond the session, to an all-the-time relationship. (This does *not* mean violating the No-Socializing principle. It means *thinking* about each other continually.)

3. Expect decisions of each other to re-emerge rapidly and completely, to no longer tolerate any influence of patterns on the conduct of one's life. Completely clean up at least one incident.

4. Re-sharpen once-powerful techniques if they become dull and sloppy.

5. Read, re-read, and re-read all RC literature continuously.

C. Leaders

1. Divide and spread the functions of leadership as far as possible *as a counseling tool,* to motivate re-emergence.

2. When a mutually-respectful, well-functioning relationship has been established between a group of leaders, *fall in love with each other.* Use counseling to remove any barriers to the process. "All for one and one for all." Express that love in tough, decisive counseling.

3. Adopt a two-legged stance, always a leader *in the wide world,*

and always a leader *in RC,* always *at the same time.*

4. Model the reclaiming of power, the adopting of new viewpoints, the interruption and contradiction of internalized oppression in every group.

5. Become and function as an expert on every group's oppression and liberation. Be the clear "voice from outside" against every internalized oppression, the "leader of allies" for every oppressed group.

II. BUILDING NEW COMMUNITIES AROUND HOMOGENEOUS (ALL "WYGELIANS") GROUPS OF LEADERS FROM EVERY SECTION OF THE GENERAL POPULATION. ("WYGELIAN" IS HERE USED TO MEAN A MEMBER OF A PARTICULAR DISTINCTIVE GROUP, E.G. WOMEN, BLACKS, YOUNG PEOPLE, ELDERS, ETC.)

A. The best counselor and leader available (not necessarily from within the group) should meet with each group, to build and develop a group of leaders who have, or will acquire, constituencies.

B. Such meetings to be held "on call," not regularly, nor, usually, often.

C. The agenda for such meetings should include:

1. Check-up on past individual commitments to leadership activity;

2. A general exchange of information on Wygelian affairs and working out programs and policies;

3. Individuals making commitments for the next period;

4. Demonstration counseling of each leader on whatever he or she is having difficulty with, *or* counseling on internalized oppression with the whole group.

D. Hold occasional one-day workshops where these leaders' groups caucus separately and then are listened to by each other.

E. Qualifications for being members of such leaders groups: They must be RCers, must be Wygelians, must be a leader or desiring to be a leader: a) in RC generally, b) in Wygelian RC, c) in Wygelian wide world affairs, or d) in wide world affairs generally.

F. Develop constituencies for all such leaders. The completely-representative RC Communities of the future (form still undefined) will develop out of these constituencies.

III. MAKE THE USE OF RC LITERATURE CENTRAL TO ALL OUR ACTIVITIES.

A. Designate literature agents and librarians for all Areas and outside organized Area classes.

B. Establish depots of *all* in-print RC literature in all new Areas.

C. Organize support groups widely for learning or relearning to read.

D. Invite even wider participation in writing for the journals.

E. Secure wide distribution and sale of RC journals *outside* RC.

F. Encourage students to report on literature in all RC classes.

G. Raise the circulation of *Sisters*, *Men*, *Working for a Living*, *Classroom*, and *Wide World Changing* to 8,000 copies; of *Present Time* to 15,000 copies; of other journals to 5,000 copies.

H. Make prompt, responsible payment for all RC literature a universal habit.

IV. "FERTILIZE" AND "PRUNE" THE COMMUNITIES.

A. Certify "hordes" of new teachers from among experienced Co-Counselors.

B. Encourage all teachers to view each Fundamentals class as the start of a new International Community. Challenge all students to become teachers and leaders quickly.

C. Establish rational financing throughout the Communities. Assist the Foundation leadership in concentrating more on raising money *outside* the Communities.

D. Insist on wide sharing of leadership functions.

E. Divide Areas that are flourishing as soon as new leadership is showing hopeful signs of being available.

F. After a whole-hearted effort has been made to counsel and invigorate the leadership, dissolve all existing Areas which remain Areas in pretense only.

G. Urgently recommend that all teachers holding credentials teach *Fundamentals* classes regularly.

H. Suspend teaching credentials where the teacher has not actively taught classes for more than six months (except in special circumstances).

I. Recognize and establish "leaders groups" as a basic organizational form in RC, comparable in importance to the "class" and "support group." Any group of leaders and would-be leaders in a common field (teachers, assistant teachers, support group leaders, Wygelians, Reference Persons, etc.) should meet at irregular intervals with the best leader and counselor available being responsible for the meeting and with this kind of agenda:

1. Report by individual leaders on successes, unsolved problems, carrying out of previously-set goals and commitments.

2. Discussion of the general situation in the area of their leadership, review of and, if necessary, revision of policy, reaffirming of previous, and setting new, goals for the group.

3. Setting of goals, making of commitments and announcement of intentions (with notes taken) by each individual leader for the next period.

4. Demonstration counseling of each leader by the person in charge of the meeting on whatever material he or she currently needs skillful, tough counseling on *or* alternatively, a demonstration of counseling on a distress common to the whole group (internalized oppression, etc.).

J. End the concept of "co-leading" or "co-teaching" in RC. Eliminate all "A-frame" leadership and replace it with "I beam" leadership. Recognize what a camouflage "co-leading" has been for helplessness, irresponsibility, powerlessness, and "blaming." Recruit and train one's own "perfect Co-Counselors" for oneself. Restrict the meaning of the word "support" in RC to a) help in doing work, and b) good counseling.

K. Organize "in-RC" support groups to be primarily for discharge on the distresses most easily discharged in the company of people with that commonality. (Recognize that some distresses for a Wygelian, for example, discharge more easily with non-Wygelians.) Keep such support groups small (under 8) to allow enough time for each member to discharge well. Refer leadership and policy discussions to leaders' group meetings.

V. ELIMINATE NUCLEAR WEAPONS FROM THE WORLD.

A. Discharge our own numb terror of nuclear holocaust.

1. Step outside, and assist each other to step outside all our distresses. Choose new viewpoints. Reclaim our power.

2. "It won't happen because..." (posture, facial expression, and tone of voice, tone of voice, tone of voice modeled by the counselor.)

B. Use and teach our tools of discharge, rational discussion, modeling and reaching agreement, in the wide-world "Preserve the World" movements.

1. Offer to conduct workshops for activists.

2. Spread the use of humorous songs, sayings, poems, speeches, both anti-nuclear-weapons and, satirically, "pro-nuclear-weapons."

3. Use your skills to solve the problems that develop in the wide-world movements.

C. Join and lead wide-world organizations and actions.

1. Whenever possible, lead by offering policies and solving problems, rather than by taking leadership posts. (Preserve, rather than compete with, existing wide-world leaders.) When absolutely necessary, take leadership posts and lead resolutely.

2. Help establish one-point (no nuclear weapons *or* no new nuclear weapons) coalitions of existing organizations as widely as possible. Propose special occasions where all such groups will listen to each others' *full* programs respectfully for agreed-upon amounts of time. Propose other coalitions on other issues for all groups who can agree on these other issues. (Keep the coalition from disintegrating from the pressure of some groups to force the other groups to support them on these *other* issues through the threat of withdrawal and attack.)

3. Work for actions rather than discussions.

4. Devise ingenious ways of appealing to *every* section of the population.

5. Devise ingenious ways of actually making the use of nuclear arms *impossible.*

6. Propose, in stages, bolder and bolder actions to actually *remove* all governments from office who insist on continuing with nuclear armaments.

7. Establish people-to-people contacts of all sorts with anti-nuclear weapon forces on *both* sides of the "Iron Curtain."

8. Win the time for us all that we need to solve all the world's other problems, as we surely can with the knowledge we now have.

VI. RAPIDLY EXPAND THE USE OF RC KNOWLEDGE IN THE WIDE WORLD.

A. Encourage Co-Counselors to teach basic RC theory and practice wherever the opportunity exists without (necessarily) labeling it "RC."

1. Encourage all Co-Counselors to teach one-to-one, from the very beginning.

2. Present RC ideas in the wide world as your own, rather than as "RC."

3. Initiate and teach classes with RC content, (or train, manage, or organize people in RC ways) using any description or title that suits the situation. (Feel free to use RC literature as "reference" material.)

B. Open Fundamentals classes to all persons who wish to attend and are not disruptive, remembering that class attendance does *not* automatically mean Community membership. (Screenings for classes and for Community membership are at very different levels.)

C. Encourage each Co-Counselor to organize "wide-world support groups," both formal and informal, at every opportunity among the people with whom he or she associates in the wide world. Necessary and desirable features are: Each person having a time to be listened to without interruption; each person helped to say something positive *first* before negatives dominate; an invitation to enlarge the group by inviting others; division of the group when it grows unwieldy. RC need never be mentioned, save to individuals who become intrigued and seek to know more. Opportunities for such "support groups" include lunch hours at work, car pools or any group riding together, tea or coffee hours in the neighborhood after the children are in school, and meetings of "the gang at the pub." (Do not drink any alcohol yourself or it won't work.)

D. Maintain and build regular (monthly?) "introduction to RC" evenings or public lectures.

1. Plan a (good) regular location and regular time.

2. Publicize these as public events.

3. Strive for repeat attendance. ("Come back next month. You are welcome to bring your friends.")

4. View these as primarily for sharing basic information with the public. Answer questions or solve problems in demonstrations willingly. View the recruitment of class members or (eventually) Community members as only incidental to the information-sharing function.

E. Write with a rational viewpoint for newspapers, magazines, radio, television, etc. on the issues confronting people. Write and publish books.

F. Collect, share information about, publicize, exchange and promote already-published books by RCers or by allies.

G. Support the writing of a new basic book giving the fundamental theory and practice of Co-Counseling in fresh language, which will mention RC only at the end "for those who wish more advanced knowledge."

What Is Our Present Position? What Do We Know? What Are We Doing And About To Do? A Summary

Schloss Heiligen Hoven I Workshop
January 1983, 9 AM

We live in an interesting universe. Some logicians apparently have proved it is the only universe. They have assumed that other universes could co-exist and have found the implications of this run into a contradiction with some known facts. So we have reason to think that it is the only universe.

It seems to be infinitely interesting. We live on a very beautiful planet, condensed out of the heavier elements in the solar cloud, and assuming a form that has been favorable towards the emergence of complex chemical interactions that could produce large, self-replicating molecules.

These simple forms of life, once begun, expressed the upward trend in the universe toward complexity and, eventually, meaning, and modified the planet in their progress to make it even more beautiful and more satisfying for themselves. The green plants solved the question of trapping energy from the sun and transformed the atmosphere into an oxygen atmosphere. We animals emerged on the support of the green plants. We gained more and more independence of the environment. We became able to move around.

We evolved into millions of different forms. We became larger and more complex. Some forms specialized to fill every nook and cranny of the environment. Some of the less-specialized forms concentrated on developing more and more complex nervous systems and some developed such central systems as made possible a great deal of freedom and individuality.

Appeared in **Present Time** No. 51.

Our species and its forerunners finally came up with nerve networks so complex as to give us freedom to create new responses at every instant.

The best scientists in the field are filled with awe and wonder when contemplating our central nervous systems. They know only a little about them, but they know that they know only a little, and they *can* tell us that our forty billion neurons—nerve cells—interact with each other in almost unbelievably complex ways. Only a few hundred of these forty billion nerve cells bring messages into the central nervous system from our sense organs. Only a few hundred of them take commands from the central nervous system to our muscles and our glands. The other forty billion neurons just sit there and talk to each other unceasingly. Apparently the most foolish act that we ever performed was a marvel of complex achievement.

From these tremendously complex nervous systems which evolved in the beautiful web of life on this wonderful planet in this interesting universe came the ability not only to think—that is, to have fresh, new ideas constantly—but also the ability to be aware, to actually notice what's going on, to think about thinking while thinking, to not only cope, but also to enjoy.

This wonderful heritage, this treasure accumulated by billions of years of universe transformation and evolution, is a gift deposited with us upon our conception, birth, and growth. To really awarely contemplate such treasure is to realize one is possessed of incredible good fortune.

A VULNERABILITY

This ability to think and be aware had a vulnerability, an Achilles' heel, from the beginning. This function is apparently so delicate that defeats or hurts of any kind cause it to be interrupted and, when interrupted, a more primitive form of behavior which we inherited from our ancestors takes over.

This more primitive form of behavior, the conditioning, or

acquiring of new patterns of behavior under stress, was no disadvantage to our non-intelligent ancestors: in fact it was useful to them. All other mammals can "learn" in a crude, rigid way through conditioning by tense experiences. For ourselves, however, able to function on the much more complex ability to think *intelligently*, such reversion to the more primitive behavior can easily constitute a disaster. We have called these reversions "distress patterns," and their effects can range from passive dullness and rigidity to the most vicious, destructive acts.

The strange duality of human behavior has puzzled thoughtful people ever since there were thoughtful people. How can human beings be as good as a baby caressing his mother and as vicious as the mass slaughterers that decorate the front pages of our newspapers? How can human beings be so creative and intelligent and right and alongside that be so completely stupid and unaware? People have tried to explain this by separating humans into categories, but that has never been useful. Someone once said that "there's so much bad in the best of us and so much good in the worst of us that it is simply up to the best of us to get along with the rest of us."

We have come to a better understanding of this in the last thirty-two years. Other people around us and in many other parts of the world have reached toward better understandings also. We in this room, and perhaps three hundred thousand more, have achieved the greatest clarity so far.

Is there a profound difference between the human being and the distress pattern which the human acquires? We have concluded: yes, there is a profound difference.

Is the rigid distress pattern behavior inherent or spontaneous within human beings or is it only acquired by hurt? We have concluded that it is only acquired by hurt, that there is nothing inherent about it.

Is the distressed behavior, once acquired, permanent, impossible to be resolved? Or is it something that can be undone? We have concluded that, theoretically at least, it can be completely undone and that any past failures on our part to undo it completely represent only ignorance and lack of resource, not any theoretical impossibility.

A BETTER VIEW OF REALITY

We have thought of our present struggles as parallel to that of some kind of developing organisms. We hatch out into a limited environment of confusion, misinformation, and stupid behavior that surrounds us. We crawl around like caterpillars, in search of our real natures, in spite of the surrounding confusion. Occasionally we get to the edge of the confusion and glimpse a little daylight from the larger, surrounding reality. We share information with each other. We encourage each other. We put together a picture of reality as best we can that contradicts and pierces the confusion around us. We put the individual insights that we acquire after discharge together with other people's insights, and more and more confidently assert that the overall picture which we construct from these insights is much closer to the actual reality than the picture of bleak confusion and distress which the society around us offers us. We have learned, even when appearances and feelings seem to justify despair, to say confident words. When we find a new way to see outside the confusion, we excitedly call to our fellows to look with us. Now some of us are beginning to insist that the time must be close at hand when we must change decisively, must *reject* all the patterned confusion that has surrounded us, and act on our own recovered sense of reality and with our full power. We propose that we do this before some very sick patterns blow up our lovely world.

THE SOURCES OF HURT

Since we assume people's inherently wonderful, intelligent, creative, good, cooperative, benign nature, then from whence came the contradictory appearances which we offer to each other? What is the source of the hurts which create this great ball and cluster of distress patterns in which we have been enmeshed and from which we struggle to emerge?

Accidents are certainly the source of some of them. A tumble off the porch, a slipping ladder, a drunken driver, a meteorite, an epidemic disease that kills a loved one—all these can leave distress recordings.

Contagion is certainly another source. We have clearly observed that the victim of a distress pattern is almost always "pulled" (whether he or she gives in to the urge or not) to search for a kind of "comfort" by passing the injury or insult on to another person. The man who was beaten when a small child for spilling a glass of milk observably feels a great pull to beat his own son when that son spills milk. This is apparently in the nature of the pattern. A great many hurts are passed on by contagion. The undischarged hurt tends to hurt another person.

The hurt is passed on in all kinds of subtle ways as well as by the gross re-enactment. There is an interesting article in **Present Time** No. 50 about a small child observing her mother crushing a beetle and suffering a tremendous loss of confidence in the universe at this murder of one form of life by another. Almost all Co-Counselors who persist very far in their re-emergence discover they must discharge a great weight of discouragement and hopelessness from their very early years, acquired just from observing how human beings' actions in general contradict the child's own picture of what reality should be.

ORGANIZED IMPOSITION OF DISTRESS

The third great source of these distress patterns is an "organized" one. Long ago, in struggling to master our environments, we agreed to organize ourselves in rigid ways in order to secure more cooperation and achieve more success. These rigid, structured, organizational agreements included an agreement by the great majority of people to submit to a small minority and be exploited by them. The agreements were imposed by violence and threat of death but apparently were continued, at least in part, because, overall, members of our species survived in greater numbers when organized that way than they did in free, independent, less cooperative existences.

The great majority of our ancestors at one time submitted to being slaves while at the same time a small minority of our ancestors adopted the roles of slave-owners and agreed to enter and live within slave-owner patterns. Both kinds of existence warped and limited the person's essential humanness. Both the slave-owner and the slave gave up a great deal of their human potential; but the population as a whole succeeded in surviving famines better.

Later, when the class society was modified, the great majority of our ancestors agreed, under pressure, to be serfs, while a minority became nobles. Both groups accepted severe restrictions on their humanness to do so but economically they exploited the environment more successfully.

Later, almost all of our ancestors agreed, however reluctantly and under whatever lashes of hunger and coercion, to become wage-workers, selling their labor as if it were a commodity in return for a part of the value which their labor produced, while a small number became owning-class, controlled the factories, mines, transport, and banks, and purchased the labor of the working-class majority.

All these societies, all of them to this day, maintained themselves (until they collapsed) only by forcing the human beings within them into rigid roles in which they would carry out the functions which the rigid society assigned them.

It is plain, once we have recognized its existence, that only the distress recording made such rigid societies and such rigid roles possible. Both the slave and the slave-owner had to be thoroughly conditioned by the installation of distress patterns before the rigid slave societies could operate. Both the serf and the noble had to be thoroughly conditioned with distress patterns in order for feudal societies to function. Both the wage-worker and the capitalist must be loaded with specific sorts of distress patterns for capitalism to function longer than a week.

So the societies which humans had invented (or floundered into) in order to master the environment and so survive better in terms of numbers became great organized forces for the systematic installation of distress patterns on the population as a matter of routine. Educational systems were contrived and maintained that educated only in limited ways but that thoroughly conditioned all young people to fit particular rigid roles in a society. It is no accident that the threat of punishment has dominated educational systems until recently (and in some ways still does). It is no accident that threats of violence, of being nailed up on a cross in a slave society, or being run through with the knight's spear in a feudal society, or being laid off work and being unable to find a job in a capitalist society, have played such key roles in the functioning (such as it has been) of these rigid societies.

So we now have a world of four and half billion inhabitants, all of whom are covered with great clusters of distress patterns, many of them submissive patterns, a few of them rigidly rebellious patterns, a few of them arrogant, oppressive patterns, systematically imposed on each generation by the past victims on behalf of the rigid, oppressive society. Much of the world's population is unnecessarily in economic distress, unhappy, confused, unaware, addicted.

TIME FOR A CHANGE

There is another viewpoint from which to take stock of our current world. Having mastered the environment as much as we have, we have tremendous resources. We are overwhelmingly motivated to do things differently. Finally, we have some interesting insights into what our real natures probably are, and at least the beginnings of a theory and collection of tools for regaining these real natures functionally. We have a chance to recover and participate in the kind of relationships which we have always dreamed of having with each other, the possibility of actual rational relationships. We can have a rational society in which no human being ever exploits another human being for economic benefit or patterned gratification. We have some very exciting glimpses that indicate that we humans are much greater, much more able, much more powerful than anyone has suspected.

I could talk at more length about various aspects of this situation, but as someone (a German scholar who was living in England at the time) once said, the point is not just to understand the world, but to do something about it.

ABILITIES INHERENT

Our ability to free ourselves from distress recordings aparently developed at the same time as our flexible intelligence did. We have every reason to think that the small child two million years ago was just as able as the modern small child to cry away or tremble away or laugh away a hurt right after it occurred and thus prevent the retention of a distress pattern, if that small child was permitted to do so. We have good reason to think that every human being that has ever lived always discharged as much as he or she could, whenever, and as soon as, an opportunity was present. We here, in particular, are in the relatively excellent position we are because, up until now, every time there was the slightest chance to discharge, we did so.

Thus our task simply becomes one of providing each other greater opportunities for discharge. Our abilities and skills as clients are already present, ready to operate. Our discoveries of how to be counselors, how to enhance and expedite the discharge and re-evaluation process in another has, of necessity, been somewhat random and characterized by early trial and error, since in great part it required our also being clients to throw off the individual and social conditioning against discharge which had been imposed on us. At this point we can be more concise and more general about what is required.

We early defined the Co-Counseling relationship well as *two or more intelligences paying attention to one person's distress*. If we can achieve that situation, we know quite accurately what to do.

The difficulty with beginners in counseling is always to get the second person, the counselor, to act undistressed and rational in the relationship with the client. At the very frontiers of the most advanced and skillful counseling we are still wrestling with the same phenomenon: how to keep the counselor's distress out of the session; how to make sure that it is *two* or more intelligences dealing with one person's distress, not one and a half, or one and three quarters, or one and seven eighths.

I will be talking about and demonstrating some advanced insights about this at this workshop. First it is probably good to review the fundamental relationship. We can summarize it much better these days than we have ever been able to before.

Most counseling knowledge has been taught and demonstrated, and most of you have learned it, in bits and pieces. In practice the counseling work we do is almost always in bits and pieces. We take a corner off a pattern here in one session and, by the next session, some other problem has become more urgent. Nevertheless, it is always helpful if we can summarize or generalize what we are doing. Such a generalized summary is easier to remember than a mass of details and to remember what we are doing is one of our principal tasks.

THREE INTERFERING EFFECTS

The distress pattern has only three strengths to use against us; otherwise it is an idiot affair, to be treated with contempt. But it *has* three strengths.

It can persist. In fact, as long as it exists at all, it does and will tend to have the same effect it always did. Many a client, having discharged a great deal of a pattern in a session, forgot to be vigilant, and very quickly was back into being dominated by the remainder of the pattern. A pattern can persist.

A pattern can confuse one. "Up" becomes "down" in the pattern's sphere of influence. The unilateral firm direction against the pattern becomes modified into confused cooperation with it.

And the pattern can make one forget. That's all the pattern can do—but never underestimate those three strengths. One of the most humorous occurrences in RC occurred around this summary. I had finally realized that one could summarize the strengths of a pattern, that it can persist, it can confuse you, and and it can make you forget, and I had said this at a workshop in California. Two weeks later I got a letter from a participant. He said, "I remember you said a pattern can do three things. I can remember that you said it will persist and it will confuse you, but I can't remember what the third thing is."

So, if we can summarize and memorize our theory, that becomes an important tool against the pattern's ability to make us forget.

Our goal in counseling is not, rigorously speaking, discharge. Our goal is the *re-emergence* of our client. There are occasions when it is crucial to remember this; but, since ninety-five percent of re-emergence depends on discharge, for practical purposes almost all of our goal for our client is discharge—more, faster, deeper, more profound discharge.

THREE WELL-DEFINED ACTIONS NECESSARY

So a central question becomes: how does one, as a counselor, assist his or her client to discharge? Three steps only are necessary and sufficient:

One: pay enough attention to the client that one sees clearly what the distress is.

Two: think well about all possible ways to contradict that distress.

Three: contradict that distress sufficiently.

The word "sufficiently" is important. If one has contradicted the distress somewhat and there is still no discharge, this does not mean that one should then abandon RC and go study Freud. It means that you should contradict the distress MORE. When contradicted sufficiently the distress always discharges. That is a great fundamental natural law, completely dependable. When the distress is contradicted sufficiently, discharge occurs.

OBSERVE

First, pay enough attention to the client to see what distress is there. One simple way to do this is to ask the client, "What is your distress?" In most cases the client will think, "I thought you'd never ask" and will tell you more than you thought you wanted to know. There are various forms of asking this. "Is there anything you feel like talking about?" "What do you like about yourself?" "Where were you born? What happened after that?" "What would you like to tell me?" "How are you today?"

It is possible to *look at the client.* Any woman who is not looking like this (models a proud, relaxed posture) is displaying her distress for you to see, her chronic distress. Any man who is not (models a proud, relaxed posture in a slightly different way) is displaying his chronic distress. Any voice that is not ringing and positive and pleased is displaying chronic distress. Any facial expression that is not relaxed, serene, and positive is displaying chronic distress. Any action that is not done awarely is displaying distress. Any ingestion of addictive substances, such as tobacco smoke, alcohol, or drugs, shows the same.

Distresses are not, in general, hidden. There is reason to think all of us have been displaying our distresses all the time in the hope that someone will at last notice and do something to help us. There's reason to think that the person who acts antagonistic and starts a quarrel is always simply asking for help. So: one pays attention to the distress to see it clearly. One of the easiest ways to start is just to listen, or ask an interested question, "How is your life going these days?"

THINK

The second step is to think of all possible ways to contradict that distress. Simple listening is sometimes very effective in achieving discharge. This is because it contradicts almost all distresses, since almost all distress includes not being listened to. If the original distress didn't include it to begin with, then by now the client has tried to get some help so many times that the pattern has acquired an additional crust of distress of not being listened to.

Sometimes beginning Co-Counselors conclude that simple listening is all that's necessary for counseling, because they were lucky and their first five clients discharged very well when they just looked at them and kept their mouths shut. That is not sufficient theory, however, because the sixth and seventh clients will probably need a little more contradiction of their distress than that.

The most common problem in Co-Counseling at this time is, I think, not thinking enough about how to contradict the client's distress.

Is it because we are uncaring people, that we don't think enough about this? I don't think so. I think each one of us is deeply caring and loving to a profound degree. I think the problem is that we have formed some habits that get in the way. Many of these habits are reinforced by distress and have become chronic patterns. Sometimes I say in a workshop, "Encourage your client to look pleased and model it for her," but the would-be counselor's face is too pre-occupied with its chronic job of looking anxious to do any modeling for the client's face. The habit of always holding out our own distresses in the hope that we can be client (even when we have agreed to be counselor) must be broken. A great part of our most advanced work currently is slowly learning to break this habit of bringing our own distresses to our client's sessions.

ACT

The last step is to contradict the distress we have observed. We have seen that our client is frightened and anxious and so we have thought, "How can we contradict fear and anxiety? Confidence and cheerfulness might contradict it." Not bad thinking! So, we want our client to have confidence and cheerfulness to contradict his fear and anxiety. Some counselors then say to the client, "Be confident and cheerful!" That isn't good enough. We need to remember the client is always already contradicting the distress to the fullest extent he or she can. Giving the client an order to do more and stopping at that is not much contradiction and may even add to the distress.

Think of your client as an avalanche victim. From one point of view he or she is just fine and so is everybody else. There is another point of view, however. Thinking of him or her as client, to free her or him from patterns, he or she is covered with a pile of rock rubble. Some barbed wire has accidentally got wound around her and is cutting into her lips and face and one bruised eye and one broken finger are sticking out of the rubble of the avalanche of hurts. So if you've figured out that it would be good for your client to dance, that it would contradict some immobility distress, and you say, "Dance!" it doesn't work. No, if we are correct, that dancing would contradict our client's distress, you know who is free to dance. Not the client, but the counselor. *If you dance,* your eager client is probably going to manage a little laughter even through the barbed wire. The counselor is the one who has great freedom to contradict the client's distress.

This is obviously true, but the counselor frequently argues. His teacher or coach says, "Look at your client with confidence and cheerfulness," and the counselor replies, "I can't do that!" "Why can't you?" "Because I'm shy."

Who just brought his distresses to his client's session? If that would work, we would all already be fully re-emerged. We are learning (and I'll talk about this later in the workshop) some ways to get us over these deep habits of bringing our distresses to our client's sessions. This morning I will simply remind you that the counselor is the one that has great freedom to contradict the client's distress.

Examine the simple tactic, which all of us have used thousands of times, of having the client repeat a phrase whose words contradict the distress. Though simple, this has served us well, as far as we've gotten. The counselor thinks of a phrase that will contradict the client's distress. The client says, "I'm afraid I'll die," and the counselor thinks, "What would contradict that?" and tells the client to say, "I'll live forever." Perhaps the client manages to discharge. If the counselor insists that the client *say*, "I'll live forever," the client doesn't usually discharge. A good verbal direction, of course, is not one the client can say; it is one that, if the client tries to say it, produces discharge. The thought of saying it may be enough contradiction to bring discharge as long as the counselor expectantly repeats "I'll live forever" (hopefully, in a confident tone of voice). The client *tries* to say it and discharges. When repeating a phrase works, it's not, in general, the client who repeats it; it's the counselor who repeats it. With some of my professional clients, I remember repeating the same phrase for hundreds of hours of discharge. Of course I acted as if I expected the client to repeat it all through that time. (The client never said it, but I truly knew it by heart after repeating it twenty million times.)

So, it is simple. Not "easy," not in the sense that "easy" means freedom from patterned resistance, but it is simple. We pay enough attention to our clients to see what the distresses are. We think of all possible ways to contradict that distress. We contradict it enough. Discharge occurs.

Now, once the client begins to discharge, old habits will pull at us to "go to sleep." (In some cases, *actually* go to sleep. This is a problem of mine. As soon as my client is discharging well, I feel safe and I sometimes go to sleep; but not all counselors close their eyes honestly like I do. They sit there and pretend to be awake.) Of course the fact that your client has begun to discharge is rationally an invitation for you to help them discharge more profoundly.

MANY WAYS OF CONTRADICTING DISTRESS

So you touch them reassuringly. You act more confident. You project greater expectations upon them in a relaxed way. You search your memory for little bits of poetry that might give them a viewpoint outside the distress. If they are discharging their terror of an atomically burned-up world, you recite something about the beauty of the planet. (Recites Edna St. Vincent Millay's poem—"Oh, world, I cannot hold thee close enough..." and Goethe's poem "Im aller Vipfelm ist Rüh....") *You* furnish enough contradiction and *the client* discharges.

This is what we'll be doing. Very advanced counseling comes very close to simple beginning counseling. How will you scorn fear in your scorning fear groups? You will pay enough attention to see what the fear is, you will think of all possible ways to contradict it, and then you will contradict it. There's nothing more scornful of fear than a contradiction. "You have a fear?" (to someone there) "To be completely alone?" (In a serious tone of voice) "That will undoubtedly happen some day. Congratulations! Solitude is wonderful. Enjoy it well." Now, if I say, in an anxious tone of voice, "Oh, you will never be completely alone," the words might seem to be a contradiction, but I'm just reinforcing his fear.

If someone tells me, "I'm afraid of dying" and I say cheerfully, "Oh, you probably will," they may say, "Hmph!" but they're probably already laughing. Contradict the distress. If you're trying to help someone discharge on early sexual memories, the incest victim, covered with shame and guilt, is saying, "My father wouldn't do anything like that," you, as counselor, can approvingly say, "Oh, you were probably so attractive he couldn't resist!"

Contradict whatever distress is there. What are some of the general concerns of our groups? Working class? What are the common chronic patterns of the working class? Just exactly what the society has jammed on them. "You're not intelligent." "Shut up and keep quiet." "Do as somebody else tells you," leading to "I resent any leader who seems to tell me what to do." So what will undoubtedly come up in a working-class group? "I'm afraid I'm stupid." How do we contradict this? The fact of the matter is that working-class people are far more intelligent than any other class. They're much more in touch with reality. They are the hope of the future. (They are the only class that has a future.) On the leadership question, you can say, "We're all going to be leaders eventually, but we're smart enough to know that whoever is our leader has to lead now. Let's go!" You contradict whatever distress is there.

We have people here whose parents were Nazis, a tough situation. What distress is going to hit people in this group? They asked us this morning, "Is there safety here?" I would ask them to say, in a confident tone of voice, "They invited us! Everybody will be encouraged as WE make it. They can't get there and leave us behind." Of course, as I ask them, I will be repeating it for them.

DARE TO BE PROFOUND

Use very fundamental contradictions. Every person must be proud of exactly who they are. Remember the great fundamental insights on the RC scroll:

"Every single human being at every moment of the past, when the entire situation is taken into account, has always done the very best that she or he could do, and so deserves neither blame nor reproach from anyone, including self. This in particular is true of you."

If a counselor isn't around, say, "This in particular is true of *me*."

Reassuring Reality

A Welcome to Re-evaluation Counseling

As you begin to learn Re-evaluation Counseling, as you begin to learn to Co-Counsel, I extend a welcome to you from those of us who have been Co-Counseling (and developing and learning Re-evaluation Counseling) for a longer period of time. Welcome to what can well be a very interesting part of your life.

Re-evaluation Counseling is not very "old." Now (in 1983) it is about thirty-two-and-a-half years old. It has been pursued continuously by some of us throughout that period and by more of us through a portion of that time. A great deal of information and experience has accumulated. I can't hope to summarize much of that experience in this letter of welcome, but I can, perhaps, offer some perspectives on it that will be useful.

NATURAL, BUT SUPPRESSED

In beginning Co-Counseling you are beginning the systematic re-learning of a very important relationship and process. This process is natural to all human beings, but most of us were discouraged from pursuing it when we were very young and have had difficulty in using it ever since. This difficulty arises in part because we were trained to not use the process but also because this process requires at least one partner to make it work, and such partners have not, in general, been available in the worlds in which we have lived.

You will be learning how to take turns listening and paying attention and otherwise assisting yourself and one or more other people to recover certain abilities which you inherently possess but which may not have had a chance to develop. Among these are the enjoyment of life, which seems to be the natural birthright of every human being, and certain other tools for achieving and enjoying excellent relationships with other people.

Most of this information will come to you in your class work, in your reading of the literature about Re-evaluation Counseling, and in your practice of Co-Counseling with your partner or partners.

NOT MAGIC

If you are fortunate, you are likely to be "enchanted" with the early results of your Co-Counseling. Even if you have some difficulty in the beginning, you're likely to be quite impressed by what other students in your class are able to achieve. It sometimes happens that a new student of Co-Counseling gets the impression that Re-evaluation Counseling is a "wonder process" that works of and by itself. This can lead the student to feel quite disappointed when hard work and difficulties appear. It is important, I think, to say to you at the very beginning that there's no "magic" involved. Re-evaluation Counseling is a workable process, but it really requires thoughtful work to make it function. It will challenge you to use your best determination, effort, and thinking in order to achieve the best results.

ORDINARY PEOPLE

Similarly, although your teachers and the experienced Co-Counselors and the leaders of the Co-Counseling Communities are, in my opinion, very fine people, you should remember also that they are very ordinary humans. They still have many difficulties that they have not yet freed themselves from. They still are capable of making mistakes. They still can have lapses of thoughtfulness. They are by no means perfect or likely to act perfectly in their relationships with new Co-Counselors, experienced Co-Counselors, or with each other. They are just people like you and I. They are engaged in a workable and worthwhile process, but for most of them (for most of *us*), they still have a long way to go. To expect perfection of them, or to think that they will "solve all your problems," or that "Re-evaluation Counseling works" would be to set yourself up for some future disappointments. Re-evaluation Counseling doesn't "work"—*it can be made to work.* You, in general, will get just as much out of your counseling as you put into it. Your gains will go as far as you persist. Though much of what you have to learn and work through will be a great deal easier for you because other people have already persisted and worked through similar difficulties and will share what they have learned with you in class and through the literature, your own progress will still require effort, thinking, and persistence on your part.

YOUR CHOICE

To date, many people have taken one or two series of classes in Co-Counseling and have Co-Counseled for a few months and then have not done any further study or further organized effort in Co-Counseling. They have simply taken what they have learned and continued to apply it as far as possible in their lives and are quite satisfied with what they have gotten from Co-Counseling. This *can* be your choice as well. You may find that you have other things to do (or even that you've not been able to make the Co-Counseling continue to work for you well enough that you are motivated to persist), and that is just fine. You are very welcome to have an introduction, or an introduction and a small amount of experience beyond that, with Re-evaluation Counseling, then take it into the world and use it to the best of your ability, knowing that those of us who persist in going farther send our good wishes with you.

It's also possible that you will go farther than that and become a fairly skillful Co-Counselor, but then, as you begin to use your skills and reclaimed abilities more in non-counseling activities, will become so busy in the wide world with your improved life and functioning that you will conclude that, for now at least, you don't have the time for Co-Counseling, that other things are more important than Re-evaluation Counseling, and will simply not keep much contact with us more persistent Co-Counselors. Perhaps you will plan to rejoin us at a later time. Perhaps you will simply go on your own with a slightly altered future and enhanced abilities and enjoyments. That, too, is just fine. You are under no obligation to other Co-Counselors to persist beyond the point where it seems profitable or possible for you to do so. In the past many people have gone just this far with the use of Re-evaluation Counseling.

THE "COMMUNITY"

There is a substantial group of Co-Counselors, however, who have organized themselves into what they call a "Community" or "Communities" of Re-evaluation Counseling. These have decided that the information, the possibilities, the fellowship, and the goals involved in working together with other people to use Co-Counseling and to advance the theory and practice are worth a persistent effort.

To become a member of the Co-Counseling Communities it is necessary that you not only participate in activities but that you make a contribution, that you share in the many, many facets of work and activity that the Communities sponsor. There are several dozen publications, for example, with special readerships and constituencies. There are workshops and support groups and leadership and publications for people of different ethnic backgrounds, different age backgrounds, different professional backgrounds, different national backgrounds. There are special workshops for people who seek liberation from particular oppressions, such as those of racism or sexism or classism. There are special relationships in the Community, and particular leaders, for women and young people and men and college professors and blacks and many other groups. There are support groups for people who share similar interests and backgrounds and come together and use Re-evaluation Counseling in special ways to solve problems connected with their background, their oppression, their professions, or their interests. There are "information coordinators." These are individual Co-Counselors who undertake to be information centers for Co-Counselors of a particular background, experience, or profession.

These activities, workshops, publications, support groups, leaders' meetings are situations in which the mastering of Re-evaluation Counseling and the use of it for personal advancement and re-emergence can be pursued intensively. To participate in them it is simply necessary that one help support and carry out these activities to the extent possible in one's given situation.

LONG-TERM COMMITMENTS AND LEADERSHIP

It is also possible that, as you feel the workability of re-emergence and the innately human simplicity of the discharge and re-evaluation process and as you sense the implications of this for human beings in the present world situation, you will become interested in making this a major activity in your life, one parallel to and supportive of your other main interests, whether they be professional, family, cultural, religious, or artistic.

To those of you who decide this and wish to explore "going all the way" for total re-emergence for yourself, for preserving the world and making the entire world situation rational—a special welcome. There is a substantial number of people already committed and functioning in this way and those of us who are in this position are eager for others to join us. We feel a great need for more people who are willing to grow into leadership, who are willing to make deep commitments and persistent address to the accelerated development of Re-evaluation Counseling knowledge and application. It doesn't matter what your age or gender or background or education or ethnicity or profession; we have need of you (if you are so interested) just exactly as you are and exactly in the situation you are in.

If you find yourself this deeply interested in the implications of Re-evalution Counseling at some point, remember also that I and others in the leadership are interested *in you* and will be glad to hear from you. We will arrange whatever encouragement, contact, and assistance for you that it is possible to arrange.

ONCE AGAIN, WELCOME

Again, a warm welcome to Re-evaluation Counseling, to whatever depth you pursue it. All the rest of us Re-evaluation Counselors are "pleased to have you aboard."

Sincerely,

Harvey Jackins

The Tremendous Opportunities of the Present

The current situation facing the peoples of the world and, in particular, the working classes of the world, though demanding attention and leadership, is one of great opportunity. There are dangers, to be sure, but these are handleable and calculable, and the opportunities for decisive progress in the well-being of the human race are without parallel in our history. Humanity is on the brink of emergence into its full role as the leading edge of the upward trend in the universe. Our present resources are more than adequate for the preservation, improvement, and care of our home planet to where it can be a veritable Eden.

Humanity stands for the first time in its history able to take full rational charge of itself and of the planetary and solar environment in which it functions, eliminate all threats, discomforts, setbacks, and catastrophes, and tend to the enhancement of the surroundings and the flowering of our own natures.

It is also true that difficulties and dangers abound. As long as humanity is still pent within the collapsing structure of world capitalism or confined within the assumptions of the old society, it is faced with energy shortages, widespread starvation, wastage of resources, pollution of air and water and soil, overpopulation, small-scale imperialist wars, and a non-functioning economic system. The governments of the major powers are dominantly reactionary and, looming over it all, is the escalating threat of nuclear holocaust. A war with nuclear weapons *could* sterilize the entire planet and reduce all life to the level of bacteria.

First reported to the Wide World Changing III Workshop, then appeared in **Present Time** No. 46.

All these are real problems tactically, and the danger of nuclear holocaust, for example, is very real, but they are tactical problems only. The same situation which makes it a necessity to sharply confront them carries with it tremendous opportunities for liberating humanity from the habits of submission to being maneuvered by destructive forces. It brings great opportunities for full-scale cooperative taking charge of our own lives, of our relationships with each other, of the resources of the planet, of our rapidly expanding knowledge of technology and science. In a short time we can bring about a real situation far beyond the most glowing fantasies of the past.

ELIMINATING NUCLEAR WEAPONS

The overriding problem facing all humanity at this time is to keep the pile-up of nuclear arsenals, concentrated in the United States and the Soviet Union, from being triggered in the "conventional" way, in which "conventional" imperialist wars are begun, into an exchange of atomic fire such as will devastate the world. The danger is very real and acute, but the opportunity to eliminate it is also without parallel in that no living human being stands to gain anything from the release of these weapons. Only the blindest of patterns could act to turn them loose. The opportunities are excellent for uniting all humanity in the broadest, most unified movement ever known—to insist that the nuclear warheads be dismantled, that nuclear arms be done away with. This gives all of us humans a chance and an overriding motivation to get ourselves together and discover the possibility of acting in concert across all divisions and national barriers. As this is done (and it must be done), the resulting organization and habit of acting effectively in our own interests will undoubtedly scoop up and bring solutions to all of the lesser problems facing us. For humanity to have the experience of successfully insisting on complete nuclear disarmament will in itself break most of the patterned barriers which alone have allowed imperialism to flourish and will end the illusion of powerlessness which is the only thing which permits the nuclear build-up to continue.

On this question we have an overwhelming need for *initiative* on the part of the people's forces. A few people everywhere are trying to put together organizations and to speak out, but also everywhere are obviously cramped by the enormous fear which they feel, the overwhelming numbing dread of the holocaust, which keeps them from putting free, flexible attention on the problem and rationally thinking about it.

Here Re-evaluation Counselors have a very special role to play in modeling and transmitting a correct perception of the situation, along with sharing the tools for dealing with the numbing terror. Even our beginning efforts in encouraging people to discharge on the repeated completion of the sentence "It won't happen because ________," have indicated that people can be freed to far more courage, confidence, and initiative than has been previously tapped.

Here is an area where we cannot wait for spontaneity, where, because of the danger, we cannot wait for the issues to come up in their turn. All of us, regardless of how hesitant we feel, must help each other quickly shed our fears in this area and move to raise the issue correctly, precisely, and effectively everywhere.

THE POSSIBILITIES FOR POWERFUL PEOPLE'S MOVEMENTS

The phenomenon of "Solidarity" in Poland has burst on the world scene like a great sunrise, ripping apart the "taken for granted" myth of the inability of peoples under oppressive regimes to organize and to take charge of their lives effectively and consistently. "Solidarity" faced all the problems which any movement can become heir to. Difficulties of organization, a repressive regime, the threat of armed invasion from other countries, over-eager simplistic proposals for moving too fast, (which arise spontaneously from within a movement as people become excited, and are re-enforced by deliberate provocation and the use of *agents provocateur* proposing super-militant unworkable solutions), the pattern of elitism, caution, and of undue compromise, which appear in leadership intimidated by threats from the bastions of the old society, fatigue from struggle on the part of some forces and an over-eagerness to struggle for struggle's sake on the part of others, the isolation of the movement from allies outside the nation; all these have occurred or are occurring to Solidarity. Its proof, however, of the main thesis, that any group of people led by their industrial working class can organize and bring together all elements of the population in indomitable, invincible organization no matter what threats, scares, and forces are running against them, cannot be obscured. Solidarity, and its achievements so far, are the great "existence theorem" demonstrating the possibility of the potential new rational society arising within the framework of the old collapsing capitalist one.

Though the Paris Commune, the Russian Revolution of 1917, and the Chinese Liberation of 1949 all temporarily took their peoples a long way toward a rational, just society, and were defeated only by the resurgence of capitalist patterns and habits of thought within the revolutionary leading bodies, Solidarity is indeed a "horse of a different color." In Poland the "capitalist road" communist party was in full power. The Solidarity movement, in acting against it, forced some purification of the party's ranks in the process and continues to have that effect. Solidarity, acting primarily on its own strength, won allies from the older nationalist forces of society such as the Polish Catholic Church, but also won the support of much of the communist party membership.

THE ORGANIZING OF THE UNORGANIZED

One of the key tasks in the United States and (to a lesser extent) in western Europe, and very much a key issue in the developing countries, is the organizing of the unorganized workers into self-reliant, membership-controlled unions with correct policies and strong leadership. The example of Solidarity again shows how clearly and quickly the rest of the population will rally and organize themselves providing the industrial workers take the lead. This has been too long neglected. In the statement, "Organize the Unorganized," which I wrote and distributed earlier, I propose throwing away the old concept of waiting on the presently-organized workers to furnish the structure and support for the organization of the unorganized and, instead, call upon the unorganized workers to themselves tackle the job. There are certainly enough aware activists with perspective that, with a minimum of organization and encouragement, a great organizing drive could sweep over the United States in particular. With this momentum and with fraternal help offered from the United States, tremendously powerful organizations could be formed very quickly in many other countries. This action is the catalyst which will permit the organization of the rest of the population in each country around the many issues that concern them (always, and in particular, the elimination of nuclear weapons).

We need to bring our notions of how to organize up to date. The models of the past are simply not sufficient. Even though we can learn much from Solidarity currently, we also need to think freshly on how to use our special RC knowledge of people's relationships. The instant print shop, the xerox machine, the long-distance telephone, and the RC support group or RC class are key new factors that could lead to rapid organization of very large numbers of people.

INTERNATIONALISM AS A FORCE

The organized movements of the future, in particular the workers' organizations of the future, must never again be allowed to lapse into the narrow nationalism which has been so characteristic of the labor movements in the developed countries until now. Any new trade union, or people's organization, or anti-nuclear organization begun in the future must, from the beginning, have a policy clearly established of international cooperation, of reaching across all national barriers, of proclaiming always and everywhere that all men are brothers, all women are sisters, that all humanity has the same goals. The present nationalist divisions, once challenged and their wrongness clarified, do not have such strength, even in patterned ways, that people will not follow better policies when offered. Such better policies can say that it is patriotic to be internationalist, that to be chauvinist on the key issues of the world is really to be unpatriotic, in that it acts against the real interests of one's own country and one's own people.

THE FEMININE REVOLUTION

Of the many attempts at people's movements in the last thirty years, the one most successful and most persistent and the one newest to the world as a major movement is the liberation of women. Here in spite of betrayals, mistaken policies, isolation and lack of allies, and all other kinds of difficulties, very real gains have been won. Things are better in the lives of women, in the respect offered them, and especially in the raising of their consciousness. Very large numbers of women are ready to act boldly and decisively whenever their leadership puts forward correct policies. The basic slogan of the women's movement within RC is to *accept no limits to women's liberation and development*, to "never again settle for less than everything." This attitude, when persisted in and supported by male allies, brings tremendous strength and effectiveness not only to the women's struggle but to the general struggle of all people for liberation.

Like the working class, the women overlap every other group, every other movement in society. They furnish allies to the liberation struggle of any group of people from every class and every geographical division. The women's movement is the most powerful ally of the working-class liberation movement. It is actually functioning thus in some ways and in some areas and can potentially do so everywhere. A tremendous force is waiting here to be tapped. With bolder leadership and more correct policies and especially with the wholehearted support of the working class and other liberation movements, the women's movement can well decide the future of humankind.

We have placed good emphasis upon this within RC and the development of women's policies has proceeded well and through many difficulties, but what we have done to date is just a small part of what is available to be done. Old habits of treating the women's movement condescendingly still continue to inhibit the release of this vast, progressive force.

ELIMINATE RACISM EVERYWHERE

White racism (and such closely related patterns as anti-Jewish oppression or anti-Quebecois oppression or anti-Arab oppression) has been systematically installed and perpetuated in the population for hundreds of years. The patterns which maintain it consist almost entirely of two kinds of distress:

(1) Fears of anyone or anything strange or unknown, i.e., "different" than ourselves or our familiar experiences.

(2) The reactive lure or "appeal" to "get into the other end of the pattern" and act out, at someone else, the contempt and mistreatment, which has been previously put upon us, with the approval and encouragement of society.

Needless to say, all such attitudes are completely destructive in their effects and are non-survival to all participants.

The elimination of racism simply requires that the unfamiliar become familiar, that the rehearsal of distress patterns be replaced by their discharge, and that the residue of internalized racism inside each oppressed group be systematically faced, contradicted, and discharged.

We have accumulated most of the theoretical and organizational knowledge necessary to do this from our experiences in the Re-evaluation Counseling Communities. The thorough application of this knowledge, both within RC and in the wide world, remains, as yet, an unmet challenge. The overwhelming need for unity across all barriers in the struggle for survival will force us to meet it.

INCLUDE EVERY GROUP IN THE LIBERATION MOVEMENT

Since the oppressive society pits every group against every other group and encourages and conditions and enforces their mutual oppression of each other, it becomes crucial for wide-world-changers in this period to apply all our knowledge and skill to achieving the unity of *all* the oppressed. This poses some practical problems. We must find ways to bring together the different groups as they are organized, help them have some practical experience in communicating to and listening to each other and in seeing each other as real people instead of as the stereotypes they have been conditioned to believe in. We need to be helpful in putting together a program which includes the needs and desires of every group.

This will sometimes meet resistance and impatience from groups which first begin to feel their power. They will want to rush ahead, demanding support for their program, but unwilling to pay attention to the needs and requests of the others. The source of this is, in part, the internalized oppression within each group. The tradition of the U.S. labor movement of downgrading the importance of women and the organization of women is an example. In part it will arise from feelings of powerlessness and panicky urgency that one can only deal with "the most important questions" at any one time.

To counter this, I think it is necessary for us to communicate, and reiterate over and over, that *there is no unimportant oppression*, that everyone needs every ally that they can get, that we must be glad to throw our support behind every group, no matter how small or unpopular, if they are actually seeking liberation, and that we'll be glad to include their proposals and demands in the general program.

UNITY BY STEPS

The already-achieved understanding, within RC, that members of each group, no matter how narrowly-defined, need to caucus and think out their program in a homogeneous, safe atmosphere before they negotiate with the other groups, will be of inestimable value. Where we have influence or leadership, we must simply insist that groups caucus separately in just as finely-divided group caucuses as they can possibly wish and only then caucus in larger caucuses where each subgroup speaks and is listened to respectfully by the other subgroups. When a general policy has been worked out in and for each of the larger groups, then and only then can all of the groups speak to each other, again with full respect and attention.

To make this a regular practice will take some leadership at first, but people must come to understand this. They must not yield their position or give up their leadership role because people are anxious for "unity" and want to ignore the necessity of actually carrying out the work which can lead to real unity or just because someone from a powerful group is impatient and wants to "take over" on a narrow basis. We must hold tough for correct policies on this procedure or we will, farther down the road, wish that we had, when the resulting narrowing of our base creates problems for us. A strong trade union movement can understandably *feel* that they can "go it alone" but as the battles get joined, the importance of having the support of young people, of physically-different people, of women, of middle-class people, of Gay people, will show up. The price paid in time and patience and understanding and in a lengthened program will be clearly seen to be well worthwhile.

ONE-TO-ONE ORGANIZATION

The actual organization of people will in general best proceed by one-to-one contact as effective organization always has done. This principle, which we've clarified in RC, needs to be widely publicized because the myth of "mass organization by calling meetings" is still widespread.

THE INDIVIDUAL AND THE MOVEMENT

Some individuals will come to the fore more easily than

others. Some are more interested, more experienced. The finding and choosing of leadership will always be a key point in the process of organization.

Our general experiences in the Re-evaluation Counseling Communities can be of great value here in wide-world organization. Some of the insights that we've developed are:

(1) The person most eager for the job is not necessarily the best person for the job (some patterns are "eager");

(2) It helps to examine the motivations of a person who wishes leadership or wants to take on a task (reactive motivations need not be ruled out, but they should be recognized and their rigidity taken into account);

(3) All the needs and the whole situation of the individual need to be taken into account and allowed for so that the strains of neglecting oneself or failing to support one's family because of organizational activity can be countered, by support and division of labor, to prevent the familiar "burn-out" of leaders.

The entire theory of leadership as developed in RC can be reviewed with profit for any work in the wide world.

NO NARROWNESS TOWARDS ALLIES

In a similar vein, it should be made clear that any movement seeks support on each part of its program or policy and that no support is rejected simply because the supportive people disagree on, or oppose, some other parts. Thus, though we will have a wide-ranging policy which takes into account the needs of all of our allies, other people must be invited to participate and support the struggle even if they are only in favor of part of the policy. A fair assumption to put to them is that we think they will feel differently if they examine the other parts of the policy thoroughly and become acquainted with the people who proposed them, but that in any case we will join with them on the points in which they are in agreement and seek to achieve these. Thus we can have a principled respect for each other's differences and work together closely without anyone being enforced to accept anything with which they disagree.

THE CORRECTION OF MISTAKES

Anyone who does anything important necessarily makes mistakes occasionally. This fact needs to be faced and held up to the light in every organization. The leader who does make a mistake can insure strong and growing support by admitting the mistake as soon as it is obvious that it is one, apologizing for it, and helping to undo any bad effects from it. Leaders often fear that if they admit to having made a mistake, they will weaken their support, but, in practice, frank admission of a mistake and skillful correction of the situation bring much additional support.

THE CARE AND NURTURING OF LEADERS BECOMES OF GREAT IMPORTANCE

As a movement grows in power and strength, the leadership is certain to be attacked from outside (and unfortunately, often from inside) by people who, wittingly or unwittingly, are agents of the oppression. Leaders will not, in general, be attacked for their mistakes, but on any basis that can be used to restimulate fears and distrust of them. If leaders and members can face this reality of wide-world struggle ahead of time and be ready to cope with it, the organization can become nearly invulnerable. (Otherwise, this sort of thing can be very disruptive.)

ASSESSING SITUATIONS CORRECTLY

The wide-world-changer, who would furnish leadership to others, needs to, and can, learn to assess situations accurately, both short-range or tactically and long-range or strategically.

One basic principle here is to not confuse the tactical and the strategic outlooks. The forces of the dying society, because of their control of all the social structures and because of their patterned habits of command, can almost always bring great pressures to bear in any limited situation and force the outcome their own way. In order to do so, however, they must always weaken themselves drastically somewhere else, and create severe problems for themselves in the next stage of the struggle, intensifying the inherent and insoluble contradictions with which they are saddled by the nature of the society itself. The wide-world-changer should never be demoralized by apparently "losing" any particular battle. Her or his opponent, the disintegrating society, has lost more in the long run.

The permanent gains of the progressive side in any non-final struggles lie almost entirely in the areas of partially-successful defense of people's well-being against the encroachment of oppression, in improved organization, and in higher awareness and consciousness on the part of the progressive forces and their supporters. This implies: constant attention to minimizing the damage done by the oppression or repression to one's own forces; a rigorous stand against any "adventurism" or panicky risk-taking; continual improvement of organization using accumulated knowledge from the history of past struggles but also the lessons from recent and current ones (flavored with creative thinking), and a well-communicated, correct, confident assessment of the tactical dangers and the strategic opportunities of the given situation.

In this period the progressive forces must necessarily play by the rules of guerilla fighters, avoiding confrontations, educating, organizing, expanding one's forces, winning small victories at the society's weak points, winning allies, and extending unity.

In assessing a situation, one must continually take into account the tremendous bias in the flood of "information" with which one is bathed in present society. Oppression, maintained in earlier generations mostly by naked force, is now largely supported by sophisticated misinformation apparatuses. Currently, the various attempts at countering the Establishment media machines are also almost all seriously contaminated by despair, rigidity, preoccupation with the past or naive dedication to once-progressive, but now regressive, political forces.

The successful wide-world-changer must learn to "read between the lines" of newspapers, radio broadcasts, and television screens. The humanness of the news people and the contradictions of capitalist competition will allow glimpses of reality to slip through, but they must be watched for and understood. The "editorializing" of almost all news accounts must be recognized and allowed for. No one's morale could stand up to accepting news media accounts as actually the news.

On any given struggle, for example, the news media will always give the appearance that the balance of forces is, long-range, against the progressives. The reality will always be that, long-range, the balance of forces favors the progressives.

NOW IS THE TIME

There have never been so many people in the world. There has never been such a variety of people and cultures in the world. There have never been such resources of technology, agricultural knowledge and equipment, scientific knowledge and culture available to people. Workers have never been so ready for organization. There has never been such clarity of policy as is today available. Never before have people had the tools for dealing with individual irrationalities and distress.

The present situation is enormously hopeful, enormously inviting. If the activists of the past, whom we admire so much, had had our opportunities, things would have been a great deal different by now. Yet we, with all our remaining patterns and misgivings about ourselves and feelings of being incompetent and unworthy, are far better able to take charge and proceed directly toward the liberation of humankind than any of our activist predecessors ever have been.

The stakes have never been higher, the odds have never been better, we've never had so much going for us. Let us take charge and set things right.

Close Friendships Between Women and Men

A clearer understanding is beginning to emerge of the nature of the inherent relationships between women and men, the cultural distresses that get in the way of these natural relationships, and what can be done about removing the distresses through counseling. Some of the confusions in this area are beginning to be challenged and some dependable guides for counseling well on these distresses are beginning to be found.

Advances began in recent months as an attempt to solve a counseling problem for a woman RC leader who felt incapable of attracting, getting acquainted with, and establishing good relationships with men. In the results and follow-up of the counseling, broader issues came to light and are still emerging. The following is a state-of-progress report on what reality seems to have been uncovered in the area of women/men relationships until now.

The *appearances* in our cultures are that women and men find it almost impossible to relate to each other on an intelligent, mutually-respectful, loving, human basis with any consistency or over any long period of time. Most enduring relationships seem to be ones that involve a great deal of pattern and oppression, including dominance and submission, etc.

THE INHERENT REALITY

The reality is that women and men are inherently disposed toward excellent, enjoyable relations with each other and only patterns get in the way of such excellent relationships.

Appeared in **Present Time** No. 44.

ALL WOMEN ARE INHERENTLY INTERESTED IN AND EAGER TO BE CLOSE FRIENDS WITH ALL MEN. ALL MEN ARE INHERENTLY INTERESTED IN AND EAGER TO BE CLOSE FRIENDS WITH ALL WOMEN. Every woman apparently is inherently attracted to every man, and every man attracted to every woman.

Why this is so is in part "obvious" (to any RCer) and in part is still the subject of speculation. We have known for a long while that human beings love human beings, and, to a woman, *men are human beings*; to a man, *women are human beings*. The general principle, "Love is the way human beings naturally feel about each other . . ." is the foundation of this attractiveness between the two genders.

I speculate that there is also an inherent interest *because of our differences*, that women always seem fascinating to men because they are different from themselves, and men also seem fascinating to women because of the difference. Some people disagree with me vociferously on this and insist that any special attraction must be patterned, but I do not think so. I think that in addition to the general attraction between humans there is probably a special inherent bond of attractiveness between the two genders.

The importance of the oppression of sexism as a barrier to, and destroyer of, these excellent inherent relationships between women and men has at least begun to be explored. Most RCers are now aware that sexism is enforced upon both males and females very early in their lives and that the enforcement itself installs a hurt which keeps the sexist pattern in place, either in the role of enforcer or in the role of victim. We have become at least somewhat aware of the pressures of the sexist conditioning on women to submit, propitiate, appease, withdraw, isolate themselves, and upon men to dominate, enforce, and oppress.

CONDITIONED MALE DEPENDENCE

What we have not, until now, taken as aware account of, are

the pressures on men which reinforce the sexism but also act independently to throw up barriers between them and women. Males are not only taught to "look down upon" or "lord it over" or "feel superior to" females, but they are also taught to regard them as the only possible source of human attention, warmth, caring, touch and human concern. Since the "big boy" and the homophobia conditioning bars males from expecting or turning to other males for any of this warmth, all of us males grow up with the usually unfaced but clear impression that only from women can we receive any comfort, warmth, or humanness.

(This conditioning is under attack in our men's work in RC. Men should be able to share warmth with each other fully, but the conditioning is deep and, in the wide world, almost fully operational.)

This places within each female's hands (although she is often unaware of it) an enormous power over males which males are subject to, even though they are usually unable to think about it or question it. This is the power of *rejection. All males in our culture live in terror of rejection by females*. If an adolescent boy goes against his embarrassment and fear enough to ask an adolescent girl to dance with him at a school dance she need only (frightened herself) toss her head and say, "Not you!" to have him plunged into an abyss of total rejection.

(His way of countering the rejection may mask what happened, as he resorts to counter-rejection, sexist language or wandering off by himself alone, but the effect is basically rejection and it is very heavy. Each such experience of rejection or, later, even anticipated rejection, adds to the vulnerability.)

ANYONE SHE WANTS TO

Any woman can attract any man she wishes to have as a good, close friend and can keep that relationship permanently if she is able to do three things:

1) Think of herself as worthwhile, likeable, and attractive

and communicate to the man that she has this attitude toward herself by look, posture, facial expression, tone of voice or words,

2) Indicate to the man that she finds him interesting, attractive, and desirable as a friend, and

3) Communicate to the man that he is not in danger of being personally rejected by her.

A woman who can do this is irresistible to any man. Cosmetics, clothes, figure, complexion, all the other supposed ingredients of attractiveness, have very little to do with the attraction which a man feels for her (they do have a bearing on patterned attraction, of course, but that's another story), compared to the deep inherent attractiveness of a woman who can communicate these three things.

To do this will generally require that a woman do considerable discharging. In the demonstrations that have been done at workshops so far, the thought of deliberately being attractive brings much laughter and shaking and tears as the invalidations that she is "not attractive enough," which have apparently been placed on nearly every woman, are contradicted and discharged. Yet in our experience so far, even a small amount of discharge seems to make a great deal of difference in the woman's handling of her male environment. It seems clear at this point that any woman can have as many good male friends as she wishes simply by discharging enough to achieve this three-pronged attitude.

A fear that is always immediately raised is, "What do I do with them once I have attracted them?" with the woman apparently visualizing a host of the usual sexist attitudes which men are conditioned to turn toward women, converging upon her.

AS RELIEF FOR MEN

I think it's first necessary to state clearly that none of us men like acting that way. A few of us are so deeply conditioned that it will take intensive counseling to break us out of it, but in general we have simply grown up being told and accepting that only an aggressive, "I'm only interested in sex and that right now" attitude is really manly or impressive enough to gain us a woman's interest. Very few of us ever succeed in acting as we think we're supposed to, and most of us feel disappointed in ourselves, but all of us have been convinced that this is what women want and expect. We were told this by the culture, by our contemporaries, by the older boys, by all the male models in the male magazines and movies. So we compulsively do our best to live up to this nonsense, even though for most of us it is a hateful, diffident activity in which we feel very unsuccessful. For all except a very few of us, a firm, clear statement by a woman as to *what she wants*, which excludes that activity on our part, will be a great relief and will bring great relaxation in our attitudes and great appreciation of the woman for "taking us off the hook" of our patterned conditioning.

To have a large number of warm, close male friends certainly provides the background for any woman to choose with much more freedom any additional relationships which she wishes to establish. She is in a much better position to choose a lover, husband, co-parent, business partner or whatever if she can choose from among her numerous warm, close, mutually-respecting male friendships.

MEN, TOO

What about the man? Can a man achieve warm, close friendships with any woman whom he wishes? In my opinion, yes. It's a little harder for me to be completely clear about this since I grew up inside male conditioning and am still affected by it. My picture here is not quite as crystal clear as it can be as a male looking thoughtfully at the situation of women from the outside, but I think, yes, that any woman would welcome relating to any man who:

1) Thought well of himself as a man, was delighted that he

was male, was proud of it and showed it by posture, facial expression, tone of voice, words, etc.;

2) Indicated that he liked the woman *as a human being* first and foremost (though the door might be open to the possibility of other relationships);

3) Treated the woman with complete respect, was "decent" in every way. He needs to make it clear that he will be her ally against any sexist oppression, including any that he still carries, himself.

I have not met a woman (I am not talking about certain patterns here) that would not be delighted to have such a man for a friend, and my own experiences as a man would bear this out.

Apologizing for being sexist has often been the opening gambit for RC men in trying to communicate their decency to RC women. Perhaps one such apology does not hurt, but to continue with an apologetic attitude is in itself patterned. Self-respect is an essential feature of attractiveness.

SPELL OUT THE RELATIONSHIP

The content of any relationship needs to be spelled out clearly and completely and agreed to by both parties. (See the article by Tim Jackins in **Present Time** No. 43, page 3.) In my opinion the spelling-out in the beginning of a relationship between a woman and a man needs to be done first and firmly *by the woman*. This is in order to counter the sexist conditioning of male dominance that otherwise will tend to intrude continually. If a woman has attracted and struck up a beginning relationship with a man, I think it is her responsibility to think out, and spell out in detail, exactly what she wants the relationship with that man to be and to communicate it to him. If he does not agree to it, then she should not accept the relationship. She should simply insist that it is necessary that he accept her terms for the friendship to be an operative one. Dramatized protest from the man can be expected to occur, but holding to a firm position by the woman, declining to temporize with the patterns but staying friendly with the person, will see the man very relievedly come around in almost every case, in my opinion.

AVOID REJECTION

If the man does not come around, then the woman should postpone any relationship but *not reject the person*. In other words, she should say that she would like to have him for a friend, and when he changes his mind she will be glad to talk to him again. She should say clearly that it isn't him she doesn't like, but only his unreasonable attitudes which she cannot accept without injuring her self-respect and which he will be far better off without. She should hold out the possibility, if he changes his position later, of then accepting him as a friend, so that his terror of rejection does not come into play.

A woman will be pulled by her own distress to compromise on her own best thinking (that is, submit in an old patterned way) or else reject the man, as the only two alternatives that have been open to her in the patterned culture. To avoid either of these two alternatives is, I think, to guarantee her having life-long male friends.

Similarly, clearly thinking out and communicating the conditions of a relationship is necessary for men, but I think the initiative in spelling-out the conditions of a woman-man relationship must lie with the woman in order to contradict the sexist conditioning around them.

DISCHARGE, NOT JUST DISCUSSION

Insights, however valuable, are never enough. It takes action, in this case effective counseling, to effect permanent changes. How can we counsel well in these areas?

The approach of asking a woman client to silently "attract" a male counselor has always brought voluminous discharge whenever I have tried it. I would guess that a male counselor, while convenient, is probably not necessary, that a female counselor would probably work well, too, if it were agreed that she is to be regarded as a "man" during the session. The converse will probably work for men, also.

For a man or woman client to take complete pride in being a man or woman is very effective at bringing discharge. In my experience this requires some boldness on the part of the counselor in modeling well the ways in which he or she expects the client to express this pride. Here posture, facial expression and tone of voice become much more important than words. In fact, I have found that words are best kept to a minimum, such as "*I* am a woman!" or "I am *all man*" in order that attention be focused on the tones, etc.

Both in modeling this and in observing the client, the counselor needs to watch out for the pull to settle for defensiveness, or condescension, or "better than" attitudes rather than real, self-appreciating pride. "Head high but chin in."

I conjecture that we need discussions by women of exactly what attractive, permanently enjoyable attitudes and behavior by men would be like, and by men of what they really would appreciate, long-range, in women's behavior and attitudes, and then a respectful communication by each group to the other (perhaps before an entire workshop).

Perhaps a randomly-chosen pair could model, before a workshop or support group or class, the "spelling-out" of exactly what expectations they will be placing on members of the other gender whom they will meet in the future.

ONLY A BEGINNING

These, in short summary, are some of the developments and thinking that have emerged in the last eight or ten International Workshops. They are certainly only the beginning of an ongoing development, and one that many people have indicated great interest in.

I would be glad to hear from readers about this: somewhat interested to hear your thinking and speculations; but very eager to hear of your concrete experiences in systematically counseling and discharging in this area.

Yo Soy Un Hombre

I am a man.
I am *all* man.
Every cell in my body is male.

I grow hair on my face
  and on my chest
  and up to my navel.

I have male muscles, a deep voice,
  enormous potential, initiative, and strength.

I have great intelligence and courage.

I was a boy before I became a man.
I was completely male then, too.

It was great to be a boy.

It is great to be a man.

It is great to be a man in company
  and alliance with other men.

It is great to be a man
  sharing humanness and power
  with young people and women.

I am a strong ally of other men,
  of women, and of young people.

I despise oppression and injustice.

I am an eager champion for the
  liberation of every human.

I rejoice in this, my universe,
  and in my leadership in it.

Call on my strength. Call on my courage.
Call on my intelligence and confidence.
I will respond.

Rejoice with me,
  male comrades, female comrades.
This is our universe.

I am a man.

Appeared in **Men** No. 2.

The Art of Listening

I and a group of my friends have, for about thirty-one years, been trying to develop and expand and improve a system for people relating to each other helpfully. For the last eleven years our efforts have gone beyond the city of Seattle and in that time have spread to nearly every state in the Union, nearly every large city in the United States, most Canadian provinces, and about thirty-eight other countries. We've had an explosive expansion. Our understanding of the subject continually improves. There are new developments all the time. It's challenging to stay on top of what we are learning.

There are many ways of approaching what we have named "Re-evaluation Counseling." One way is to ask you to look at what happens whenever people are together and have a chance to talk, at times when they're not completely preoccupied with their jobs or other activity. If you will think back to the coffee-shop, picnic table, or similar situations, you will remember that people are, everywhere and at all times when in the presence of each other, either trying to be listened to — talking every chance they get — or waiting patiently or impatiently for a chance to interrupt any other person who is talking and start talking themselves.

Think about this. You will find that whenever people are together, they're making an effort to be listened to, and *are* very seldom listened to because the person that they are trying to get to listen to them is waiting desperately and impatiently for a chance to be listened to himself or herself.

From a talk to the Merced County Mental Health Association in California, U.S.A., on November 7, 1981. Appeared in **Present Time** No. 46.

SOMEONE MUST LISTEN

If we were to encapsulate what we have learned to do in a sentence or two—and there's much more, there are many complicated applications that come from it—it is to explain to people that what they are trying to do all the time, this trying to be listened to, is a very profound process. It will have profound results if it ever gets a chance to operate and it will operate, *if they will take turns*. They need to just take turns, and agree, "Yes, I *will* listen to you and really pay attention to you for a while, if you will give me a chance to do the same thing later on." We call that "Co-Counseling." The awkward word "counseling" meant "giving advice" to most people when we first started using it, but it has now come to have a good deal of the meaning we've used for it in the intervening thirty-one years, which does not mean "giving advice" at all, but basically *listening and paying attention*.

This inherent process that we're all equipped to use has been, in general, frustrated, simply because it takes another person outside of ourselves really paying attention while we talk and think about ourselves, and re-experience the distresses that we have accumulated, for it to work.

OUR ESSENTIAL NATURE IS FINE

The reality seems to be that human beings are essentially quite wonderful, and they climb their way back to practicing that wonderfulness whenever they get a chance. It's true that we've inherited a physiological set-up from our pre-human ancestors that has a lot of instincts and physical determinants in it, but we've also developed a mind, an ability to think, that is almost unique in the kingdom of life on this planet. (Some of us assume, of course, that we have older brothers and sisters somewhere out there in the Galaxy who will arrive in a space ship any day now and give us a hand, but they haven't gotten here yet.) This ability to think is quite remarkable.

We define "intelligence" as the ability to come up with a brand-new, accurate response for each new situation, to never use an old response for a new situation, because a new situation is new, and if you try to use something that worked fine for a previous situation, it's not going to quite fit the new situation, which never occurred before. There aren't any identical entities in the universe, not even two electrons are absolutely identical, and so two environmental situations for a human being will never be exact replicas of each other. There will always be something new. When we're functioning on this particular human ability, this flexible intelligence of ours, we're quite capable of taking in all the information of a situation, comparing it with the information from past experiences that we've understood, noting the similarities, noting the differences, putting together a response that is similar to what handled similar experiences in the past, but is modified to allow for the differences in this situation, and, being exactly accurate, handling each new situation well.

This ability seems to spring out of the colossal central nervous system we have. No one yet really knows how it works, but we're creeping up on it. Scientists who have spent their lives examining the central nervous system are beginning to get some vague idea. It's worthwhile noting that of the forty billion neurons (forty billion or so—I don't think anybody's counted them exactly) that each of us possesses, only a few hundred are occupied in bringing information in to the central nervous system from the sense organs, from the excellent battery of sense organs we have. Only a few hundred of these neurons bring information in, and a few hundred more transmit orders out from the central nervous system to the glands and the muscles. The rest of the forty billion sit there and talk to each other. There's a tremendous interconnection. We're very complex. We're all justified in feeling quite good about ourselves, because the goofiest mistake we ever made was really an enormous triumph of complex behavior. There's nothing simple about us.

OUR INTELLIGENCE CAN BE INTERRUPTED

This ability to come up with fresh, new answers, this rational human intelligence of ours, gets interrupted by situations of stress, of painful emotion, or of pain. Any kind of physical hurt or emotional hurt interrupts this, to a greater or lesser degree. Under those situations, the information coming in from the environment, which ordinarily is handled very easily and in great volume by our tremendous intelligence, doesn't get sorted out, doesn't get understood, doesn't get compared and contrasted with what we already know, nor filed away to be useful information. Instead it congeals, and this unevaluated information becomes, in effect, a recording of what went on during the bad times, and this recording persists. It includes the ineffective behavior, the distressed feelings, *and* the shutting down of our thinking.

We have the abilities to take such a distress recording apart (that's the principal message I have, how to take it apart, or how to encourage its being taken apart, since the process is quite spontaneous and inherent), but since this recovery ability, the recovery mechanism, the healing process is usually interfered with by social conditioning, the congealed, not-understood information from a distressed experience instead remains a recording of bad feelings and a compulsive pattern of behavior. When reminded of it enough (the folk saying goes "It reminds me too much of,"), by similarities in a new situation we are thrown into a repetition of the inability to think that the original hurt caused, and so we act rigidly, unsuccessfully, uncomfortably, and, usually, unawarely in the new situation. This allows additional distresses to accumulate and mount up.

PEOPLE ARE GOOD

This notion of the distress recording, the congealed results of an experience of distress that was not allowed to be taken apart and re-evaluated, is a very simple but very profound explanation of all the things that have puzzled us about people. Each one of us knows—and I remind you of this—that he or she is really a good person. You have been told you're not, and in the presence of fresh criticism you get to feeling you're not, but in your heart of hearts you know you're a good person, that you've always done the very best you could, *and that is true.* Each of us knows that he or she is much smarter than he or she can often show, that he or she has a lot of intelligence that doesn't come out in the tension of the final exam, or the upsetting situation, *and this is true.* I now tell you that what you know about yourself is also true of everyone else. This profound knowledge that you've hidden to escape ridicule; that you're a good person, that you always do your best, and that you're much smarter than you sometimes act or than people think—*this is true, not only of you, but of other people as well.*

THE RECOVERY PROCESSES

This wonderful nature of ours that gets obscured in this way would resurge, can resurge, and will resurge, if particular processes are allowed to take place. These are what we call "discharge." "Discharge" is a general word to encompass some very profound processes that are dependably characterized outwardly by tears, by crying, by trembling, by laughing (in many forms), by angry storming, by yawns, by non-repetitive, eager talk. These processes melt the rigidities of the distress pattern and turn its contents back into the useful information it should have been in the first place. These processes also free this tremendous intellect of ours, this flexible behavior of ours, to operate. Any discharge—any tears, any trembling, any laughter, any storming, any yawns (yawning is the dependable indication of the release of physical distress)—tends to move us back to functioning on our original nature, which is that of a genius-sized intelligence and a very good person and (more and more we're realizing this) a very *powerful* person. The powerlessness with which most of us feel infected ("I can't," "I wish I could," "I have to wait," and "Somebody will tell me I can someday") is all acquired. We're all conceived, and most of us are born, with a sense of being able to do anything. This is closer to the actual reality, and only the social conditioning has obscured this—the tremendous amounts of oppression that are ladled upon us systematically.

ACCIDENTS AND CONTAGION

The distress patterns that we acquire, the inhibiting fences that get built around us, come partly from accidental hurts. There are such things as slipping and falling and hurting oneself. In greater volume they come from the contagion of this distress. The person who was hurt is pulled by the resulting distress pattern, in some situations, to hurt someone else. The little boy who was beaten by his father is pulled, when he becomes a father himself, to beat his son in the same way and pass the hurt on. There's a certain contagion in the distress.

SYSTEMATIC OPPRESSION ALSO

More and more as we explore the phenomenon, and find our way out from under these intimidating loads of distress, we realize that there's also a *systematic* process of imposing hurts operating in this society. An oppressive society systematically places hurts upon people in order to condition them to fill certain rigid, submissive roles, or, in some cases, certain dominating, oppressive roles. We've learned in the last few years, and can now state with great confidence, that no one would submit to being oppressed if distress patterns were not first installed. We would not permit being placed in any of the roles of oppression (and we're all oppressed—we're oppressed as workers, we're oppressed as women, we're oppressed as children, we're oppressed by racism, we're oppressed by many other oppressions), none of us would accept a role in any of these oppressions except that we were first hurt as children so early that we were unable to resist and the groundwork of distress patterns was laid in for imposing new oppressions as we grew older. More than that, and this is very hopeful, no one would play an oppressor role otherwise. No man would act in a sexist way to women, unless he had first been hurt and then manipulated into the other end of the oppression. No aristocrat would ever condescendingly mistreat the common folk if not first mistreated while young. (In England this shows up very strikingly. The young aristocrats are sent to special schools and deliberately hurt there to prepare them for their roles when older. It's always easier to see in somebody else's society than it is in our own.)

MANY ARE LEARNING

This great weight of distress patterns that has limited us and has frustrated us and that hangs over us like a pall—every once in a while getting us down real hard, and then lifting somewhat again as we climb out again and function—always limiting us, always making us feel that we must accept some limited role in society because we're female, or because we're young, or because our folks worked with their hands, or whatever the oppression is—all this can be and is being thrown off by an increasing number of people at this point. Since Re-evaluation Counseling spread beyond Seattle, we have reached in some fashion—through fundamentals classes or lectures or support groups—about a half-million people. It's been a very rapid development.

We've transcended many barriers. We had no written literature to start with. Now there are twelve or thirteen books. We publish twenty-five magazines irregularly. There is a special magazine for women, a special magazine for working-class people, for blacks, for Latino/as, a magazine for people of Asian inheritance, a young people's magazine, one for mental health workers. It's called *Recovery and Re-emergence,* and it exchanges information among Re-evaluation Counselors who are working in the mental health field.

We've learned a lot; but all we've learned rests on this fairly simple re-discovery, and all the progress is based on this foundation—if at least two people will take turns, and one or more of them will listen, remarkable and good changes will take place with the person who is being listened to.

CONTENT IS UNIVERSAL

Every time we take Re-evaluation Counseling into a new country or cross another language barrier or begin to work in a new culture, we are likely to be told that this "doesn't fit into our culture." It's true that some of the trappings that we bring in from the United States culture don't fit—we're often unaware of them until the new people point them out and help us peel them off—but also it's true that the fundamentals are universal. I was told very seriously that we could not reach Arab people by talking about the need for men to cry, because Arab men don't cry. (There's a certain point to that warning, because talking about Re-evaluation Counseling is often not the way to communicate it—you want to demonstrate it instead.) I have given about twelve Arab men their first counseling session, and ten of them cried very hard the first time.

The content of this healing relationship is universal. All humans are human. The cultural differences are interesting and rich, but any *divisions* between us on the basis of culture are completely unjustified. All of us are very, very human. I remember working as a counselor in the developing years of Re-evaluation Counseling. Many of my clients were women, and as they opened up and told me all about themselves, I realized with growing surprise that women are just like men. I had never suspected that before! We're engaged currently in trying to break down the barriers that have developed between men and women, and are working to achieve closer friendships between women and men. Women are listening with amazement as they discover that men are just like women!

If you can just listen, that's good. Beginning Co-Counselors often cannot listen well, because of the internal pressure to talk themselves. When it's their turn to listen, they say, okay, go ahead, but are still very inattentive (demonstrates bad attention). Often the persons they are "listening" to are so desperate to be listened to that they pretend the other person is listening, and they have a great session! Later when better listening is needed, the second person has had a session and is not quite so inattentive, and the process improves. Co-Counseling is a sort of a mutual "take-turns" bootstrapping process. You can't lift yourself by your own boot straps but you can take turns lifting each other. It works, and of course it works in larger groups than two, but for the economy of time most Co-Counseling is done in pairs, switching roles between the first person who is listened to and the second, who listens. That's about what it amounts to.

PEOPLE ARE PEOPLE

We've tackled some very tough and complicated problems along the way. One was that we had to verify the generality of the recovery process. For a period in the early years of Re-evaluation Counseling I accepted very distressed people as clients. I had to guess as to how to handle them and made many mistakes, but I learned a great deal. Basically what I was trying to find out was, is there one kind of people who get put in mental institutions and another kind of people who can handle their lives? I had to find that out in practice. Theory wasn't enough. I'm very pleased to know, as I'm sure all of you already intuitively know, that there's only one kind of people. The person who seems to be in another strange category is someone who has been hurt very deeply, someone on whom a large load of distress has piled up, who has been, and often continues to be, oppressed very seriously. Given enough help (the word *enough* is important), anyone is able to climb all the way out to elegant functioning. Making that statement is fine, and I make it very positively. Doing it, of course, is another question, because it takes a lot of resource to support someone making a long climb back. This is no news to you who work in the "mental health" field.

HOW TO COUNSEL

We can say much more clearly now than we used to what it takes to be an effective listener for someone whom you wish to help (one-way), or with whom you wish to exchange help (two-way, as in Co-Counseling). It's very simple to say, and I'm pleased that I can say it this clearly after thirty-one years of saying it in many other ways. If you wish to help someone that you're going to listen to, plain listening is fine, but there are distresses that take a little more than that, and the more you can do beyond that, the more effective you will be.

You (a) pay enough attention to them, that you notice accurately what the distresses are. One of the ways of finding that out is to ask, "What's bothering you?", and then listen and they'll tell you. They'll never fail you. "What about yourself would you like to change?" "(Sigh) Well, no one ever asked me that before, but __________ ," and they will tell you.

If there is an inhibiting pattern in the way of them speaking out clearly to you, you can simply look at them, and the expression on their faces, the one that they wear when they're not crying or laughing or discharging in some other way, will tell you about their distress. It's a perfectly familiar expression, but it's not their's. It's the expression of a chronic pattern that has grown there from the distress that has become chronic. It may be like this (demonstrates) or it may be like this (demonstrates) or whatever, but, whatever it's like, it will tell you something.

Look at the posture. Apparently the natural posture for a man is very close to this (demonstrates). How many men do you know who stand or sit like that? Most of them have been beaten down to a submissiveness posture. A few of them are stuck in defensive postures (demonstrates). How does a woman stand? Something like this (demonstrates). Yet, how many women stand so proudly? If you see one like that in a crowd once in a while, your eyes are drawn to her almost immediately. Almost all of us in our postures tell the chronic distresses that we bear and try to resist all the time. There are other clues in a person's appearance as well.

So, (a) you pay enough attention to the person to see what the distresses are. (b) You think, "How could those be contradicted?" That's demanding. You must actually think about him or her. Think, think. How can these distresses be contradicted?

(c) You contradict them. Just that. You contradict them. The person will discharge. He or she will talk eagerly, decidedly, alively. (Not "blah, blah, blah"—that kind of talk is just the rehearsal of a pattern with words in it.) They will talk eagerly, alively, or they will begin to laugh, they will begin to cry, they will begin to shake, they will begin to yawn—something will begin to happen if you do that. If these things don't happen, you haven't contradicted the distress enough, that's all.

For many situations, simply to be listened to with interest and attention is enough contradiction. When was the last time anyone did that for you? Often discharge begins to occur simply with that. Beginning Co-Counselors sometimes have marvelous results with each other just by managing to keep their mouths shut for a little while. There's more to learn also, of course, and we're learning more all the time.

ATTITUDES TO ADOPT

There are certain additional, general things to learn, if you're going to be a good listener/friend, (and I assume you are at least considering the possibility). There are certain general hurts that people have suffered from that can also be contradicted generally. There's a certain battery of attitudes that, if you can adopt them, will make you a more effective listener and friend than if you just sit there and clench your teeth to keep silent. These may be hard to adopt at first, but if you even try to act as if you held these attitudes, it will help. It will bring you out of some of your own ruts, and it will make you much more attractive and appealing as a listener to the person that you are listening to.

What are some of the attitudes that we can extend toward the person that we are listening to that will generally contradict their distresses? One of them is *approval*. I now look approvingly at you. Which of us ever felt very hurt while someone was approving of us? It may happen, but it's not common. Another is *delight*. I shall be delighted with you. Who was ever hurt at a time when someone was delighted with them? (Voice from audience: "Not me!") I won't say that I won't find an instance someday, but I haven't found one yet. Take an attitude of *respect*. Listen as if the person's words and what they have to say and how they are feeling are worthy of full consideration.

Almost all distress carries with it disrespect. Certainly all the oppressions, which probably put a majority of our distress upon us, all carry disrespect at their core.

In working with teenagers, the internalized oppression which takes places with every group that has been oppressed was so heavy that we were looking for a way of interrupting it. (This first occurred with a group in England, but it's worked with every group of young people we've tried it with since.) We asked them to make a promise to each other, and the wording is, "I solemnly promise that, from this moment on, I will never again treat any young person, including myself, with anything less than complete respect." We've never had a group of young people together where more than two of them have made that promise before everyone in the group started crying, got their arms around each other and sobbed. Lack of respect is a crucial element in the mistreatment which young people endure.

It's also at the heart of every other oppression. What's at the heart of sexism? A woman being treated without respect. What's at the heart of racism? The non-white being treated without respect. What's at the heart of ageism? The elder being treated as a cast-off. "Oh, grandma, now you just go sit down." Lack of respect.

So, if, as a listener, you can adopt an attitude of full respect, let the person you are listening to feel that whatever he or she has to say is important, you will be more effective. What you hear should be listened to with respect, because either it will be thinking, and everyone's thinking is worthy of respect, or it will be some distress that the person is trying to voice in order to get it out there where she or he can see it and begin to take it apart, and that's very deserving of respect, also. If you can adopt an attitude of respect and keep adopting it until it becomes second nature, becomes a good habit, then your listening becomes more powerful.

CONFIDENCE FOR THEM

What else? What other hurts are so general that we can set

up a general attitude to contradict them? How about confidence? How about being confident that the person you're listening to can attain what he or she wants? The person says, "I wish I could ______," and you say, "I think you can do it. I think you're just the person who can do it." If you maintain this attitude, can't you imagine the lift that will give? Very few people have had much confidence expressed in them. Even our beloved parents, who wanted so desperately to give us the best start in life they possibly could, had been so hurt themselves that often when they went to express confidence and support to us they instead gave us warnings. "Don't go too far," and "Don't stick your neck out," and "Try to get a good, steady job and hold on to it," and statements like that. We got their fears instead of their confidence. So, if you can express confidence, if you say to the person, "I know you can do it, I'm sure you'll succeed," it's going to help almost every time.

HIGH EXPECTATIONS

What other attitudes can we helpfully adopt? I think high expectations is one. Over and over I hear from clients, "I wasn't expected to do anything. I wanted to become a nuclear physicist, but everyone told me it would be a waste of time because I'd just get married and have a family anyway." So I offer the expectation—"Now your family is grown, you can go back to school and be a nuclear physicist if you want to. Don't you dare settle for anything less than what you want." I express that kind of attitude.

COMMITMENTS

On the drive up from Fresno, I helped someone practice a commitment. The commitment is a very powerful tool. It has to be just the right commitment. It has to be the person's own commitment. This commitment was: "I solemnly promise that from this moment on I will never again settle for anything less than everything." Sounds a little ambitious, doesn't it? But try it a few times. You'll be amazed at the thoughts that come winging through your head. In your role as the listener, in your role as the good friend, remember to have high expectations.

(Not reproaches! They're already too plentiful. "Why didn't you get a higher grade? Only an A+? Why didn't you get better than that?") Offer instead the confident expectation "If you want it, you can get it, and I'll back you all the way." "You're not sure you can think well enough? I know you can think. Can you do what you want to? Yes, you can. There's no question about it."

If you remember that your goal is to be a good listener/friend and remember what a powerful force listening is, and if you then think of the attitudes you always wished somebody had taken toward you, you'll know what to do. You'll know the attitudes that your friend is waiting for. Confidence, respect, delight, safety, approval, awareness, reassurance that the person has always done his or her best, natural physical contact. Commitment. "I'll be with you. I'll stick with you, I won't abandon you no matter how hard the going gets." That may feel like an awful load, as if you listen to five people and you commit yourself, then you may have to be washing everybody's dishes next week—but it's not the same thing. If a pattern comes in to demand that you wash the dishes to prove you're really with them, you say, "I'm sorry, that's not what I really meant. I'm for *you*, not for your dirty dishes." The danger isn't as great as you may feel it is.

LOVE

There's a big attitude which we're all going to be awkward and scared about at first: love. Love. If you can look at the person you're listening to with full, warm, unabashed love, then all kinds of things become possible. Something happens (and I suspect some of you at least already know about this) when you listen really well to someone. As he or she opens up and is crying just as hard as he or she can, the real person shows. It's as if a screen rolls back with the tears or the laughter or trembling, and you really see the person, and you find yourself falling in love. That's good. Don't be scared. Be careful, but don't be scared. Don't be afraid to fall in love with each other. We have rules in the Co-Counseling Community that if you meet people as a Co-Counselor you do not go into business with them, you do not try to sell them life insurance, you do not romance them, or go off and marry them. But love them, yes. Love them thoroughly. The attitude of love improves your listening. Most of us are suffering from an inadequate chance to express love. Most of us are pent up with love that we don't have enough opportunity to express. It will be good for you.

The need to love is a much bigger rational need even than the need to be loved. Our culture emphasizes people needing to be loved, and that's real, but it's a small thing compared with the need *to love*. If you don't really let your love out, you're going to turn sour inside. So add the attitude of love to your listening. Work at it carefully, cautiously. Don't confuse it with doing each other's dishes. Just keep it what it is, just love, and it will improve. Some of you are mental health professionals, I'm sure, and you've been trained to sit on the other side of a desk and not get "involved" and I don't want to invalidate your training, but if you can have this overall attitude of love, it doesn't matter. You can stay on your stepladder if you have to and still love them, and every one of your clients or patients or whatever you call them, is going to know the difference right away. They're going to be emboldened to pick up their feet and walk right out of the swamp with great speed compared to what they would do otherwise.

Generally, I don't talk to people about one-way listening. That's a special problem. Generally I talk to people about *exchanging* this relationship, and that's the way I want to talk to you, too. Because, even if you have big case loads that you're working on, you won't do this very well unless you also have a supportive *peer* relationship with someone else. If you get interested in Co-Counseling and want to learn to do it, you can pick up any of the magazines here. (There's lots more that I didn't mention—there's *Heritage* for Native Co-Counselors, there's *Colleague* for university and college faculty Co-Counselors, there's *Classroom* for teachers in the primary and secondary schools, and there's a lot of others.) But you won't become a Co-Counselor out of a magazine alone. What you read is interesting, but you need to set up a natural relationship with someone else on a peer basis. Do it with another worker in your field. Do it with a neighbor. Just agree to take turns listening. You'll do it sloppily to begin with—everybody else did that, and I don't know why you should be an exception—but it will get better, and something that you've needed all through your life will begin to become a reality.

I do not say to you that it's "easy." I do say that it's simple, but the simplicity continually gets obscured by the distress itself and by the restimulation which ordinary living piles on us all the time and the lonely little oppressions and the discouragements. It *is simple*, however, and, persisted with, it makes a huge difference in a person's life.

WORTH DOING

Co-Counseling has been outside of Seattle for only eleven years, and it's been a very hectic eleven years. I've worn myself frazzly trying to travel all over and do workshops and lectures and get Co-Counseling Communities started; but it has been very satisfying. In the last few weeks I made a long trip to the East Coast. In two of the workshops I did—one was for Jewish leaders and one was for women leaders—I noticed a phenomenon. A lot of the people at each of those workshops were "old-timers." They were competing a little bit as to seniority. "I've been co-counseling nine years," and "I've been in ten"—like that. These people had changed profoundly. This was so plain. These people were in charge of their lives, had complete confidence in their associates, knew what they were about, and were ready to tackle some problems that most of the population is simply too numb with terror to think about, such as the fact that we have to eliminate all nuclear weapons or we're all going to be dead in about twelve years. These people were actually able to think about that. They knew how to discharge their fears and were making plans to insure that their grandchildren had a chance to live.

So I would encourage you to explore Co-Counseling if you can. Explore it through the literature. Do it through participation in the Co-Counseling Community if you can, but if not, use the knowledge that I've reminded you of this morning.

You've always known everything that I've told you this morning, but it's been obscured. Hang onto it and put it to use, and organize it to the extent that with at least one other person you make some kind of commitment to take turns listening, and to try to improve your listening.

It won't work like a magic wand. Just when you start to feel very much better because of your initial successes, you will decide on some level to bring up a deep distress and see if you can handle that, and for a while you'll feel all frazzled because you've got more in the frying pan than you can fry; but, if you persist, life will get more meaningful. You will regain a much better perspective. You will regain again the picture you had when you were young of the way life should be. You will reacquire some confidence about making your life that way. You will take full advantage of this wonderful, beautiful life that we have a chance to live. You will not live so much of life absorbed by the distress, or let so many days and hours go by in fogs and funks and discouragements and despairs and confusion and terror. You will take charge. More and more you will take charge of your own lives. Just incidentally, you will be much more effective "mental health" workers.

REALLY LIVE

It's our life. We haven't been told that. We've been told the opposite, but our lives belong to us. I sometimes say to advanced students, "There are no 'should's' in the universe." Sometimes they look at me with horror and ask, "If I don't have 'should's' to guide me in what I do, how will I know I'm doing the right thing?" But there are no "should's" in the universe. Your own intelligence is quite satisfactory for guiding your life. You're not obligated to anyone. I thought for years that I was obligated to my children at least, and I couldn't get past that.

Then one day, after some Co-Counseling, it occurred to me that anything that my children needed done for them by me, I would do because I wanted to. I didn't have to be obligated.

There are no "should's." It's your life. Take charge of it. Have fun.

Corrections, Changes, and Reminders

The Re-iterative Decision As a Tool for Change

A Correction of a Distortion and an Apology

In the last two years or so, I have been emphasizing the effectiveness of making a firm decision (or making a "commitment" or a "solemn promise") as a tool for contradicting distress and achieving its discharge. In urging this upon people, I have often given the impression, and have often had the impression myself, that to do this is always possible and sufficient, that if one could make and keep a clear and strong enough decision, then emergence from any pattern could take place very rapidly. I am sure that I have often given the impression of considerable impatience with Co-Counselors who failed to make or keep such commitments.

When first introducing the use of commitments, I allowed for the necessity of "practicing" the commitment and recommended that the counselor formally release the client from the commitment at the end of the session until the client had been able to think about all the difficulties to be faced and had practiced the commitment enough that he or she was reasonably sure that he or she could keep the commitment before it was made a permanent, binding one. For myself, however, and for other leaders of the Community, I fell into the position that once a commitment was clear, it should be kept.

Later, when I publicly made a commitment myself *and then did not keep it,* I rationalized the situation to myself by saying that I had failed so far but had really only postponed the time when I would keep the commitment perfectly. I kept "trying" to fulfill the commitment, but didn't give myself any credit for the effort, and kept thinking to myself that "soon" I would "really" keep the commitment.

THE "SUPERVISED COUNSELING" WORKSHOP

At the "Supervised Counseling" Workshop in 1982, we attempted to locate the source of, and begin to work against, the gap between counseling practice, even by the best Co-Counselors, and the level of theory available. We concluded that the primary reason for this discrepancy was an apparently-very-long-time habit of all people of paying attention to their old distresses all or nearly all the time. We interpreted this as an attempt on our part to have our old distresses readily available in case we were ever able to find adequate attention and support from another intelligence so that we could begin to discharge them without delay. We agreed that this had clearly not been workable but *was* understandable. Later discussions led to a conclusion that we deserved appreciation rather than reproach for having done this, since it was an indication of our determination to emerge when no other possibilities for discharge seemed possible.

The persistence of this patterned habit into the times people were in the counselors' role apparently was at least a principal explanation for the failure of much of our best counselors' *practice* to live up to the level of their theoretical understanding. In beginning to undo these patterned habits of keeping some attention on our old distresses at all times, we were forced to the realization that to change these habits would take *repeated* decisions on our part. It would take discharge to support these decisions, but repetitive decisions would be necessary. These repetitive decisions have already shown their value as a tool for the ending of this habit and the improvement of our counseling. In making and re-making and re-making this decision to take and keep my attention away from my old distresses, I came to realize that the commitment which I had "failed" to keep (had kept only partially) had nevertheless served to improve my functioning considerably. That is, I had moved in a definite, important way toward my goals even if I had not achieved them all yet, nor maintained them perfectly.

It seems clear to me at this point that my anxiety to overcome my obstacles and my eagerness to move quickly had led me into a distortion of some theoretical understanding that I had previously grasped well. It had also led me to present these distortions to others as "theory" in a way that was not helpful to them. I apologize to the Co-Counselors whom I may have confused or discouraged by doing this.

I had previously been well aware of, and had spoken and written quite clearly on, the fact that the dynamic universe, continually in change, accomplishes this process of change in alternating modes. That is, small quantitative changes accumulate, often over a long period of time, before rapid qualitative changes take place. Also, when qualitative changes do take place, they usher in another period of quantitative changes which tend to be gradual and accumulate slowly in comparison to the dramatic rapid activity of the qualitative change period.

(A common illustration of the alternation of quantitative changes and qualitative ones is the change in physical states of water with increasing temperature. The gradual change in the temperature of ice when it is warmed from a low temperature gives way to a rapid qualitative change in its state at the melting point. That is, the molecules vibrate faster and faster in the crystal lattice of the ice as the temperature increases, but at the melting point they break free from the crystal structure and begin to slide over each other in constant movement and activity typical of the molecules of a liquid. As the temperature of the liquid water into which the ice has been converted continues to increase, the quantitative changes are expressed in more rapid liquid motion of the molecules. This changes gradually and quantitatively until, at the vaporizing point, the motion of the molecules changes dramatically from sliding over each other to flying apart and becoming molecules of a gas.)

Thus, I need to re-balance my emphasis on encouraging and improving Co-Counseling. In this recent period I think I have distorted my effectiveness by putting undue emphasis on qualitative changes in counseling, on the dramatic commitments, the sharp break-throughs, the corner-turning sessions. To correct this I need to reassure myself and others that the slow work, the steady improvement, and the accumulation of small gradual gains is also valuable and necessary.

In the universe as a whole, in all the dynamic processes we have any knowledge of, "creep" alternates with "leap." This undoubtedly is also true with such complex processes as discharge and re-emergence. The "undramatic" session in which one simply "thinks out loud" about current events and gains a better perspective is probably quite important. In one sense it is as important to the upward trend and to the individual's re-emergence as the dramatic session which frees a "whole chunk" of our thinking and leaves us re-evaluating excitedly and joyfully for weeks afterwards.

Not only do the quantitative gradual processes, the "creep" processes, necessarily alternate with the dramatic, quick-change, qualitative-change, "leap" processes, but it is probably essential that they do. Both kinds of progress need to be appreciated and encouraged.

Reminders from the 1981 World Conference

The theory of Re-evaluation Counseling promises, and raises expectations of, an effectiveness of counseling which our practice in general fails to live up to. Though our practice continually improves, the theory advances beyond it at all times. This is a desirable condition.

It is possible, however, for people to become "disappointed with" RC because of the expectations aroused by the theory and the difficulty in finding counseling effective enough to fulfill these expectations.

All Co-Counselors should remind each other that the job of making counseling practice improve and advance toward the theoretical possibilities is in all cases a job for everyone and, in particular, for "first person singular." It is not something for someone else to achieve and bring to the individual Co-Counselor ready-made, without his or her participation and effort.

Appeared in **Present Time** No. 46.

THE WAY YOU WERE TAUGHT RC IS NOT *THE* WAY RC IS TAUGHT.

***The* way RC is taught is the way *you* teach it, if you think about communicating the basic, universal content in a way that *your* friends and fellow-workers and neighbors and associates can hear and understand it and use it, not repeating any non-essential words or practices just because your teacher or other RCers used them.**

Co-Counselors who become RC teachers should understand that they are expected to teach, not just wear the title of "teacher." New RC teachers will receive the accumulated literature on teaching RC to begin with, (except where a language barrier exists) and are expected to pay for it and to read it. All RC teachers will receive regular "teachers' packets" of newly published RC literature, (except where a language barrier exists) and are expected to pay for and read such literature themselves and, in addition, organize the promotion and sale of such literature and other RC literature to their students.

Every RC teacher is expected to offer in each RC class three scholarships to young people under 21 years of age, and two scholarships for Third World persons. The RC teacher should not expect compensation from Outreach Funds for these scholarships but regard it as her or his personal contribution to human liberation and to having a more interesting class.

A teacher who is not introducing liberation theory and the techniques for counseling on and discharging oppression distress in all roles in the oppression, is giving an incomplete or inadequate version of RC theory to his or her students. Counseling on and discharging oppression distress is an integral part of Co-Counseling theory and practice.

Community members need to think about and practice support of leaders. Leaders are a valuable asset to members. Leaders need good counseling. Leaders need encouragement and support. Leaders need sharing of the work and help in carrying out the jobs of the Community. Leaders still need the thoughtful consideration accorded any individual Co-Counselor. Leaders need all the respect accorded any Community Member. Leaders need prompt and decisive interruption of the attacks, both from within and from outside the Community, which will tend to arise and be directed at a leader simply because she or he is a leader.

Our theory is at present already adequate for full re-emergence. Our practice is mainly inhibited by the effects of the distress patterns themselves. Patterns confuse us about theory. Patterns persist more than we persist in efforts to discharge them. Patterns make us forget the theory and fail to use it.

The remedy for all this lies in the great ef-

fectiveness of the "second person's" words. If we remind each other of theory consistently and if we require persistent, dependable progress of each other, the practice of Co-Counseling will quickly advance toward the present level of the theory.

EVERYONE CAN BE ENCOURAGED TO READ RC LITERATURE, to be in non-RC support groups, to learn to Co-Counsel informally, or through formal RC classes, or through classes with an RC content but not an RC name.

BECOMING A COMMUNITY MEMBER, HOWEVER, IS A RESPONSIBLE PRIVILEGE. When Community membership is offered to a Co-Counselor, the responsibilities for being a Community Member should be clearly stated.

A Community Member is a Co-Counselor who is able, willing and acts to take responsibility for the integrity and consistency and correctness of RC theory and practice, for the growth and well-being of the RC Community, and for the keeping of the agreements among its members, such as are embodied in the *Guidelines* and policy statements.

Attendance at Regional and International RC Workshops should be assumed to be limited to Community Members except in special cases or special circumstances.

People from groups who endure burdensome oppression should have the activity expected of them in being Community Members take their special circumstances into account.

AN RCer CAN INTEREST PEOPLE IN HEARING BASIC RC INFORMATION, BY FIRST ACTING AS A RESPECTFUL LISTENER AND MODEL OF A RATIONAL HUMAN.

Basic RC knowledge such as:

people are good except where they've been hurt,

discharge helps people think better and feel better,

everyone has always done the best he or she could at every moment of the past,

listening has more effect on people than telling,

children and all people flourish under praise and validation and wither under criticism and fault-finding,

everyone needs to be touched and to touch,

love is the way people naturally feel about each other,

etc.,

if communicated widely, makes an RCer's environment much safer, much more sup-

portive, more enjoyable. It is a pro-survival act to disseminate RC knowledge and practices widely in the environment, and every opportunity to do so effectively should be grasped.

A CO-COUNSELOR is a person who exchanges Re-evaluation Counseling with one or more other persons to the best of her or his growing ability.

A COMMUNITY MEMBER is a Co-Counselor who is able, willing and acts to take responsibility for the integrity and consistency and correctness of RC theory and practice, for the growth and well-being of the RC Community, and for the keeping of the agreements among its members, such as are embodied in the Guidelines and policy statements.

A LEADER is a Community Member who is able, willing and acts to see that everything works right, with no exceptions.

Leadership in RC consists, in great part, of modeling the practice of RC for the people whom the leader presumes to lead.

EVERY EXPERIENCED RCer IS URGED TO ORGANIZE AT LEAST ONE SUPPORT GROUP OF NON-RCers among

neighbors, in a car pool, with people with whom one works, with people with similar interests. Such a grouping does not need to be called anything, not even a "support group." The necessary theory should be communicated informally by the RCer's practice of it until people ask for a formal presentation. The leadership of the RCer will consist of seeing that everyone has a turn at being listened to without interruption, that each person is encouraged and persuaded to talk of something positive before dwelling on difficulties, that new people are occasionally added to the group, and that the group is divided and a new leader helped to lead the group when the original group becomes too large to give each person time enough for a good turn.

Why Not "Unlearning" Racism?

The phrase "unlearning racism," developed and used by one of us (Ricky Sherover-Marcuse) in her workshops with non-RCers, seems to have been useful in that the phrase seems to dampen the guilt feelings that people associate with their conditioned racism and encourages them to dare to attend a workshop, listen to theory, and begin to take some directions which can lead to discharge of some of the racism. Used in this way, and backed by skills and dedication, some good results have been achieved.

Its use inside RC is leading to some problems, however. Part of our theoretical clarity in this field has been exactly that racism *is a distress pattern*, that people inherently know better than to be racist and that they have to be hurt in the presence of racist treatment or racist attitudes for these to become part of their behavior. In general, we know that racism has to be grafted onto adultism, by early oppressive and non-respectful treatment of young people, as is the case with so many other oppressions. In this sense and considering the way that we have used the word "learning" in RC, the use of the phrase "unlearning racism" in RC represents several contradictions. A pattern is not "unlearned." It is discharged. Racism was not "learned" in the beginning but was imposed or conditioned by the hurt and by the installation of a pattern by that hurt.

The value of the phrase has apparently been to disarm the defensiveness of people and keep them from shutting down over their fears of being blamed for their racism and has led to more courage on their part in approaching discussions on the

Appeared in **Present Time** No. 51.

topic. There must be a way to preserve this advantage without inviting theoretical confusion or drifting back into a "liberal" attitude toward racism such as has been so ineffective in all the wide-world work up until now.

A similar difficulty can attach itself to the terms of "target group" and "non-target group." They are euphemisms that may make it easier for us to start thinking in the area, but if they bypass our recognition to the oppressed group *that they have been oppressed*, that is, that they have been subjected to systematic, one-way mistreatment enforced by the society simply because they are who they are, we are likely to leave them prey to the familiar patterns of internalized oppression, blaming themselves and each other for the continuing oppression. Similarly, if we reassure the people outside the oppression that they are simply "non-target," without in some other way motivating them to do the necessary work to become *active* allies of the oppressed, then we are allowing them to perpetuate a kind of passive racism for their own comfort. That, I think we would all agree, is not a good idea.

We challenge RCers to come up with verbal clarity in this field. Can we, without losing the clarity of the "oppressed" and "oppressor" characterizations, find words and terms that do not provoke defensiveness and offer some of the encouragement necessary to begin to discharge such as has resulted in wide-world work with the use of the "target" and "non-target," "learning" and "unlearning" phrases?

—Harvey Jackins
—Ricky Sherover-Marcuse

The Purpose of Support Groups

In many Communities, we need to clarify our concept of support groups. They have often been large groups, meeting infrequently and trying to fill leadership and policy functions as well as communication and discharge functions.

I propose that we think of support groups as *places where we can discharge the distress that is difficult to discharge if the group is not of similar background and experience.* As with all RC meetings, they should also include a review of previously-heard theory and up-to-date information on new theory, but discharge should be their primary function.

This means that support groups should be small, from two to six people. Implied is that each person presently active should form her or his own support group and recruit it largely from the wide world, making the support group an introduction to RC for many more people.

The leaders of Jewish support groups, in my opinion, should meet occasionally with other Jewish leaders and with the top leadership of the Area or Region (Jewish and non-Jewish) and *this group* should discuss policy and provide leadership for introducing the tools and concepts of RC to all sections of the Jewish community. This group should also plan the work of educating non-Jewish RCers of the Community to be good allies, and should plan parallel workshops which bring all Jewish RCers together and, separately, all active allies together to work out their respective roles and policies and then to exchange their thinking with each other in a final, joint meeting.

Appeared in **Ruah Hadashah** No. 5.

Changes in "Support Groups"

The concept of "support group" has changed a good deal since it first developed within Re-evaluation Counseling. I think it is time to clarify the concept further. This type of organization is likely to be the vehicle for much of our outreach and our re-emergence in this next period.

A support group is a meeting of people with similar interests or similar backgrounds, who use the discharge and re-evaluation process in the favorable environment of the support group.

We have had *liberation* support groups of many kinds. In these, people who have endured similar kinds of oppression meet together. Often in the past, these have been used for discharge, but we have also tried to use them for working out policy, for writing articles, for developing leadership, for solving problems, and so on. I propose that we redefine the support group as a group *for discharge* and call other meetings and set up other groups for these other functions of leadership, policy, and so on. This would certainly mean that people who endure similar oppression, people who work at similar jobs or in similar workplaces, or in the same workplace or live in the same neighborhood will come together in support groups and take turns being listened to. This means that support groups will be kept to a small enough size that there is discharge time for each individual in each meeting, or, if there is some particular advantage in the group being larger, to be sure that it divides for most of the meeting time into smaller groups to allow each person time for discharge.

This also means that we do away with the former stricture

Appeared in **Present Time** No. 45.

that "one must be in a regular class in order to be in a support group." It is perfectly possible for the support group to take time to review some existing theory and get up-to-date on new theory and still leave most of the meeting time for discharge by the individual members.

It can also mean that support groups be a point of introduction to Re-evaluation Counseling for new people. Such new friends will thus be able to see Re-evaluation Counseling work and enjoy its practical results without having first to surmount their fears of strangeness, of theory, and of commitment. Their interest in theory and in organization will arise naturally.

To implement this and in accord with the decision of the 1981 World Conference that each Community member function as a leader and build a constituency in the wide world, I seriously propose that *each experienced Co-Counselor* set up at least one support group of two to eight members from among the people with whom she or he lives and works.

These support groups should not, in general, carry the label "RC" but should carry the correct content of RC. It will be sufficient that each person have a turn, however informally, to talk about what has been good or satisfactory in her or his week or day and what she or he has done well, and then, what has been hard or what has been difficult. The RCer leading the group should guide this to take place without any announcements but just by asking the right questions of people. This kind of support group can meet quickly after work, in tavern or car or locker room, or, for homeworkers, in the mornings when the children are at school. Such a group, which can be called a "getting acquainted group" (if it needs to be called anything), will fill an immediate need for the people in it and will also interest them and attract them without any big explanation or commitment. It will also serve the needs of the experienced RCer who is forming and leading it. None of us ever gets enough of this kind of group attention often enough in our lives.

The experienced RCer leading the group may have to resist the familiar pressures for everybody to talk at once, to interrupt each other, or to plunge into negatives without first remembering something positive, but this is certainly not beyond the skills of even an inexperienced RCer to handle.

A closing point at each meeting should be deciding which additional people the whole group can agree to invite for later get-togethers.

If these support groups grow rapidly (and they often will), then one finds an assistant to lead the second section when the group divides in order to provide time for everyone. The assistant will want information on how to do it. The evolvement of new leadership is thus begun.

The people who first become ready for a more profound use of RC theory and practice will make themselves known through asking questions and being curious. They will be a natural source of additions to the body of Co-Counselors and, in some cases, to the membership of the RC Community.

Clearing Sexism From the Counseling Relationship

In the discussions at the World Conference about repudiating and eliminating the disruptive attacks on leadership which had preceded the Conference, some attention was given to *why* the restimulation had confused as many people as it had, in the face of all the usual assumptions of fairness, respect, etc.

One matter that came to light was the apparently widespread but, until now, little-reported phenomenon of some male RCers making sexist sexual overtures to female clients *while in the counselor role.*

We have previously had widespread discussion in the Communities of the principle that men should not exhibit their sexist material at women counselors *while clients.* There has been general agreement on this, and it has increased the safety of women RCers in the Community. Apparently it is time to firmly and clearly enunciate the other half of the responsibility. Men RCers *should not* exhibit their sexism, including sexual suggestiveness or seductiveness, while in the counselor role, either.

(A number of men [and women] have contacted me since the discussion to say that dramatization of sexual distress at male clients by female counselors also takes place, and I have no doubt that it occurs and should be stopped. This is not the same or comparable, however, to male counselors harassing a female client, which is part of and becomes reinforced by the heavy sexist oppression of the society as a whole.)

Appeared in **Present Time** No. 45.

Let's have an immediate end to dramatization of sexual distress in counseling sessions. Let's use our counseling tools to require any misbehaving counselors to be client on this distress and eliminate it.

Please share with others in letters to the journals the good experiences and successes you have had in eliminating this kind of clutter and achieving loving, respectful Co-Counseling attitudes as a result.

Leadership

Grasp Wider Leadership

Introductory Report to the Regional Reference Persons' Meeting—June, 1980

Each of us is a very ordinary and a very extraordinary human being. We hypothesize, but also we have a lot of evidence, that all human beings are very much alike, basically. We are all good. We are all very intelligent. We are all very powerful. We are all very curious, eager, cooperative, and a whole series of other positive characteristics. As we emerge from the distress into which we have been stuffed, more and more of these similarities appear. We are more and more reassured. As we work with deeply distressed clients, as we work with intensively oppressed clients, with victims of incredible multiple oppression, as we work with clients from cultures which are very different from our own, it is a common experience to realize how very much alike we all are.

Any important differences seem to be acquired. Our whiskers may grow differently inherently, but that's all. The distressing differences are simply the results of different mistreatment, of different conditioning. The great variety of our creativities is simply because this is a very complex and beautiful universe that we have evolved into and different ones of us have taken an interest in and assimilated knowledge of different portions of this universe. As we get into communication with each other, our creative differences are very rewarding and enriching.

Differences in opportunity vary widely. Each of us in this group has had some different opportunities and as a result, some different experiences.

I hope that this meeting will signalize a grasping by each in-

Appeared in **The RC Teacher** No. 16.

dividual here of the totality of the world situation and assuming of individual responsibility for guiding the upward trend on this planet through the next period.

Perhaps some of us will not pursue that path, no matter how much I wish that each one will. Perhaps the distress will snag one of us or something will distract one or more of us. It would be reasonable, I suppose, from our past experience, to expect that one or two of us might decide to do something easier, might embrace a pattern and live with it the rest of their lives and defend it, might settle for a less challenging future than I have in mind for you. That will be all right, I think. I have no business imposing my goals on other people; so if it turns out that you wish to take what insights you've gathered from your experiences in RC so far and live happily and snugly in a limited way ever after, you certainly have a perfect right to do it. I have no business telling you what to do with the rest of your life.

I will tell you, however, that I am confident that each of the twenty-four Regional Reference Persons who got here, and the three Liberation Reference Persons who are sitting in with us, can, if she or he so wishes, determine the future of the world. I offer you this alternative.

It is only fair, if one person challenges another person to a course of action, that the first person be prepared to model it. I cannot say to you that I have completely modeled what I propose to you, nor even that I will be able to, although it is my firm intention to do so. I am not outside the aging and physical disability distresses enough to be sure that they will not interfere, although I have every intention of overcoming them.

But, I have modeled somewhat. I would propose to each of you that you do at least as much as I have done so far. Beginning as an individual, without financial resources or outside approval, I have enlisted enough people in re-emergence to clear the pseudo-reality away from a lot of the reality of the world. I would estimate that a good third of a million people have been significantly influenced by RC ideas, by ideas which came from RC. (I am not including the parallel ideas which arise spontaneously everywhere in this historical period.) The resources which I had to do this with were and are no greater than the resources which each of you possess.

I was thirty-four years old when I got the first glimpse that crying helped rather than hurt people. That was all there was to start with. Most of you are now older than that. Each of you has had a far more rapid, accelerated access to our body of knowledge than I had. I don't think I am asking you to do anything in this first step that I haven't already done, nor in any later steps, more than I intend to do.

I propose that each of you, in a fairly short period of time because of the resources that are now available, plan to have at least as many Co-Counselors in your Region as there are presently in the world. Difficulties? I think they are all subjective. I don't believe anyone here has a Region without sufficient population to reach that goal. Probably the least populated is New Hampshire and Vermont and there must be a couple of million people there, aren't there? All of you have numbers of people available equal, roughly, to the numbers of people who have already come into RC. I don't think any of us has a Region (or a constituency, for the Liberation people) that is short on numbers or consisting of people any more difficult to reach than the present participants in RC. So I propose that you consider accomplishing this directly, that you assume leadership and responsibility for this.

There are some good growth rates. I don't know what the numerical growth rate in The Netherlands is, but the way new teachers in new cities appear on the map, I think there is very substantial growth. As far as I can tell, a key factor responsible for that is Joke's gentle but determined insistence that people will do the sensible thing. She's not free from resistance. There are as many patterns in The Netherlands combatting her leadership and her policies as there are anywhere else I know.

You may have other personal goals, and if you think there is a conflict, I certainly have no right to object if you decide the other goals are more important, but in general I don't think your good goals are in conflict with this. If you have goals that point you in a lesser direction, I would suggest a session or two on it to see if they really matter more to you. Certainly, from some of the reports of the Regional people we've heard, the singing sound of people having found what they want to do, I can't conceive of anything as satisfying.

Just in the last couple of weeks, I'd had one of these generalizing insights that I treasure as I come to understand more of the Universe around me. This is about art and about creativity in general. What do we like in a good novel or a good technical book, or in a painting or in a piece of music or in a stage play or in a movie or in a song? I think what we thrill to is intelligence. In a good novel we meet intelligence on its pages. In a good scientific article, we recognize a mind. A long time ago, in trying to explain why people love people naturally, that love is the way people naturally feel about each other, I said, "People love people because, though the whole Universe is all delightful and appreciable and beautiful, there is probably nothing else in the universe sufficiently complex to really interest a human mind except another human mind." I think this intelligence is what we like. Why do I respond the way I do to Mozart's music? Because there is a mind there in the music putting those vibrations together so elegantly. There is no question that human intelligence did that. The creaking of a rusty hinge or the song of a blackbird, which resembles the creaking of a rusty hinge, are pleasant, but you can't be content with those very long before you go prowling for the sound of a human voice, hoping that it will make some sense. It is the same in a lecture, a magazine article, in a painting. How do painters know when a painting is good? I think it is because they recognize a mind in the paint. They can tell that intelligence has left its tracks in that painting. Whether it is an abstract or a landscape or whatever, there is sure recognition of intelligence. This is the really satisfying part of the Universe to us. This interaction with other human minds takes the compression off our own. We flow out.

To free human minds to be themselves must be the most satisfying activity one can do. We now know how to lift the weight off the pinned victim, or in the words of the song, to "free the spirit from the shell." So, I challenge or invite each of you to liberate humanity from its only real serious handicap, its vulnerability to irrationality, its susceptibility to the imposition of the distress pattern. It is now possible to free humanity from the existing distress, to stop the systematic imposition of additional distress and to finally achieve such liberation of our awareness as will prevent any distress from being re-imposed except temporarily by accidents. Such accidental distresses will be removed the next hour by the immediate converging of fellow humans to achieve the discharge necessary for prompt re-emergence. I challenge each of you individually to do this, enjoying and glorying in the parallel activity of the others who will be doing it, using the resource of mutual aid and mutual discussion, but not depending on it, not making it the precondition for your own full initiative.

At leaders' meetings at workshop breakfasts I posed the question: "If a peculiar virus suddenly attacked the world which was fatal only to people in RC, but you happened to be immune, and so, in a period of a day, all other RCers were dead, and you alone escaped to tell the story, would you start RC over again world-wide, and if you would, how would you go about it?" Pulled outside their usual ruts to think, almost everyone concludes they would do this, and they come up with a great variety of the most brilliant and sensible plans for getting started. I suppose at least half the people said, "I would immediately put a guard on the present stock of RC literature and use it to the fullest." A large majority of people at these meetings proposed good, sensible, brilliant plans.

If they can plan this way now to start the international community over again, why aren't they doing it while we are all still alive? This is one question we have to answer here. Why are we not individually seeing that other people take their own initiatives, that other torches catch fire and shed at least as much light as we do and pass the fire on into the outer reaches of the darkness.

What peculiar phenomenon is occurring? How can we change the fact that achieving responsible leadership seems to block the emergence of additional responsible leadership, that training and involving one hundred or two hundred Co-Counselors in an Area seems to stop the process of attracting and permanently involving a larger number of Co-Counselors in that same geographical setting? It's as if there was only room for so many rational people in the world. That notion is ridiculous and dangerous. Some patterned caricature of this must be limiting our growth. We have to find it and take directions against it. I invite you and challenge each of you, individually, not as a group. (Groups are important, groups have their function, but the idea that a group can substitute for individual initiative is very much in error. It has to be you, the first person singular, that does this.)

I invite each of you to say, "I promise to find a way to remove any blighting effect I am having that has so far led someone else to fail to take over, not my job, but the comparable one he or she should be holding. If my present attitude is blighting the emergence of people who will play leadership roles, I promise I will find a way to change it and I ask help in changing it, so that others do not continue to hold back from taking full responsibility in the same way that I expect me to."

Please, each of you, build and lead a community of one-third of a million Co-Counselors. If each of us did that there would be quite a few Co-Counselors around. This is fantasy, of course, but just for a moment speculate. Let's see, there are twenty-four of us here. If each of us did that, that would be eight million Co-Counselors. Imagine eight million people unitedly saying no to war plans, with the influence that Co-Counselors have when they use it. We could pretty well guarantee some nice things happening.

I had a couple of thousand very loosely committed followers in 1970, but they were mostly very dependent. I don't think there was anyone around me in 1970 before Buck Creek I who was playing one-tenth the role that each of you is playing today. So, in ten years, this much has happened, and our resources, our communication network, our publications have changed dramatically in those ten years. I've had that chance. It's your turn. Act like a musician and "take it"! I just finished my chorus. Now each of you grab your sax or trumpet and "take off."

Learning to Organize

The June Liberation and Special Interest Reference Persons' Meetings began with reports from each individual on his or her work. These reports will appear in various journals. Harvey's report, below, followed:

Listening to these reports tells us how far we've come, not only in the details that were reported, but in the type of reports, and in the confidence of the people making the reports. Some of our newest Liberation Reference People haven't had time to do more than count their three or ten constituents, but it is evident from the people reporting and their attitudes that things will be happening.

I think we have three key jobs to do at this meeting. One is to really understand the role of a Liberation Reference Person and begin to define it better. We have enough experience accumulated that we can fill out our original projections or guesses about the role. Two, we need to get very, very clear on the relation of Liberation RC activities to the regular community geographical structure and how we as individuals relate to that.

Three, I think that many of us need a seminar on how to work, how to do good work. Enough good work has been done that we can learn a great deal from each other, and enough mistakes have been made that it would be good to look at them and learn from them. Members of this group need to learn the fundamentals of how to organize. There are such fundamental concepts—they have been talked about in relation to Wide World Changing. You find some of them written up in the

Report to the 1981 World Conference. Appeared in **The RC Teacher** No. 16.

Wide World Changing magazines. This particular job is a new kind of organizing, a different kind of organizing from what has ever been tried before. We need to discuss and exchange a lot of information about this. If this weekend can accomplish these three things, it will be very successful.

This meeting should mark a turning point in our understanding of ourselves as Liberation Reference People in RC and what we do, and hopefully in the understanding by the whole community of the job of Liberation Leadership. We had to start off with guesses, but now we've had experience. Enough has occurred that the fundamental laws of Liberation Referencing in RC are beginning to surface. It's true that any important activity will turn out to have its own laws and only with practice will these laws begin to appear, but the intervention of intelligence is a very important part of the process. The occurrence and revelation is spontaneous, but aware grasping and holding the laws up to awareness is a function of intelligence. This is what I'm going to try to start this morning.

THE LIBERATION JOB

The job of the Liberation Reference Person is to eliminate the isolation of his or her group from the general population, and, conversely, to eliminate or break down the isolation of the general population from the group. It's a two-way responsibility.

The isolation has been accomplished by the imposition of distress, and in all our groups, by the *systematic* imposition of distress through oppression.

Some steps for breaking down this isolation are:

(1) Recovering pride;

(2) Recovering power;

(3) Achieving allies;

(4) Participating in furnishing general leadership.

Part of your job as Liberation Reference Person is to accelerate the recovery of pride by the members of your group. We could write a book about the ways we have found of doing that, but I'll just mention it for now.

On the recovery of power: Certain liberation movements in the wide world have put a great deal of emphasis on recovering pride, but in the process have neglected the recovery of power, and have gotten caught in unworkable pretense.

The achieving of allies is crucial for liberation leadership because the distress continually pulls us back toward isolation, back toward thinking it's "us against the world," back toward attacking other groups. (Often there will seem to be ample apparent reason to do so. If you've been in a knife fight at a Los Angeles high school with several hundred on each side, then it can seem that you have obvious reason to distrust and hate the other group and be antagonistic to it.) Liberation leadership must continually find ways to bring forward the necessity of alliances. Unity inside the group, alliances outside the group.

The liberation person must keep in mind, and facilitate, participation in furnishing general leadership by members of the group. I say to a particular liberation group when I meet with them, "Take over the Community. Insist that a black be your Reference Person, insist that a Chicano become Regional Reference Person." This is shorthand talk. In a careful theoretical statement, we should say, "Participate in furnishing leadership for the general population." Unless and until there are black leaders, until there are Chicano leaders and Native leaders, until there are Chinese, Filipino, Japanese, South Asian leaders, until there are women leaders of the whole Community, liberation will be very limited, very insecure. It is a necessary achievement that a Mike White and a Sundreya Smith and a Judy Imai and an Aftab Omer and a Lorenzo Garcia become Area Reference Persons as well as liberation leaders.

How do we break down the isolation? How do we do these

things that I've been listing? Well, we set up and encourage group sharing—within the group—of pride and of difficulty. This has been one of the most powerful experiences of any liberation group when they first get together and tell what it's been like to be a "Wygelian." (I'm inventing here a general term for an oppressed group that won't identify with any particular group. All right? It's actually the name of a lovely pink bush, a Wygelia, but the bush won't mind.) The first time a group of Wygelians gets together and shares what's been great about being a Wygelian, and then what's been rough about being Wygelians, there's a tremendous breaking-down of barriers and a great relief because, in practice, every Wygelian, with a great deal of help from outside, has blamed himself or herself for all the difficulties. This revelation that it was outside oppression that systematically installed Wygelian difficulties is a great raising of consciousness for everyone.

Within the group this is a powerful tool. It is a preliminary tool: it isn't enough, more must follow, but I don't think it is a step that can be skipped. There are certain signs that indicate when you've done enough of it and it's time to move on. If you don't move further, the group starts getting sour and people quit attending.

It isn't enough even in the beginning in an RC group, although it would appear to be for a couple of meetings. Our general insight, that every meeting of RCers must include a review of old theory, getting up-to-date on new theory, and at least some modeling or demonstration of individual re-emergence, applies to any meeting. Even the newest group of Wygelians should include these three elements. The theory doesn't have to be called theory, it just has to be given. "I realized yesterday...," something like that. The furnishing of theory and the practical demonstration of re-emergence will give perspective and future to a pride-uplifting and experience-sharing meeting. There will be ample opportunity to secure discharge and demonstrate re-emergence.

This experience-sharing is a necessary but not a sufficient step. It is a necessary early or first step in the organization of Wygelian liberation ("Wygelian" again standing for whatever your group is). The collection of the group, and early within the group the exchanging of experiences, leads to the realizing of commonalities within the group both on the pride and enjoyment side and on the oppression side.

This group need only be as large as two. There is a great deal of invalidation around us in the society that is likely to enter our head, that says that it isn't good or important unless we have a *big* group, that otherwise we're not doing anything important. *This isn't true.*

An RC class of two is just fine. I taught many classes of two people in the early years of RC. I tried to get more and sometimes I did, but I frequently had as few as two. I've done many introductory public lectures with only one person showing up. I decided in each case to go ahead and do a public lecture for that one person. I gave them the best I had. Guess who got up in front during the demonstration? Guess who participated in RC from then on without fail? A class of two, taught responsibly for eight weeks, not only brings two well-trained people into RC, who have had lots of discharge and lots of practice, but the teacher emerges. I learned a great deal in my two-member class that I could not learn in a class of fifty-six that I taught once. The general rule is, however many show up, do your best job for that number.

A well-taught class of two will lead to a class of sixteen. An abandoned class of two leads you back into your discouragement with only your tail feathers sticking out of the shrubbery. This is true particularly in liberation work where the more your group has been oppressed, the more untrustful, suspicious and discouraged they are. Promises of attendance by twenty-two people often lead to one or two showing up. You've had this experience, I know. Don't be demolished and discouraged when only two show up. Actually, if you move correctly with two, you will win the confidence of the twenty-two after a year, perhaps. It may not come fast, but it will work. For the leader who is also a member of the group, it is also important to remember that the group in which pride is shared and difficulties are shared need be no larger than two. A group of two is simply an opportunity to do intensive work. When you have a group of twenty, you will have to shift gears, and handle it as a group of twenty, which involves different skills. This you will learn to do well.

Once the group has begun to share pride and share difficulties, then it's necessary to begin to point toward a speak-out, where people outside the group listen respectfully and keep silent while the members of the group say to the outsiders the things they have discovered in their experience sharing.

[Editorial Insert: Experiences since this meeting have led to a powerful format (see **Present Time** *No. 41, page 36). Members of the oppressed group appear before the majority group as a panel, and each in turn tries to say to the majority, "I'm going to assume that you are my allies," and then each speaks to the three topics:*

"What I wish you knew and understood about me and my people."

"What I want you never to say or do again."

"What I need from you as my allies."]

We have been very lucky in RC in some of our initial experiences in liberation work. God must have had her eye on us or something. At liberation I and II, for example, some correct decisions were made of whites keeping their mouths shut until the Third Worlders all had spoken fully. Once it had happened, we realized what a powerful tool we had stumbled on. Now we systematically move toward providing a forum of people outside the particular oppression for people in the particular oppression to speak to.

If necessary, a speak-out can be one-way. Sometimes great good will come from this. The people spoken to, if it's understood that they will just listen, are likely to hear the fourth speaker say, "Please get off my foot!" instead of what they thought they heard the first three speakers say, which was blame and reproach. That wasn't what was said, but they're likely to hear that the first three times. If they keep quiet and listen, about the fourth time they're likely to hear—understandably emotionally, but reasonably—a request to "get off my air lines, quit shutting off my air." You know that story about the emphysema patient?

The doctor came to visit the emphysema patient who was breathing through an oxygen tube. As the doctor stood there talking, the patient became very agitated and began to struggle and the doctor said, "What's wrong? What's wrong? Tell me, tell me. I'll do anything but tell me, tell me...." Obviously on the verge of collapse, the patient finally reached out for a pencil and paper and scribbled something and fell unconscious. The doctor picked up the scribbling and it said, "You're standing on my oxygen line."

This is often what the message of the person in the oppressed group comes down to: "Quit making my life so difficult when it's so completely unnecessary and doesn't do you any good. Just move your heavy foot to the left two inches, please!" Even in a one-way speak-out, this is likely to happen.

If you can arrange a mutual speak-out, it's better, much better. All the people present in the oppressor roles are also oppressed. If you were to gather the whole population and listen to everybody, everybody would obviously be oppressed. (Even the owning class. If we let the owning-class people speak last, we'd discover how enormously oppressed they are, what victims they are.) It becomes apparent that there are no human oppressors—an insight that is very precious and that we reached with considerable effort. There are no human oppressors. Only the structure of the pattern oppresses. If we can have a mutual speak-out, where many oppressed groups listen to each other with respect, we get this powerful thrust toward alliances, toward understanding, toward mutual support, toward supporting each other's program. The speak-out, if necessary, can be one-way, but if possible it should be mutual.

RATIONAL ORGANIZING

We need to know how to organize rationally. This is basic knowledge for every part of RC, but is certainly needed here. It is, in general, not available in the wide world. Most organization in the wide world is for the purposes of oppression, and the theories of organization that are available in the wide world, except in small details, are not useful to us. I have learned from other liberation movements, in particular political liberation movements, but most of what I have to say here comes from my own experience. Added to experience, RC can be powerful. I won't try to tell you everything I know about organization, and I don't know everything about organization. This will be just a start, but I think a good start.

ONE-TO-ONE

How does one organize in a pro-people direction? Very fundamentally, one does it one-to-one. In spite of all the jargon about "mass" organization, "mass" meetings, putting out leaflets, making speeches, in spite of the usefulness of printed literature (and it is very useful), effective organization is always done one-to-one. I called many "mass" meetings and did much of that kind of activity in my years as a labor and political organizer, but, looking back, all the permanent results, all the forces that kept on going (and some of them are still going on though their directions have gotten a little funny), came from personal friendships that I made with individual people, in spite of my shyness and my lack of knowledge. The people who mattered, the forces that mattered were the ones who somehow established personal friendships with me.

This is parallel to something that needs to be said about counseling. I didn't say it this week and I now wish I had: counseling is not ever "role-to-role." We talk about it that way. We say, "counseling the client," and it is easy to get the impression that two roles go into a room and hold hands and something happens. (Sometimes it does, in spite of that. People make it work.) But any effective counseling is person-to-person. I'm never really effective as a "Counselor," but only as "Harvey." In the estimations that we did of the demonstrations all week, those of you who were here remember people over and over again saying, "You made yourself personally available," as if it were a startling thing. I don't think that you can ever do very good counseling except as "Harvey" or "Diane." Diane has to be aware of me. I have to be aware of Diane. It is a personal relationship.

The analogy of this in organizing is that you have to make the friend. A real friend, not for the purpose of organizing, and it has to be one-to-one. Occasionally, you will find someone who has found their way so close to a correct program that a pamphlet will push them over the edge. When **The Human Side of Human Beings** first came out, I think six people came rushing down to the office, waving their copy of the book. Now about two dozen people a year write me saying, "This is what I've been looking for all my life, I found this book." But this is out of thousands that are contacted. Those people are just the little lucky profits of chance. In general, the law is, if you want to win a co-worker, you make a friend first. If you want to win more support, you make personal individual friends.

How do you do this? You like them and let them know it. I could repeat that over and over and still not emphasize it enough. You like them. What is the greatest single difficulty for all of us in doing effective work? Patterns of shyness, of being afraid to show we like someone. I've tried to think if there is a culture from which we can borrow. To some extent, Hawaii is. In spite of the tourists, you are still likely to walk out on the street and be greeted with a smile by the first five strangers in the morning. "Hello, how are you! Aloha!" It's a little surfacy, a little bit glassy, but it is better than the glum face of the mainland. Another model I think of is the Southeastern United States. I remember when I first went there, I was amazed at the culture. Again, it is a little rigid, but nice. "How are you this morning? Did you sleep well? Nice to see your bright face. Come, I would like you to meet my friends." There is something good to learn here. Basically, of course, you can't borrow a welcoming feeling from anywhere else; you have to get rid of your blocks and get back to your own natural friendly feelings.

We model for the persons we want as Co-Counselors, we encourage them, love them confidently and listen to them. We provide just enough structure to assist the contact, just enough, not more. We don't try to drag them into a strange, unfamiliar structure. We choose the structure that is familiar enough that it doesn't feel too difficult. How many here have been inducted into the army? This tremendous strangeness of going into the army and its completely hostile environment is designed, of course, to scare you so witless that you are conditioned quickly into a numb killer, an automaton. It's a horrible thing. To go into a very strange environment is tough. Choose a structure that the person can accept.

S. made the first contact with Palestinians by arranging to meet several Palestinian men for dinner in an Arab restaurant. This was something they could do; they didn't have to step clean outside their patterns or their culture to do it. She figured that out and did it. Now she has them come to her. We've noticed that our classes and our workshops are often very frightening to people when they are set up for one culture, say for University "busy, busy" intellectuals. When we try to bring a working-class or Third World person in, they tell us afterwards it was a chamber of horrors because the unfamiliarity was so frightening.

LITERATURE

Use literature. A written communication is almost always more rational than an oral communication because the patterns infest our oral speech and, though we devise ways of getting around the patterns by the way we look and the way we wave our arms, they are vulnerable to misinterpretation. To write something, in general, tends to strain out the patterns. This is because we are likely to look at and read what we've written, to edit it and cut it down. We're likely to ask someone else's opinion of it.

Use the literature, but offer it cleverly. "You'll enjoy this" is not the way to offer literature. Nor is, "You need to read this book," or "I want you to read this." This installs blocks. I have a roomful of books that people have given me and told me I ought to read. I think I've read two. Don't offer literature that way.

There are better ways. You can leave the journal open in a place where there is nothing else to read and people are going to be. That's better than telling them that they should read it. I don't say it's the best way, but it's a little better. The best way I've found is to ask someone if I could have their opinion of the article or book. "Would you take a look at this? I'm uncertain in my own mind about it. I'm not sure I understand it and I don't want to swallow it unless it makes sense. Would you take a look at it and give me your opinion?" I have never met anyone who could resist having their opinion asked.

Use the literature in other ways, of course. Do a "commercial" in your class or workshop. Use the literature. It will keep on working while we sleep. The literature is working all the time. It will work and work and work and work. If you figure your time is worth $3.00, note that a $2.00 journal will go on working days and nights on two dollars. Sometimes it will say things better than you could.

ASK FOR HELP

How do we organize? We ask people for help with small jobs that they are easily able to do without becoming intimidated, without feeling oppressed or exploited. "Would you give me a hand with this?" "Could you pick up this spent kleenex?" "I am meeting this person and I want to get their opinion on something, but they seem a little uneasy when they are with me alone. Could you come sit in with me?" If the person will help you by sitting by while you explain RC to someone else, you know who is in a relaxed position to hear what you say.

Ask help with small jobs. Ask people to give you a hand. This is very fundamental. Ask everyone's opinion. There is no one whose opinion is not worth hearing. (Even if it's pure pattern, you at least know what pattern you are dealing with after that.) It's only rarely that you won't get a worthwhile opinion, but that's only the beginning of the value, because look what's happening to the person who is giving the opinion. They have engaged their thinker in this area. In order to give you an opinion, they have put thought into the area where you want to have them start thinking. This is the profound result.

USE INTERESTED LISTENING

Use basic counseling all the time—outside RC, but also inside RC. Do not wave labels, do not label it as "counseling." Do not turn on the self-conscious red light that says, "I am counseling you." That's distracting. Inside RC or outside RC, be a good, interested human being, which is all that basic counseling is. Listen, be interested, ask questions, listen. Nobody is going to call that "counseling." Listen, be interested, ask questions, listen. It's the most powerful tool in the world. You organize by listening. By being interested. By asking occasional questions to indicate your interest and steer the thinking. Listen some more.

HELP PEOPLE RELATE

As you begin to collect people together, you'll begin to be alarmed that you have too many one-to-one clients. You will become alarmed about it long before you need to be alarmed. You may fear being surrounded, having no time for yourself. You may fear that you're not building a mass organization this way, or that you're not really a good organizer. Your fear will come in long before it is a real problem that you have too many one-to-one relationships, but there will come a time when, of necessity, your organization must take a group form. In other words, the people who have come to depend on you must learn to depend on each other. It's analogous to putting the rim on the counseling wheel which we have been trying to do. The hub and spoke type of counseling, where the hub person can counsel everybody, and everybody waits for a chance to be counseled by the hub, is replaced by everybody going around the rim of the wheel, every spoke turning for counseling to the next spoke.

Again, begin this wider contact on an "I need your opinion" basis. "George, I'd like your opinion on how much time I should spend with Joe and whether Joe would make a good participant in this project that I am thinking about. You have good judgment about people. I am quite interested in him, but I don't want to make up my mind without some other opinion. Would you meet us and have dinner?" Say the same to Joe and introduce them and facilitate the meeting and they will take careful stock of each other and, probably, if you chose well at all, say "I think he's all right. I like him. " The friendship is begun. If they say, "Nah, not that one," you ask, "What would bother you about him?" and you listen out the block and you get there more slowly, but you get there.

This may be hard to remember, but if you can do this much, do what I've said so far, with considerable ease, I think that, good organizer that you are (and you *are* a good bunch of organizers), you will almost immediately be ten times as effective. Look at someone who is extremely effective in a group. Look at P. There are other factors in P.'s effectiveness, but part of it is that, regardless of how she feels, she does this. I suspect that P. often feels shy and sometimes I think she feels shyer than anybody else in this room; but she has made up her mind: when she sees somebody who should be organized, her shyness is trodden underfoot. Her determination simply rides over the difficulty and people respond to her, by the hundreds and the thousands.

DON'T SUBSTITUTE NOVELTY FOR CREATIVITY

As part of taking leadership, all of you are or will be leading workshops. Tommy will be leading a workshop with a hundred and fifty ethnic Chinese in it before very much time has gone by. There are some things to learn about taking leadership in RC. All of you are or will be leading workshops. I talked before about the urge to go abroad where you can get lots of glamour and applause instead of staying home and building your own constituency. There is also a pull, when you feel insecure and feel you are a failure, to do "something," and the easiest way to do this is to think up a workshop to lead. That's *not* a good enough reason to schedule a workshop, especially if it has to be supported by Outreach funds.

The same kind of feelings, which often include undischarged fears of making friends and really relating to people who live around us, will sometimes tell us that the thing to do is to be "creative," to come up with "new" things. That's good. We want people to be creative, but there is a trap, a big ditch, that's very easy to fall into, and that's the substitution of novelty for creativity.

Creativity itself is risky. Any important decision you make is, by definition, one you cannot know ahead of time is right. If you know ahead of time you're right, it's not really a very important decision, although it may seem so to other people. The basic challenges to your thinking are when you do the creative best you can and hope you are right (but watch carefully as the decision goes into effect in case you need to catch a tree before you fall into the lake in case your decision turns out to be wrong). Even creativity is risky; but there is a patterned business of innovating for some kind of patterned satisfaction. Perhaps this is to "push things faster," or to get a little applause, to show someone that you're doing your job well, or to avoid the fearful work of really organizing people personally. All kinds of sneaky patterned motivations can come in.

You're in a very dangerous position, each one of you. Even if all you have so far is a title, and you don't have any constituency yet, you still have a title. You are in a very dangerous position because patterns abound; hopeful, wistful, dependent patterns, that will conclude that you are the solution to all their problems of dependency. If you have a title, then you must solve their problems. Such faith is touching but exhausting, and to try to live up to it is irrational. You show people how to help each other, you don't let them lean on you.

As soon as you get a leadership title, you are regarded as the font of wisdom and if you goof, your mistakes will be copied. Long ago we clarified the principle that "set exercises" are not good counseling, that you must do the particular thing with the particular person that your best judgment says is best at that particular time; but because the great pull of the distress pattern is not to think, the patterned urge is to find some formula to use. You've seen people try to rigidly copy every thing I do. Don't think you're not subject to the same mimicry.

Your job as Liberation Reference Person is not to make a big splash, your job is not to prove you can "innovate" or "invent new theory" or anything of the sort. I don't want to limit your creativity. You've got to be creative like everybody else, but *apply it to your job,* which is to end the separation of your group from the general population. Be a little modest about your leadership or attempted leadership on any other point than this. Use a little modesty, a little caution. You're married to Caesar now. "Caesar's wife must be above reproach."

REGIONAL CONFERENCE REPRESENTATION

Diane: Does "representative Regional Conferences" mean that, if a limited number from those populations that are highly represented in the general wide world is available to the conference, the other groups will be restricted in their numbers to come?

Harvey: No, it means that now we get busy and see that no group is under-represented and that if we approach the conference with a shortage still there, I will urge the Regional people to do what I did at the last World Conference, i.e., give the Regional people permission or encouragement to reach out and bring in additional working class, Arabs, Third World groups, physically different, elders, young people, and so on. We will buttress up the number of such participants at the Regional Conferences, so that their voices, the voices of the less-well-represented, are amplified for those particular deliberations.

Any questions or discussion about that? It is clear we don't know how to do it but is it clear what we're setting out to do? Take a Los Angeles region, for example. Just imagine what a really representative meeting would be there with that enormous diversity of population—about 60% Third World now.

The effect of doing this at the World Conference was remarkably good. We want to get the same phenomenon in twenty-eight Regions. Start now. That's the whole point. If we don't start now, we'll have missed half our effectiveness.

Any question about that? You will be the ones who will have to be the Regional people's consciences. Just send friendly notes saying, "How are you coming at improving the Japanese representation in your Region, Jackie?" Or, "I knew, Joan, when I met you that I could have confidence in you, that an important question like this wouldn't be delayed. I just thought I'd check in with you and see how many new black RCers there are. I'd be happy to write them a note and welcome them into the sisterhood of black RC," and so on.

Diane: I have a question regarding the major function for Liberation Reference Persons being to eliminate isolation of your group. If you're functioning as a minority group in a particular country it's clear. But let's say if you are Asian but in Asia—and so in the majority—your job would be to put your people into an international context—but why would that be the major function? I also think of women, who in a human sense are isolated, but live in close contact with every sector of the population.

Harvey: I think you are right. It does need clarification. I said "isolation from the general population," and I think it should be "isolation from the general liberation forces." Women are still overwhelmingly isolated from the liberation forces.

EACH GROUP LEAD EVERYONE'S LIBERATION

That reminds me of one thing I meant to say to this workshop and almost forgot. Observably, every group, as they get together and find the commonality of their oppression, without exception falls into one particular ditch. They don't always verbalize it, but the feeling is plain from the other things they say.

Each group settles into a feeling that they are the bottom of the totem pole, that their oppression is really worse than anyone else's. What's worse is that they draw the implication of powerlessness. "We, the most oppressed, deserve to have those other fortunate people take some initiative first and come to our support, and then (maybe) we'll go to their support later."

Do you hear what I'm saying? Every group tends to feel this way and you see the track of the oppression that paralyzes us right there. If nobody can go first, nobody's going to go. We have to see this clearly. "Who else had as tough a life as we half-Norwegian children living on small isolated farms? All the rest of you were really advantaged. *You* complain about what happened to *you*, but you see, *I* was the one who *really* had it rough." This is an observably universal tendency in every group. The implication is that "we" have to wait until somebody else gives us some support. See? First help us, then maybe we'll think about somebody else. It has to be a pattern.

I think the direction against this is exactly to move first on the basis of our pride in being who we are. "Who else but we Wygelians should help lead everybody's struggle? We Wygelians can lead all liberation."

The best viewpoint is, "Of course my group will act first!" "It is obviously up to us Wygelians to lead everybody's liberation."

"Who else but people like us should lead the whole thing?" I think this falls for each one of you with equal logic and much greater results than "We ain't gonna do it until somebody else gives us a hand," or "We're not going to be interested in them until they show interest," or "When they support me, then I'll support them." "What the hell did they ever do for us?" You hear this in every arena of struggle. Mike?

Mike: White racism has pitted every Third World group against every other Third World group. What can be done to un-button this?

Harvey: I think this is already beginning to happen spontaneously, which is good. First of all, we need to build the support groups of the individual Third World groups, and then arrange joint meetings. Make it a festivity, a great occasion where the black support group meets with the Asian support group (or eventually the Japanese support group). Form an evening to listen to each other. Just that. Use the model we accidentally fell into at Liberation I and II—the separate caucusing, the joint respectful listening. It cuts through the confusion. There are a lot of other things you can do once that happens, but I think if you try to do anything else first, it will end up mostly hot-air and dramatization. The respectful listening to each other's heritage and situation must come first.

Understanding and Combatting
The Operation of Internalized Oppression
When Directed Against Leaders

Our success in combatting oppression and its results was greatly increased when we began to recognize the operation of *internalized oppression.* The oppression coming from outside leaves distress recordings which, when restimulated, push the individual to mistreat himself or herself in the same way that he or she was mistreated by the outside oppression originally (invalidating himself or herself, accepting powerlessness, etc.). Alternatively, the pattern can turn on other members of the group (attacking, invalidating, competing, being non-supportive). Thus, the internalized oppression carries on and perpetuates the damage originally inflicted by the outside oppression, reinforced occasionally, of course, by fresh oppression coming from the outside.

We have begun to combat this internalizing process. The internalized oppressiveness directed by the individual against himself or herself can be challenged and directions set against it now that we can identify it for what it is. Divisiveness within various liberation groups can be handled better when we realize that it is internalized oppression that brings up the competition and the disunity.

ANOTHER KIND OF DAMAGE

We have been slower to deal with internalized oppression *directed against leadership.* We have moved a little. We have noted the damage done to the women's movement by the "trashing" of leaders and that movement's effort to deal with it. Those of us with experience in the labor movement have remembered that

Appeared in **Present Time** No. 45.

during labor struggles we came to expect union leaders to be slandered in every possible way in the media, with wild charges made against them to divert the membership from supporting their leadership or the struggle.

We have grappled somewhat with the tendency to abandon the Co-Counselor *as client* as soon as she or he takes a position of leadership, and have tried to deal with this through the "Golden Circle" and the "group counseling the leader" techniques. We have learned to "offer a session" to Co-Counselors who hang their "resentment of authority" on RC leaders. We have at least partly recognized these anti-leadership phenomena as expressions of internalized oppression, weakening the Community as a whole, and hindering the re-emergence of individual Co-Counselors.

We also need to learn to deal with attacks which affect the whole Community and the theory and practice of RC, but which claim to be only attacks on or "criticisms" of an individual leader or leaders.

EVERY WORLD CONFERENCE

Every World Conference (or, previously, the Area Reference Persons' Workshops which filled the same function) has seen some kind of highly restimulating attack on the leadership of RC. The months before the 1981 World Conference saw an intense and persistent campaign of this nature.The "internalized oppression directed against leadership" operated to some degree in a number of places in the Communities, and allowed confusion and restimulation to spread and be magnified. The World Conference discussed the situation at length and unanimously condemned the attacks and completely supported the leadership. The delegates learned a great deal about combatting this kind of internalized oppression and returned home to clarify to their Communities that such attacks should be handled as the patterned phenomena that they are.

Almost all RC teachers and leaders, and nearly all Co-

Counselors, would actively and intelligently defend our right to practice Re-evaluation Counseling, and would support the enhancement and development of our theory and the building of strong, supportive Communities. To do this well, however, requires leadership, and leadership needs support.

SOCIETY ATTEMPTS DIVISION

The oppressive society, in order to survive and perpetuate its oppression of the population, must, of necessity, seek to alienate us from each other. It must seek continually to sow suspicion of each other among us, to make us appear to each other as inhuman and untrustworthy, to pit us against each other and to tell us that "the others" are incapable, irrational, or evil.

In RC we consistently push to recognize and claim the humanness in ourselves and *in each other*. We seek to learn to trust each other, to learn to cooperate. We remind each other continually that within every pattern there is a person—good, dependable, and a natural ally of ourselves. We seek to promote unity among the various groups that have been divided from each other by the operation of the oppression.

MISREPRESENTATION A CUSTOMARY TOOL

In the world of patterned conflicts it is customary that the person or group is seldom charged with actual errors or mistakes, but instead is charged with accusations that will arouse prejudices against them and will be difficult to answer without antagonizing someone by the answer. "Have you or have you not stopped beating your wife?" was the classical example from U.S. folklore. Restimulated by the attacks, some RCers questioned, "But what about patterns? How do we know it isn't the leader's patterns that are being accused?" This highlights the internalized oppression nature of the response. If we feel any Co-Counselor is acting badly from a pattern, do we attack him or her or do we stand aside while he or she is attacked? Don't we rather interrupt the attack and go to the person with counseling tools? If we suspect that leaders are operating in a pattern, do we not organize counseling support for them?

The phenomenon of internalized oppression against our leaders must be understood and eliminated from our practice if our leadership is to have safety to function and if our Communities are to flourish.

Why Leaders of RC Can Expect To Be Attacked And What To Do About Such Attacks

Anyone who undertakes leadership can expect, at some time or other, to be the object of "attacks," or at least to "feel attacked." These attacks can arise from a number of different sources, each needing to be viewed and dealt with differently.

A REACTION TO MISTAKES

The first source is a response to mistakes the leader, himself or herself, makes. Since no one has yet been wise enough to do anything significant, or give significant leadership, without making some mistakes, such mistakes do happen. Other persons, inside or outside of the leader's constituency, will often feel upset by the mistakes and will respond with, sometimes rational, or, more usually, patterned, criticisms of the leader which will often appear to the leader as attacks.

The best way of handling this first kind of attack seems to be to admit the mistake openly, to not defend it or excuse it, to take responsibility for it and apologize for it, and to promise to not persist in it or repeat it. (One should certainly make such a promise privately. Often it will be helpful to make it publicly as well.) Depending on circumstances, it may then be helpful to counsel the persons who are upset, if possible, and sometimes, in the process, convert them from criticizers or attackers to supporters.

UNAWARE CLIENTING

The second source or origin of attacks is the compelling, often desperate, desire of some persons to use the free attention

Appeared in **Reference Point** No. 21.

(or even the imagined free attention) of the leader in order to seek discharge of their distresses. Unable to ask for counseling reasonably or "nicely," often completely unaware of their own motives, these persons seek to be counseled by rehearsing the invalidating role of their own old distresses at the leader. At some level the attackers are hoping that the object of the attacks will be a powerful, confident-enough counselor that they themselves can discharge. More often, of course, both in the wide world and in RC, the leader becomes bewildered and rehearses a defensive, submissive, frightened, or angry distress recording of his or her own back at the attacker.

To handle this kind of attack well requires the integration of theory into the leader's thinking well enough that the decision not to be restimulated is second nature and nearly automatic. To respond to the attack with relaxed, friendly, persistent validation of the person is, usually, to contradict the pattern enough to bring discharge. (Sometimes, in special circumstances, one can "out-dramatize" the pattern and secure discharge.) To do this well keeps the leader in charge in situations which have, previously, generally been regarded as "unhandleable" and can lead to great gains for everyone. There are several strong, effective leaders of the RC Communities who are my close allies and supporters today, but with whom my first introduction was a violent, completely unjustified, and unprovoked attack upon me.

"YOU RESTIMULATE ME"

The third source of attacks is a variation of the second source. It has tended to show up often in the Co-Counseling Communities. On an unaware level this is, "I can't stand you." "You disgust me." "You disappoint me." "Ugh! Men!", etc. Slightly more awarely, it often goes, "You restimulate me! Boo hoo!" or "Nobody has that kind of a haircut except Marine sergeants and football coaches." Again, the person is seeking to claim a session as client on the basis of "restimulation."

Our fairly recent insight that "restimulation" is not, as we so long assumed, "the involuntary confusion of the past with the present" but always, at some level, a deliberate decision to bring up the distress (in the ancient, persistent hope that someone will help us with it) removes the theoretical justification among Co-Counselors for this sort of behavior. However, I expect that it will still tend to occur and that every counselor, but especially leaders, will have to deal with it. (As you know, "positive" identifications can cause just as much difficulty as negative ones.)

How to handle these "attacks" will depend in great part on how willing and able you are to assume the role of counselor to the person who hangs the identification on you. You are *not* obligated to, and unless it is a free, relaxed decision on your part you should probably not do it. If you decide to counsel the person as they are "asking" you to, then the familiar tools for "breaking" identifications or using them for discharge come into play. If you decide not to, you can pleasantly reject the identification, evade it, avoid the person as tactfully as you can manage, or refer the person to someone who will wish to counsel him or her.

There is a phenomenon around this kind of attack which can be confusing. This is a kind of "delayed restimulation." Things have gone well for the client as a result of a particular session or discussion—or series of sessions or discussions—but later (even years later), having "dug up" more distress, the person decides to blame the leader and accuses him or her of being hurtful in some way connected with the previously appreciated session or discussion. It is important for the leader not to buy into this, but to remember that the client is, unawarely, just trying to secure some more counseling by manipulating any old guilt patterns the leader may not yet have discharged.

VANDALS, RAPISTS, AND ASSASSINS

The fourth source of attacks also has its origins in the second source, but has become qualitatively different in its rigidity and operation and needs far more effort and caution to handle. It is very familiar that the victim of restimulated distress often feels a pull to endure the replay more "comfortably" by acting out a different role in the recording than his or her original role. Thus the person who was originally invalidated now invalidates others—the beaten child, grown-up, beats others, etc.

Severe distress and undischarged resentment can lock such a person into a chronic pattern of compulsively seeking to hurt and destroy, with or without any "excuse" in the current situations. These people become the vandals, the senseless destroyers of art and property, the "muggers," the rapists, the assassins. Increasing numbers of such desperate people roam the world, seeking opportunities to "get even" for early mistreatments by hurting someone else. These chronic-pattern-ridden individuals become much more numerous in times of a collapsing society such as the present.

To handle the abuser or the assassin pattern is a very different matter than the previous cases. The safety and protection of the person attacked must receive first consideration and action. Avoiding vulnerable situations requires constant care. "Do not walk in Central Park alone at night." "Work to make the streets of our cities safe for women at night, but do not pretend that they already are." Install peep-holes in your front doors. Move through dangerous areas in groups or with bodyguards. Ask for protection. Carry a police whistle. Learn karate. Practice yelling for help. Have two of your biggest and best-muscled friends pay a warning call upon any identified threatener or harasser. Do not "argue" or "reason" with such a pattern. (It is possible sometimes to distract it or out-dramatize it.) "Do not try to permissively counsel the rapist." Yell loudly for help, counter attack and/or run.

TROUBLEMAKERS

Where the patterns do not involve physical violence but seek to injure by slander, machinations, or "making trouble" in various other ways, it is generally necessary to expose or organize effective pressure on the person to interrupt the pattern, stop the attacks, and (rarely) reach the human behind the behavior.

Our program for trying to reach into prisons with RC is intended, long range, to begin the re-emergence of some individuals from such patterns, and to acquire information for dealing with all of them well when the oppressive society is finally stopped from producing them in such numbers.

The decisive question in the current situation is to avoid and prevent any opportunity for such attacks. We have many good reasons for our policy of "keeping a low profile" for RC, but one of them is to avoid drawing the attention of the aggressive patterns in the world which are "looking for something or someone to attack."

AGENTS OF REPRESSION

The fifth kind of source of attacks upon leadership is the oppressive society itself, expressed through its organs of repression. This is a "whole different ball game" although such government agencies or their representatives often use or manipulate individuals from the previous categories, particularly from the fourth.

Many of our RCers are necessarily naive about the way the society really operates. They have been told in school that "democracy works for all" and have little awareness that the poor, the working class, the cultural or racial minorities, and other singled-out groups are all subjected to intense individual attacks if they begin to protest and organize.

People who have been through labor struggles are generally familiar with slanderous attacks on leaders and with "frame-ups." They have been standard weapons against labor organizers for many generations. Traditionally, police, sheriff's departments, prosecutor's offices, and private detective agencies have carried out this kind of activity.

The FBI, CIA, and other "spook" agencies, in the U.S. and in other countries, have carried on a great deal of these assaults against progressives in the last few decades. The vast networks of "informers" and unpaid "helpers" that these agencies recruit through "getting something on them" and then holding prosecution over their heads if they do not do the bidding of the agency, have given them a huge supply of "witnesses," perjurors, and provocateurs to manipulate as they need them.

The role of these agencies in the U.S. was somewhat exposed by the Watergate scandals and by the revelation that the FBI had tried to blackmail Martin Luther King into committing suicide at about the same time that he was being considered for the Nobel Peace Prize. Similar, as yet unpublicized, campaigns against progressive leaders undoubtedly have occurred tens of thousands of times.

On Tuesday, March 8, 1983, the Associated Press reported, under the headline "FBI given more scope":

> *"Attorney General William French Smith has given the FBI broader authority to infiltrate and monitor groups....*
>
> *Smith issued new guidelines yesterday...replacing curbs imposed by Attorney General Edward Levi in 1976.*
>
> *Levi had issued the rules to halt abuses disclosed by congressional committees which found that the FBI infiltrated anti-Vietnam war groups, civil-rights organizations and the women's-liberation movement during the 1960s and early 1970s, and attempted to disrupt their activities and discredit their leaders.*
>
> *...Specifically the new rules will:*
>
> *—Authorize the FBI to infiltrate or put informants into groups during preliminary inquiries, where 'there is not yet a reasonable indication of criminal activities' warranting a full investigation. Levi had restricted these techniques to full investigations.*
>
> *—Permit the FBI to continue low-level monitoring by informants of groups which...pose no 'immediate threat of harm.'*

... —Allow the FBI to collect publicly available information on groups or individuals who are not under investigation, if the Privacy Act is not violated...."

ATTACKS ON RC LEADERS

Even though we have attempted to keep RC to a low profile in the wide world, its profoundly progressive nature and its effectiveness were bound to come to the notice of the repressive forces and their agents at some time. This has happened, and a number of our best leaders have been and are being attacked and harassed, in ways and with a persistence that would be difficult to explain except by the involvement of government agents.

The repeated attacks which have been made on me since the 1979 World Conference (and perhaps those earlier) have pretty clearly revealed themselves as agency-inspired and managed. Individuals who were only peripherally involved in RC and without financial resources of their own suddenly were launching expensive mass mailing campaigns to everyone listed in **Present Time**. Individuals who required government approval to remain in the U.S. as students took weirdly intransigent positions against me at the 1981 World Conference. Every attempt was made to represent the attacks as coming from inside RC and a few foolish and distressed individuals lent themselves to this appearance, but the World Conference, acting for the whole RC Community, rejected the attacks and put an end to such pretensions.

Once the attacks had been defeated at the World Conference, the organized, outside RC, nature of their sponsorship became plain. Smearing publicity began to appear "out of the blue." Former clients of mine from ten years back, whose pasts made them vulnerable to agency blackmail and cajolery, appeared on television programs in Seattle repeating slanders against me. The programs juxtaposed me with unsavory characters and known criminals. Some weeks later a weekly newspaper repeated the same slanders. The newspaper shortly went out of business. Then a few weeks later another weekly newspaper parroted the earlier stories.

Legislation was introduced into the State Legislature that would have, in effect, outlawed RC. The same slanders, the same people appeared in legislative hearings (often making fools of themselves). The legislation never got out of committee and was dropped for that session. The legislator who sponsored the legislation was defeated at the next election.

Last summer an obvious agent appeared at a workshop of mine in Ireland, having persuaded one of the London ARPs to okay his application. He came equipped with photocopies of all the attacking letters and news accounts, both from Minneapolis and Seattle and circulated these to RCers at the workshop, attempting to organize an attack there. When no one supported him, he advanced a number of other stories to account for his being there, and finally, asked to leave, announced that he would write a series of exposés for English newspapers of the things he had heard in sessions at the workshop.

DON'T DEBATE SLANDERS

Many provocative attempts have been made to get me to "reply" to the slanders circulated against me. Our considered judgment has been that to do so would be only to play into the attackers' desire for continuing publicity for their slanders. (One cannot prevent *some* damage being done by such unprincipled smears, but one can contain it and limit it.) Other RCers and friends have spoken out and written to the media and, when their statements were printed, have been effective.

Now the attacks upon me have begun again in Seattle and Washington State. A number of other leaders in the U.S. are being harassed in weird and wonderful ways. Various pretexts are being used in the various cases, but in each case the RC leader is being vilified in some very restimulative way and their connection with RC is being attached to the defamatory allegations.

In Washington State there is a repeat of the same ex-RCers making sensational allegations to the press and television stations and attachment of this to attempted passage of a bill in the Legislature which could make the use of RC difficult.

Active speaking out by RCers and their friends is needed. The slanders against me and other leaders need to be rejected, and the value and good name of RC needs to be asserted and re-asserted. This should not be left up to the attacked leaders to do.

NEW SKILLS TO LEARN

Handling this type of attack well will require improved maturity, consciousness, and awareness on the part of our leaders *and* of our Community members. The first requirement is facing the reality that these kinds of attacks *will occur* and will be made on any leader who reaches a certain level of effectiveness. The leader must expect and be ready to handle them, not be bewildered and lost in indignation or dismay at "the unfairness of it all." Other leaders and Community members cannot afford to sit back passively and watch to "see how the leader handles the attack" or, as has, amazingly, sometimes happened, join in a "discussion" on the "merits" of the attack. The leader (and the RC Community which is the real object of the attack) deserve immediate, counter-attacking support. This support must not be defensive, but needs to be indignant toward the attackers and wholeheartedly validating toward the person attacked. The leader *is the Community members' leader, is the Community's leader,* and it must be clearly everyone's battle from the first hint of attack.

It needs to be made immediately clear by other RCers that no "vulture" can attack an RC leader without losing some tail feathers in the process.

The "dirty tricks" experts who plan such attacks and harassment count on naive attitudes among us. It costs them little effort to have their agents suggest or imply slanders which will push people's buttons. If we allow this kind of restimulation to take place, we can get caught in the illogical "How do we *know* the leader isn't guilty of the slanders?" or, "I'd better dissociate myself from the leader before I'm contaminated by the association."

The fact is that the leaders have earned our confidence and support. They also need it precisely at the time of the slanders and attacks. Self-estimation and estimation by the group are desirable processes for improving leaders' functioning but *no leader deserves to be attacked.*

The general attitude that "an attack on one is an attack on all" and that "the best defense is a fierce, indignant counter-attack" needs to become endemic and aware throughout our Communities.

We will save ourselves tremendous resources of energy, time, and confidence if we learn to deal with attacks this way and examine any "weaknesses" or "corrections needed" only after the attackers have been defeated and driven off and our unity re-affirmed.

Disabled Persons' Leadership in RC

Talk at the Leaders' Topic Group
of the Disabled Persons' Workshop
October 12, 1982

I'd like to talk about some problems I see as leader of the International Community. A number of these were brought up: the logistics of the situation, the real difficulties as well as the familiar inhibiting patterns, and the high expectations of RC.

This last is a problem I'd like to lay to rest. It shows up as a difficulty everywhere in our Community.

A number of people who have some exposure to RC and use it well, and then drop out, do so because RC "disappoints" them. It doesn't meet their expectations. Since everybody in RC, like everybody else, has always done the very best they could at any given time, there must be something wrong in the expectations. I think we're beginning to see what it is and to do something about it.

Our theory has developed and been clarified and been expressed well in print, on tape, and on videotape. The theory is well-developed. It is clear and promises much, but the best practice seldom reaches the theory's level and a lot of the practice is far behind.I think we need to find a way to tell people when they first come into RC that the theory is valid but there is a great gap between what we know and what we, as yet, usu-

Appeared in **Complete Elegance** No. 8.

ally do. We need to tell them that knowledge of the theory, by itself, isn't enough to bring the practice to a satisfactory level. I think we have to tell them also that that gap is going to persist, that as we bring our practice toward where the theory is now, we're going to keep advancing the theory also, and that it's very important that we do so, that the theory needs to lead the practice. We need to keep moving the theory ahead.

One of the biggest achievements of the last fifteen years or so is that we've actually been able to get so much theory into print. I remember very well when there was nothing printed I could give to people. I had to talk and do demonstrations in order to teach people anything about RC. That's all the communication there was. When a student in an early class suggested that I could draw a diagram on the blackboard, that was a novel idea. When we printed the first manual, it was a little inky mimeographed thing, so small you could put it in your shirt pocket. It had about ten directions in it. The first pamphlet, "The Communication of Important Ideas," was mimeographed in 1961. We were amazed that we at last had something in "print" about theory.

Since then, thirteen books have been published, twenty-seven magazines started, a host of pamphlets written, good audio cassettes (like "Affection, Love and Sex at the University of Maine," which would be a best-selling record if they ever put it on a disk) made, a lot of videotapes issued, and color videocassettes are coming up, which are going to communicate a lot to many people.

This is a great achievement. Yet somehow people identify this theory with what they can already expect in the Community. When we describe in theory what a human being is really like, we somehow create this illusion that newcomers can come into RC and expect people to be already functioning like that, instead of realizing that they're on their way but still cluttered by the patterns and discouragements and the hopelessness and forgetfulness and all the other patterns which still impede us.

I don't think there's any rational reason for people to be disappointed. We need to encourage people's high expectations. That's a part of good counseling, to have high expectations of people. Yet we need to explain to each other continually about unreasonable expectations, or confusing theoretical ideals with present practice. They are two different things. Each one is perfectly valid and all right, and we don't get into trouble unless we confuse the two.

On logistics, we do have some Area Outreach Funds and we have an International Outreach Fund that's not very large. It is carefully collected from 1/16 of what people pay for classes and 1/3 of what is left over as a net on any Regional or International workshops. There are about thirty fairly-well-organized oppressed groups in RC, organized well enough to have their own International Liberation Reference Person. All of them need special financial considerations to operate. Because the wide world is so uncooperative in general, and society is so busy oppressing people, but never giving them a hand out of the oppression, because if groups of people do get grants from non-RC sources, the grants are not, in general, thoughtfully given, even if people do sometimes make thoughtful use of them, somehow the expectation arises that since RC is against oppression, then we should have already eliminated any financial difficulties for the group. If there's any oppressive attitudes among RCers, that is something to be disappointed about. There is disappointment about the levels of counseling and also disappointment that we don't immediately have solutions to logistical problems—the lack of money, the lack of ramps, the lack of facilities, the lack of physical assistance, in this group's case.

Consider the young people. In general, young people don't have money. In trying to get some from their parents, they collide with adultism. Even if the parents are wealthy, it often takes longer for one to talk the well-to-do parent into paying for a child's or a young person's attendance at an International workshop than it would to go out and raise it elsewhere oneself.

So there are all these expectations and, as yet, very little internal resource. In general we've made good use of our resources and I'm very glad that every oppressed group speaks out and makes demands and makes requests. This group, the disabled, I think has not been demanding enough.

A solution is always there. There's a general principle that we have seen clearly enough to make a scroll out of it, that "there's always at least one elegant solution for every real problem." That's true.

The key statement that I would make to this group about leadership is that *no one else is going to do it.* The society's conditioning on every group is that they're helpless, or nearly so, and that if there was any justice somebody else would come in and lead them out of the oppression. Of course every oppressed group feels that they have worse oppression than anyone else, without exception. One can understand that, with the oppression pounding them on the head every day; but there's no one else capable of leading, of leading well enough, or furnishing the leadership that your group needs, except yourselves. You're the only ones smart enough to do it. You're the ones who have the motivation, in spite of all the discouragement, powerlessness, and logistical difficulties you're confronted with, to break through.

You *can* have allies, and I promise right now that I'll be your ally, to every extent that I can be. I made a commitment a long time ago to be a complete ally for any oppressed person or any oppressed group, and I will be.

As far as using the resources that the Community has, I can help. I've been around since the beginning. I have no power, but I have prestige as International Reference Person. Go to your Area Reference Person or your teacher or your support group leader, or whoever, and if they give you an unreasonable time, throw ridiculous difficulties in your way, it's perfectly possible to get on the phone and call me. If you're broke, call me collect. I will not rebuke or remove that person, I will not denounce them for their attitude. You don't develop leadership that way. But I will ask them some questions, and they will, in general, listen to my questions, out of respect if nothing else, and we will see if something can be changed. Your Regional Reference Persons, where you have them, will, generally, be thoughtful allies. If you run into difficulties and tell them, they will, in general, do something. If they don't, call me. I can't promise to solve any particular difficulty, but I am committed to try.

Getting the job done will be up to you. What do *you* have to do the job with? I think you know this theoretically but you can't be reminded of it too often. You have your intelligence. You are the smartest people in the world.

You have a central nervous system with about forty billion neurons in it, a few hundred of which bring in information from the sense organs, a few hundred of which send commands out to the muscles and glands, and the rest of them sit there and talk to each other, making tremendously complex computations, that seem to be the basis of flexible intelligence. I would say to each of you, your mind is capable of solving any and all problems. I'd like to remind you of that ten or twelve times a day.

Look at the oppression, the tremendous invalidation and discouragement that's been put on disabled people. Yet sitting here are J-, an Area Reference Person, S-, an Area Reference Person. In your folder is the draft program by M-, Regional Reference Person. M- came into a Community that treated her unawarely. When she first came in, they all treated her as if she were splendid, cute, and not too much of a nuisance. But M- has a mind. At our first workshop together I told the workshop to keep an eye on her as Regional Reference Person material. I got some pained letters scolding me for "putting undue expectations" on "dear little M-." M- is now Regional Reference Person and she runs a tight ship in her Region. You, too, have all that intelligence.

M- made some decisions in the middle of enormous oppression; she made some decisions that she was going to keep her mind working, and that she was going to accomplish things. There's no one smart enough to do it for you.

I'd like to say further that I don't think that you can plan to lead the liberation of disabled persons unless you set your sights on leading everybody. I think this is quite important. If you don't have the goal of leading the whole Community (I'd eventually include the wide world, but right now, the whole RC Community), you will be torn by the difficulties in the RC Community that you don't take responsibility for because you're "only" leading physically different RC. You need to assume that you're the "head cheese of the whole shebang," at least in your own mind. You need to adopt the viewpoint that whenever difficulties show up in the general RC Community or in the wide world, you're going to think about them, work out a tentative solution, get in contact with the right people and lead the move to correct the problem. Otherwise your failure to take total leadership will come back at you as helplessness, will discourage you too much in the area of leading disabled people.

You need to trust your own thinking, not because it will always be right, but because it's the only thinking you have. If you trust your thinking and make a mistake, the feedback resulting from your mistake will very quickly tell you that it was wrong and incorrect. If you accept somebody else's thinking and you make a mistake, then you have already turned off your thinking to accept theirs and the feedback saying it was a mistake will be ignored for a while. That will make a much more serious mistake out of it.

You have to make mistakes. You can't learn much, you can't do anything important unless you take that risk. So trust your thinking.

In terms of leadership, I would encourage each of you to plan to lead *all* RC as the first step toward building everything you need *in* RC. If you make this sort of decision, it makes things very different. You may forget it for two or three days, but then you remember it again. It makes a tremendous difference. The commitment which we've been using in RC which says I'll break the habit of paying attention to my old distresses actually turns out in practice to work as a series of small steps. If you make the decision, then you often forget it. You make it again, you forget it again, you get discouraged because you don't seem to be able to keep the decision, but then you turn and look back and you've traveled a mile. It's through the effort of repeatedly re-making the decision that you made the gains. That's advanced knowledge, part of what came out of the "counseling-with-supervision" workshop last month.

A word about getting good counseling: I've heard from a number of you that you didn't know where you could get good counseling, particularly on your distresses around your physical disabilities. Well, all the good counselors there are are the Co-Counselors in the RC Community. You have the choice of getting your counseling from other Co-Counselors who are also physically disabled, or getting it from other counselors who aren't physically disabled, or at least don't admit it. In the first case you'll both have to do some work on internalized oppression in order to keep the counseling with the physically disabled counselor going well. In the second case, you'll have to counsel your non-physically-disabled counselors on their attitudes toward the oppression. You'll have to make them work on it in your session, sometimes, because that's the option. When it's the client's session the client gets to work on what he or she wants to, but when you as client want to give the counselor a session, you have every right to say, "I want to give you a session on what's getting in the way of counseling me." Since it's your time, the counselors have no basis for objecting and you can pin them down and pursue them. It may seem hard to give up your chance for a session that day, but if it was going to be a poor session anyway, you can best invest the time in improving your counselor as a counselor.

You will have to train your counselors. You will have to require them to improve and train them. It seems like such a hard, difficult process. It seems so unfair that we should have to do it, it really does. All of us deserve a completely rational counselor. We need one. *But* there is no such person yet. We have to train our counselors.

We've gotten a long way on a kind of "pyramid" counseling. The new student leans on the experienced student, the experienced student leans on the assistant teacher, the assistant teacher leans on the teacher, the teacher leans on the Area Reference Person, the Area Reference Person on the Regional Reference Person, the Regional Reference Person calls me. This "pyramid" counseling is good. It complements the "peer" counseling in Co-Counseling pairs. It is good to lean and be leaned on. Here's a person, J-, working hard. J- is so responsible, does such good work, but I don't know where she goes to lean and discharge about how hard it is. I invite you, J-, to lean on me. I require it of you. Especially if you become Regional Reference Person, use me, use the fact that I'm there.

The longer-range solution is training our counselors. Should we have to? Is it fair? No. It's just necessary.

We need much more organization among disabled RCers. I don't know how many disabled people there are in this country, but it must be in the millions. All of them need the knowledge of RC, the skills of RC so their lives will be bearable. Rarely is the physically different person's life made unbearable by the physical difference, but by the oppression. It's the pattern that makes life tough.

Any life is great. It's better to be alive, if only for a moment, even if in agony, than never to be alive at all. It's true. For the high quality of life, for the life people deserve, physically different people need RC tools.

To the extent I can offer it, there will be financial support.

There will be a fair share, whatever that is, of the financial resources we have available, for outreach to disabled people.

I also offer you confidence and encouragement. Any hopelessness of yours just seems ridiculous to me out here. (Any hopelessness of mine, of course, seems ridiculous to you.)

We have a pretty good Community after twelve years of work, in spite of all the defects. To have a Community like ours is really an achievement. If we keep our expectations geared to what's actually present and possible instead of what the theory promises eventually, I think we'll avoid getting stuck in disappointment.

I need each one of you to become a powerful leader. I invite you, I challenge you to think of taking charge of everything, step by step. Step by step, take charge of things. You are the only people smart enough to run your own re-emergence, which will please everybody. You're the only people knowledgeable enough and motivated enough to look after the interests of disabled people.

Four Leadership Positions

An AREA REFERENCE PERSON'S primary job is to make decisions for an Organized Area Community when consensus is not reached quickly enough through the regular procedures of discussion, discharge, and communication. In addition, an Area Reference Person participates in the approval of teachers' credentials, gives the official approval (after consultation) to the use of Area Outreach Funds, and is responsible for correct content of Area newsletters. She or he is free, if she or he wishes, to serve as organizer, theoretician, model, and heroine or hero.

A REGIONAL REFERENCE PERSON'S primary responsibility is developing new and old leadership, advancing people in leadership with counseling, encouragement, tradition-breaking, and all other means available. The RRP also participates in approval of credentials for teachers and makes decisions about workshops which go beyond the boundaries of any one Area. The Regional Reference Person serves as the personal representative of the International Reference Person in the Region.

Appeared in **Reference Point** No. 21.

A Regional Reference Person *may* play the role of organizer, pioneer, inspirer, confidence lender, heroine or hero, as he or she wishes.

The Regional Reference Person *does not* act as a "super" Area Reference Person or take over any of the functions of an ARP (unless he or she is also an ARP).

An INTERNATIONAL LIBERATION REFERENCE PERSON is a spokesperson for the people of his or her constituency, sees that their interests are not neglected or suppressed by unaware oppressions or traditions penetrating into the Community from the wide world, encourages and helps in the establishment of a network of groups of leaders and support groups of her or his constituency and advocates the organization of International workshops of her or his own constituency when indicated. The International Liberation Reference Person serves as the personal representative of the International Reference Person to her or his constituency.

In general, the Liberation Reference Person is expected to participate in wide world activities relative to her or his constituency and to keep the general Community informed of these.

The Liberation Reference Person may or may not lead workshops, may or may not help develop and revise draft liberation policy statements, may or may not organize, pioneer, model, inspire, or be hero or heroine, as she or he wishes.

The INTERNATIONAL REFERENCE PERSON speaks for the International Community between meetings of the World Conferences, makes decisions, when such decisions cannot be reached by consensus quickly enough, interprets the Guidelines when controversy arises, is editorially responsible for the content of all International publications, gives official approval (after consultation) for expenditures from the International Outreach Fund, participates in the approval of teachers' credentials, approves International and Regional workshops, and must approve of leaders leading workshops outside their own Area or Region.

"Janie Appleseeds"

Some competent Co-Counselors and RC teachers are asking for a greater variety of experiences in their lives and for exposure to other cultures than their own.

At the recent Midwest, USA, Teachers' and Leaders' Workshop, I offered to help guide such individuals in six-month or one-year "sabbaticals" to places in the world where RC is needed but not yet established. The workshop, to avoid too much identification with "Peace Corps" or "missionaries," named such people "Janie Appleseeds." (Johnny Appleseed was a USA folk hero who begged apples from established communities and planted the seeds out past the frontier in unsettled places so that later pioneers might find apple trees already in fruit when they arrived.)

Many individuals have already "planted" RC in new places this way, but only on their own initiative. Encouragement, preparation, and community support may work even better.

I will be glad to hear from individuals who are interested. Competence is essential, and this must be demonstrated by all-round community-building where you are at present, to qualify you. Language, health, physical vigor, self-reliance, and emergence from any blocking patterns must be mastered in advance.

Financing can surely be solved. Suggestions are welcome.

Appeared in **Present Time** No. 48.

Draft Policies

Draft Policy for RC Mental Health Workers

A great variety of "mental health workers" have become members of the Re-evaluation Counseling Communities and/or Co-Counsel regularly. Among us are psychiatrists, clinical psychologists, other psychologists, therapists of many specialties, counselors in many fields, administrators, nurses, orderlies, and attendants. All of us began Co-Counseling for our own benefit. In so doing, all of us have been struck by the contrast between the elegance and effectiveness of RC theory and practice and the confusion, irrationality, ineffectiveness, and destructiveness of many of the activities we participate in, or see going on around us, in the mental health system and its professions.

We would like to be able to apply RC, not only to ourselves, but to our patients and to the mental health system as a whole.

As a step towards this we are drafting this policy statement. We invite mental health workers, mental health patients and ex-patients, and the general Community to join us in revising and re-revising this statement until it becomes an accurate and workable program and policy for the transformation of mental health systems and activities everywhere. Our goal will be to clarify theory, to expose and eliminate destructive attitudes and practices in mental health work that exist presently, and to achieve a firm program for rational and successful transformation of the field of "mental health."

Appeared in **Present Time** No. 48.

NO THEORETICAL LIMITS TO HUMAN FUNCTIONING

The viewpoint of Re-evaluation Counseling is that we can accept no limits to human functioning, no definition of "normal" or "good" mental health. We have reason to think that the best functioning adult that has ever lived has achieved only a part of the potential inherent in every newly-conceived human. The best that people have functioned may not be "normal." We can, however, tell when humans are misfunctioning, when they are acting in non-survival ways.

So-called "mental illness" can be best understood as a misfunction of the person. Misfunctioning in humans arises only from mistreatment or other damaging experiences: physical injury, genetic malfunction, poisoning from drugs and other chemicals, and *emotional distress* experiences. The source of most misfunctioning is the *distress experience* which is left undischarged.

UNDERSTANDING THE ROLE OF THE DISTRESS RECORDING

Throughout human existence people have searched for, and invented, explanations of why human beings act irrationally. The RC concept of the *distress recording* offers the first adequate and complete explanation of this, until now, puzzling phenomenon of human irrationality. The undischarged distress experience leaves a *distress recording* which can take over and dominate human behavior and feeling when a *sufficiently similar* new experience triggers the replay of the recording. Restimulated sufficiently, the distress recording becomes chronic and dominates the behavior and feelings of its victim.

ANY DISTRESS RECORDING CAN BE ELIMINATED

The distress recording is removable; its resulting misfunctions can be eliminated through "discharge" and re-evaluation. Discharge is dependably indicated by tears, trembling, perspiration, laughter, "live" storming, reluctant talk, eager, non-repetitive talk, and yawns. Discharge occurs whenever the distress is contradicted sufficiently, usually when one or more other persons pay attention to the distressed person. Any such distress recording can be completely eliminated and the misfunction will be completely eliminated with it—no matter how severe or permanent the misfunction has appeared to be.

ALL LIFE IS WORTH LIVING, TO BE RESPECTED AND PRESERVED

Some damages are, at least with our present knowledge, irreparable (brain tissue destruction, for example). No damage or resulting misfunction, however, from whatever source, leaves any human "better off dead." Any life, under any handicaps, is worth living and should be preserved. Only the oppressive attitudes of society and the accumulated distress patterns themselves ever pull people to think otherwise.

ELIMINATION OF MISTREATMENT

Since misfunction is solely the result of mistreatment, then it must follow that any long-range view—any thoughtful perspective—must include goals for the *elimination* of mistreatment, for making the practical operation of the environment more benign and for interrupting the cyclical process whereby mistreatment of one generation leads to misfunction of that generation, which imposes mistreatment on the next generation. A rational approach to dealing with the misfunctions of humans must include prevention as well as cure. Prevention will need to be part of our thinking at all times, not to be pushed aside by the emergency nature of the need to "handle" any current misfunctions.

SOCIETIES HAVE MANY UNWORKABLE TRADITIONS FOR DEALING WITH HUMAN IRRATIONALITY

Humans have always been aware of irrationality among themselves and have tried to deal with the phenomenon. Every society has evolved some kind of "mental health" structure to eliminate or suppress or isolate the misfunctioning people. There have been many approaches tried for restoring such individuals to functioning well enough, at least, that they do not bother their fellow citizens. Such activities as exorcism, witch-doctoring, or community pressure and support were sometimes helpful. From the perspectives of RC we can now understand the reasons why. The exorcist, for example, didn't blame or reproach the victim but said the evil (the pattern) came from outside the person, offered confidence that the separation could be made, and, undoubtedly, permitted and assisted much discharge during the exorcism rituals.

Most past approaches have been unworkable, unproductive, and destructive. Among these have been neglect, abuse, isolation, punishment, and imprisonment. Present unworkable practices include all these, plus drugging, shock treatment, and psycho-surgery.

THE SOURCES OF SUCH VICIOUS MISTREATMENT CAN BE UNDERSTOOD

Why did these vicious, destructive attitudes, procedures, and structures with which our societies are presently burdened arise? At least three sources of this destructive mistreatment of misfunctioning humans can be identified.

1) The first possibility is that, in very primitive conditions, the apparent economic necessity of abandoning or destroying infants, aged, or handicapped people because of lack of resources left a *distress recording* on the participants and witnesses to such cruelty. Such distress recordings, when restimulated, led to repetition of the cruelty and to repeated contagion of such patterns down the generations.

2) Second, irritation, confusion, and panic are often restimulated in the surrounding individuals by the irrational behavior of the misfunctioning humans. It is a familiar step to shift over into the abuser role to get out of the discomfort of the victim role in one's own restimulated distress.

3) As exploitative societies have developed, they have labeled the misfunctioning human as "unproductive" and thus to be dispensed with. In a further vicious development, the label "mental illness" has become used as an excuse for the suppression and destruction of rebels, non-conformists, and dissidents.

PRESENT OPPRESSIVE SOCIETIES DEFINE "MENTAL HEALTH" AND "MENTAL ILL HEALTH" IN OPPRESSIVE WAYS

We must face the fact that much of what is called "mental illness" by the oppressive society is healthy and at least semi-rational rebellion *against conformity*, against submission to, or cooperation with, *oppression*. The "mental health systems" in our present societies are almost entirely instruments of oppression in spite of the good intentions and the basic humanness of the practitioners who act out their roles in the machinery. Mental health oppression is invoked and used to force submission, to enforce conformity, and to imprison and destroy rebels and non-conformists.

The mental health establishments include thousands of therapists who are good, well-meaning human beings, who are well-intentioned and wish to be of help to their fellow humans, and who have a wide range of amounts of available attention. The mental health establishments include elaborate institutions, expensive equipment, and highly "trained" personnel. Mental health therapists of all varieties are frequently afraid of their own irrationalities and are conditioned to be afraid of their own need to discharge, and thus project these fears on their patients. The mental health establishments are also, in general, almost completely lacking in a workable theory or philosophy or procedures to actually eliminate the misfunction. Where they secure good results, they do so because the intuitive humanness of some of the individual mental health workers breaks through and has a successful interaction with the distressed human, *in spite of* the theories, institutions, and structures, *rather than aided* by them.

WORKING COMPLETELY FROM RC THEORY

Theories of human behavior which evolved prior to RC, which fail to differentiate sharply between the person and the pattern or ignored the spontaneous attempts of the person to discharge, can, at best, be respected as *historical* phenomena, now that these concepts have been revealed and clarified. Present RC *theory* is adequate to guide the complete elimination of any distress recording, no matter how severe or restimulative.

Re-evaluation Counseling *resources* of excellent counselors, however, are still limited and are not yet necessarily available enough to cope with or eliminate any particular distress recording. The rigorous use of RC theory is still often obscured by permissiveness towards dramatizations and other distortions that have passed for RC in poorly functioning Communities.

When difficulties are met in the use of RC, it is *better practice* of RC which needs to happen, not dilution with other theories or practices. The attempts to mix contradictory theories with RC arise only out of confusion or distress at "giving up" one's miseducation and mistraining in which one made such heavy investments and acquired with such great effort.

ROLE OF RC MENTAL HEALTH PROFESSIONALS

1) Our role as mental health professionals is to introduce the basic concepts of "RC" into mental health practice. These include respect for the human being, clearly differentiating between the person and the pattern, understanding the therapist's role as that of helper rather than a person who "thinks for" the patients, chooses goals "for" them, or manipulates them, understanding the central importance of discharge, the use of "the word from outside," protecting patients in the mental health system from any use of drugs, shock, or psycho-surgery and keeping clearly in mind the concept of the whole, undamaged human being existing underneath the distress.

2) It is important that as RC mental health workers we use

RC fully for our own re-emergence; that we become skilled clients as well as counselors; that we use the knowledge that we have not only to assist our patients but to assist and retrain our co-workers. It is important that we carefully examine our attitudes and practices, that we give up contradictory theory, practices, and "habits," no matter how much time we put into learning them or how much "prestige" they have brought us. We must face and acknowledge the oppressive role the mental health system plays and become dependable allies of the mental health system victims and survivors. We must clearly insist that a "cure" is a return to full functioning—not just the suppression of symptoms or "getting by."

3) Other mental health professionals will be more open to RC than our fears and timidities expect. The structure and resources of the mental health systems can be tapped and used for good purposes, if the mental health workers within them can be reached, retrained, and organized. It is in their own interests that this be done, so, if reached correctly, they will respond. Support groups, classes, and literature are key ways of doing this.

THE RC COMMUNITIES ARE NOT REPLACEMENTS FOR THE MENTAL HEALTH SYSTEM

In the RC Communities our teachers should continue to screen carefully for the persons they can accept into classes and train with their present resources. Classes can be and have been effectively taught within the mental health institutions. Members of these classes can learn to work effectively with each other—but should not be brought into the RC Community until they can function fully on that level.

RC Communities may have to use the resources of the mental health establishment for their failures in screening or for the opportunist patterns which, at rare intervals, "flip out" at workshops in an attempt to extort extra attention and discharge for themselves.

The RC Communities cannot *substitute* for the mental health systems in coping with severely distressed behavior. RC theory and practice *can* transform the mental health systems into positive and helpful forces.

Draft Plan for Arab Flourishing

This is the second draft of the "Plan for Arab Flourishing." The changes from the first draft are the result of discussions at the First International RC Arab Workshop, held on Cyprus, August 14-19, 1980. Please send your suggestions for improvement to Yasin Balbaki, M.D., the International Arab Reference Person, at 15 Hobart Terrace, Newton, Massachusetts 02158, USA, or to me at 719 Second Avenue North, Seattle, Washington 98109, USA.

Harvey Jackins
International Reference Person
for the Re-evaluation Counseling Communities

1. The Arab peoples are powerful, splendid human beings with a brilliant common culture, history, and tradition and a variety of rich and important subcultures within the general culture.

2. The Arab peoples have contributed greatly to human progress at many periods in the past and, at some periods, have been the decisive leaders in human affairs. They have produced outstanding artists, political leaders, military strategists, scientists, mathematicians, philosophers, poets, authors, musicians, and business persons.

3. The Arab peoples in the recent historical periods have all, without exception, been victimized by various non-Arab powers. This has not been for the benefit of the peoples of these countries.

4. As a result of domination by the foreign powers, the social and political progress of many of the Arab peoples has been frozen and retarded, and the Arab nations have been locked into out-of-date social and political systems to the great detriment of the Arab peoples themselves. Poor governments have been fastened upon many of the Arab peoples, and these political institutions and governments have continued to hold back their people.

5. The former colonial governments, of foreign powers in Arab countries, have left residues of internalized oppression, class division, admiration of "foreign" things, national divisions, and a tendency toward assimilation. For example, in Lebanon, French rule offered special favors to some Lebanese and made them agents of French rule, so there still remain sharp divisions between Arabs in Lebanon, divisions which do not serve the interests of any group. Serious divisions were installed between the French-dominated Lebanese nation and the Syrian nation, and these differences still continue to create difficulties for the populations of both countries.

6. True independence for the Arab peoples will mean freedom, not only from the domination of the non-Arab powers, but also from the old ruling forces within Arab society.

7. The conquest and colonization of Palestine was supported by the non-Arab powers as a weapon to protect their interests in exploiting the oil and other resources of the Arab lands for themselves. It could have been possible for Jews to live in the Middle East in peaceful co-existence with their Arab cousins; but the price of support by the Western powers was that Israel suppress the Palestinians and serve as the agent of Western power against Arab people's movements for liberation.

8. Israel was seized upon by backward Arab governments as a diversion against people's freedom movements in their countries. In the name of "unity against Israel," progressive movements were suppressed. The United States and Russia

furnished modern armaments to Arab governments ostensibly to use against Israel or to "keep a balance in the Middle East" but actually to use to maintain their own rule.

9. The governments of Israel acted as oppressors of Palestinians. Palestinians were killed, their land taken without compensation, they were driven into exile by the millions. The Palestinian peoples were divided, with part condemned to refugee camps living on a United Nations dole, part exploited and manipulated by backward Arab governments in the countries of their exile, and part living in Israel as second- and third-class citizens.

10. The role of Palestinians is crucial in Arab liberation. The Palestinian people have no illusions about Israeli rule, about Western intentions, or about Arab "nationalism" as represented by any present Arab governments. The Palestinian people are a force for freedom, for the liberation of all Arab peoples.

11. The minimum requirements for Palestinian liberation are the recognition of a free Palestinian nation and complete equality and full citizenship for Palestinians in Israel. The clock cannot be turned back nor can all the past injustice be rectified, but the denial of a national homeland to Palestinians and the oppression of Palestinians in Israel cannot be continued.

12. The solution of the problem of establishing a free and independent Palestinian state and its relationship to Israel requires direct negotiations between the Palestinian people through their chosen representatives and the Israeli people. This question cannot be brokered or solved by the United States or any outside power. It must be solved by the people themselves in a spirit of realism and mutual respect.

13. Arab oppression exists today in at least four broad forms. First, there is the oppression of the Palestinians inside Israel, robbed, exiled, persecuted, and treated as second-class citizens by a government which avowedly excludes them. Here certain-

ly the granting of full citizenship and full rights, the prevention of future injustices, and the correction of past ones must be a minimum program. Palestinians living within the state of Israel, must have full citizenship and full rights equal to that of the Jewish Israelis in every respect.

Second, intense oppression of Arabs in Lebanon is a grievous model of what can happen with too much foreign intervention and denial of independence to the Arab peoples. Arabs are oppressed by Arabs in a state of anarchy and armed terror in Lebanon, and the intervention of Syria and Israel and the United Nations has not solved this problem. The initiative of the Lebanese people themselves must become channelled to achieve a minimum program of unity to end the terror and destruction. Attempts to impose rule by conquest on one group of Lebanese by another group must cease.

Third, Arabs in the Arab states are oppressed by reactionary Arab governments who received their power from the retiring non-Arab colonists and who act in the interest of a small clique of people at best and mostly as agents of foreign exploitation. The end of the reactionary governments and the installation of true people's governments in all the countries of the Levant and Mahgreb is an important step for Arab liberation.

Fourth, Arabs who have emigrated or who have been exiled to non-Arab countries are oppressed there by pressures to assimilate, to divorce themselves from Arab culture and by the discrimination faced by them in many such countries (the United States, England, France, Germany, Turkey, Iran, to mention only a few). Here Arab liberation requires an end to the discrimination, the proud retention of one's Arab background, culture, and language, and full acceptance of this as an important contribution to the culture of the host country.

Assimilated Arabs or persons of partial Arab ancestry who have become assimilated into other cultures have a right to full pride in, and recovery of, their Arab roots and traditions. They will be welcomed completely as Arabs by Arabs living in the ancestral Arab countries.

14. Real liberation for the Arab peoples can only be achieved through real unity of all Arab peoples. The present governments of the Arab states are not likely to achieve such unity, although the pressure of people's movements can force them to move somewhat in a direction of unity.

Unity cannot be achieved around the goal of the destruction of Israel. It can be achieved around the goal of a free, liberated Palestinian state.

15. True liberation of the Arab peoples will require equality between men and women. The liberation of Arab women is an important part of the liberation of all Arabs.

16. While recognizing the unique strengths and richness that Arab cultural and family traditions bring to our lives, we also recognize the need to end the oppression of sexism and the social oppression and rigidities that inhibit each individual from his or her unique flowering.

17. The tools of Re-evaluation Counseling are useful for all peoples, in all situations of human contact and living. They are indispensable for successful liberation work in this modern situation, in helping to avoid acting from distress instead of from rational decisions, in solving conflicts between allies and potential allies, in achieving unity between all oppressed peoples, and in working together to pool these strengths.

18. The role of the Re-evaluation Counseling Communities, with respect to Arab liberation, is to make the tools of RC available to Arabs as widely as possible, to assist in communication between Arabs everywhere in setting up a rational program for liberation and in making it come about, and in assisting in finding and informing non-Arab allies about Arab liberation, and in encouraging their support.

19. The Re-evaluation Counseling Community will, to the extent of its resources, offer counseling, classes, and workshops to Arabs everywhere. We will seek to train teachers and leaders for communicating Re-evaluation Counseling widely and for Arab liberation work. We will seek to put liberation-minded Arabs everywhere in touch with each other and with RC knowledge.

20. Co-counseling skills are crucial for the individual re-emergence of Arab Co-Counselors and the mastery of these skills is an important task before all Arab RCers so as to make the most effective counseling available to each other.

Although Co-Counseling skills will not directly solve the many problems of the difficult relationships at present existing within and between the Arab countries, the application of these skills by individual Arabs can greatly assist in expediting the inevitable working-out of these difficulties.

21. Though RC, in becoming established in Arab countries, will face differences with many of the cultural patterns of these countries, these differences are, in general, not greater than the contrast between RC and the cultural patterns of the countries where RC has already become established. Flexible thinking, distinguishing between what is essential RC and what are non-essential characteristics picked up during its practice in non-Arab countries, will be important. Distinguishing between the positive aspects of Arab cultures and the patterned aspects which must be gently and eventually resisted, will make it possible for an "Arab RC" to become established, clarify itself, and flourish in all the Arab homelands.

Draft Policy for RC Physicians

Since the very beginnings of intelligence, human beings have sought to defend themselves and ensure their survival against the difficulties caused by injuries, disease, and genetic malfunction. They have appeared to have at least two goals in this regard—the prolongation of life and the improvement of the quality of life.

Self-care has always been a major part of these efforts, but because of the dependency and feelings of helplessness likely to accompany health difficulties, *the health care of others* has always been a subject of preoccupation, specialization, and social attention. The "medicine man" or "medicine woman" occurs early in all cultures.

Social and individual efforts toward health have always included both prevention and treatment. Exercise, rest, nutrition, personal hygiene, sanitation, isolation from infection, and morale-building as prevention measures have received persistent, but varying, amounts of attention in different periods of individual and social history. Manipulation, dosing, isolation, bed-rest, surgery, sweating, entertainment, and ritual have figured prominently in the area of treatment.

TWO ATTITUDES

Two different attitudes toward the *social problem* of the poorly-functioning or dependent individual have appeared throughout human existence, and are plainly evident today.

The first attitude is one of caring concern by others for the

Appeared in **Present Time** No. 48.

individual's recovery and/or survival. This includes persistent care of the individual as an infant or convalescent, special honors and assistance to the handicapped, the veneration of the elderly, and the assignment of major economic resources toward health care and for research into health care improvement.

The second attitude includes the "mercy-killing" of the injured fellow-soldier, abortion, exposure of new-born infants, abandonment of the aged, decisions as to whom to attempt to treat in crowded battle-front hospitals (triage), execution of the "insane," capital punishment of criminals, neglect or exclusion of the poor or indigent from health-care resources, euthanasia, and "pulling the plug" on modern life-support systems.

The first attitude seems to be based on our inherent human natures and the operation of individual human intelligence. The second attitude seems to arise from individual distress patterns and the enforcements of oppressive societies, often internalized by the individual as "inherent necessities."

A BASIC CHOICE

The RC Communities, and RC physicians, must firmly choose and model the first attitude. Reverence for life, and in particular for human life, must replace any internalized traces of the judgmental attitude. In a rational society, our resources are ample to support the human attitude fully.

CLASS SOCIETIES, ECONOMICS, AND HEALING

All societies operate as dictated by the basic economic relations of the society, but through a superstructure of culture which has a limited independence and momentum of its own, and which tends to reflect, in some degree, the conflicting interests of the different economic classes of which society is comprised.

Healers of many different approaches were used in slave societies, and, though their status was usually that of a slave or vassal of the slave-owner, leadership in developing the knowledge of healing was sometimes taken by free citizens and even by individuals of aristocratic slave-owning lineage.

Doctoring was often a sideline of the barbering trade in western feudal societies (the modern barber pole is a representation of an umbilical cord), but medical knowledge came more and more to be associated with intellectuals.

When capitalism replaced feudalism, it tended to replace all previous standards of judgment and human activities by the standard of profitability. Capitalism has more and more pushed the physician toward the goals of being a "successful businessman," making a large "investment" in early training and receiving a very large salary from his (or her) patients and perhaps a very large profit from the employment of other people and the extraction of surplus value from their labor once "in business."

THE CONTINUING CONFLICT

Traditions of selfless dedication to the healing of the sick (Hippocrates) and to his or her role as a scientist, which accompanies his/her extended technical training, persist in the culture of the individual physician and remain at war with the pressures of modern capitalism on him or on her to be a successful exploiter. Physicians are under great pressure and endure great conflict. They have usually chosen their profession in order to "serve the people" and are, on their human side, devoted to the well-being of all people and especially to their patients. On the other hand, they are pressured to act as "authorities," to function through dictatorial domination of staff and patients, and to judge themselves successful or not primarily in terms of their money-making.

SOME NEW VIEWPOINTS

Re-evaluation Counseling theory can look at the healing arts, and the practice of medicine in particular, from several valuable viewpoints. We are aware of the body's capacity to heal itself. We realize that the modern environment is not primarily crafted for the well-being of people, but rather for the extraction of profits. We are confident of the deep humanness of the individual physician and aware of the authoritarian, oppressive, patterned conditioning which he or she has been forced to endure during his or her medical training.

We see the operation of *distress patterns* leading to illness in at least two ways. One is the restimulation of a recording of a previous injury or illness, making the individual ill once more. The other is the interference with the body's inherent ability to recover from injury or illness by distress recordings which block or hinder the operation of the immune systems, the circulation, or other bodily functions. We have, by now, much experience that discharge and re-evaluation—the re-emergence process—can be of powerful assistance to healing and recovery whenever the illness or injury of the patient involves either of these two phenomena. We know that the well-being of any person, including patients, is greatly enhanced by being respected, cared about, listened to, and permitted and assisted to discharge.

THE INTERACTION BETWEEN RC AND PHYSICIANS

The RC Community comes to physicians with respect and appreciation. The powerful tools of modern biology, biochemistry, and medical science make enormous contributions to the well-being of humans everywhere. Physicians equipped with these tools can be a decisively benign influence if their goals are clear and their commitment is to humanness.

Re-evaluation Counseling must seek to support and influence physicians for their own well-being.

Physicians in general, and RC physicians in particular, need to clarify their commitment to life and survival. We need to take a clear stand against *needless* use of mind-numbing drugs or anesthesia which result in damage and distress to the individual. We need to model and express a reverence for human life as contrasted with assuming the power of making life-and-death judgments of survival. We need to insist that organized medicine take responsibility for the larger issues of the *prevention* of illness, the *maintenance* of good health, the full use of the capacities of all human beings, the ending of oppression, and the attainment of a free society.

We need to insist that the narrowness of main-stream medical practice be broadened, that a holistic approach be taken to the patient, that *exercise, nutrition, manipulation,* and *touching* be integrated with medical and surgical practice.

We need to support respectful alliances of western physicians with non-western healing disciplines and their practitioners so that both groups may learn from each other.

OPPRESSION IN TRAINING AND PRACTICE

It is plain that in almost all medical training establishments intensive oppression of the medical student, the intern, and the resident goes on in order to convert the idealistic, human, and loving student into a practicing physician who will function in the mold of the business-oriented, authoritarian "boss" of all other health personnel. There is pressure on every medical student and physician to become a straight-jacketed "martinet," to lend support to reactionary political causes through the medical associations, to prescribe mind-numbing drugs (or general anesthesia when local would suffice), to act carelessly and with contempt for patients, to be unwilling (or unable) to consult with patients or include their judgment and intelligence in devising the most effective and most economical treatment for them, to participate in a spiraling cost of health care that places it beyond the reach of much of the population.

THE BATTLE TO STAY HUMAN

Most physicians try to resist these pressures as best as they can. They work desperately long hours in an effort to serve their patients well. They study at every opportunity in an effort to keep abreast of new developments. They care about their patients and express this caring in many thoughtful ways. They assume awesome responsibilities because no one else is ready to assume them.

RC physicians, in particular, have grasped eagerly at the possibility of a completely human, rational approach to the healing of humans and have taken many initiatives toward an integration of these ideas with their practice.

A clear, ever-evolving policy, and effective contact with each other organizationally, should assist RC physicians, and people-minded physicians generally, to become much more effective in these directions.

PROPOSALS

We propose that all medical students join together and organize support groups, discussion groups, and Co-Counseling classes to preserve their humanness during the difficult student years. We applaud the improvements in medical training atmospheres that have occurred at some medical schools and propose such improvements in all the other institutions. We urge all present medical students to master the powerful tools of modern medicine, surgery, biochemistry, and allied arts, and to integrate them with the theory and practice of Re-evaluation Counseling to enlist to the fullest extent the abilities of the patients themselves to enhance their recoveries.

We encourage all practicing physicians to speak out against the pressure for distortion of medical ethics and competence by reactionary social and political forces. We suggest that physicians at all stages view other health workers as their respected allies and peers, recognizing the decision-making role and competence of the physician, but treated as members of a team and encouraged to develop confidence in their own fields.

We call for a complete reversal of the spiraling cost and complexity of medical care, and for the involvement of patients and all varieties of health professionals in discussions to accomplish this.

We propose support groups for physicians only, and support groups for all health workers including physicians.

We propose that physicians themselves take the lead in insisting that the present barriers to non-white persons becoming physicians be attacked and removed by decisive affirmative action, individual sponsorship, and large-scale scholarship programs.

We welcome the current entry of large numbers of women into medical practice and call for the complete elimination of all remaining discrimination against women, both in the training and in the practice of medicine and surgery. We call for research into and publicizing of the ancient roles of women as healers and midwives and recognition that their exclusion in the intervening periods has been a blow to the well-being of all peoples.

We hail the beginnings that have been made by practicing physicians, residents, and interns to integrate RC theory and practice into their medical practices. We ask that these experiences be shared widely with other RC physicians and with the RC and medical communities. We suggest that the experiences of RC classroom teachers in integrating RC into their classroom practices be exchanged with the physicians who are attempting a comparable effort.

We propose the upgrading of the RC journal **Well-Being** and its more frequent publication.

We will make increased efforts for international communication between RC physicians and health workers in different countries, and for special assistance to physicians in a position to influence the development of medical theory and research and the training of new physicians.

We applaud the leadership taken against nuclear armaments among the population as a whole by physicians and medical students through the Physicians for Social Responsibility and its affiliated student groups. We call upon all physicians and medical students to redouble their efforts and their leadership in this struggle to preserve humanity and the world of life from nuclear extinction, the most crucial "health problem" the world has ever known.

The Wide World

RCers in Non-RC Organizations

Many RCers find, as they reclaim their intelligence and power through their counseling, that they become interested in broader issues and are pulled to be active in other organizations and in the wide world. This is certainly all to the good. There often is unclarity and timidity, however, about *how* to be members of other organizations, about *how* to work in the wide world.

RCers are different than any other people in the world *only* in their possession of RC concepts and tools, which they freely offer to everyone. RCers in other organizations are there to relate to *all* other members of the organization, not to huddle together as a group of RCers in that organization. RCers should participate fully as members of other organizations and should participate in working out policy and making decisions in the organization, but including *all* members of the organization in the process, *never acting as a group of RCers*. To act as a group would be a violation of RC theory and practice, another expression of fearful patterned huddling, and would be disrespectful to our fellow-members of the organization.

It is important that RC concepts and skills be offered to *all* sections of the Jewish communities. RCers reclaiming their Jewish heritage can join and participate in all organizations: religious, community, social, political. To huddle in only non-RC activist groups is to act out of the internalized patterns of isolation which are the mainstay of Jewish oppression.

Appeared in **Ruah Hadashah** No. 5.

Past Wars and the Danger of Future Ones

—Talk at the Workshop Schloss Heiligen Hoven I Lindlar, Germany, January 7, 1983

I want to add some perspective to our discussions and discharge about the Second World War. I'm very pleased that the German RCers here began to face their own history and terrors and discharge their hurts, including their guilts. What happened last night is exactly what we have wished for. People who have been talking to me since, however, have indicated a great deal of confusion that I may be able to clarify. I did not realize until after the discussion that I'm the only person here who was an adult during World War Two. Everyone else at this workshop was a small child during the war or was born afterwards. I think this gives me some perspective that those who came later lack. I was already a grown man and a leader before World War Two. I was called up for military service three times. Although, for different reasons, I never served, I spent a good part of the war outfitting naval ships and sailing on them with Navy crews on "shakedown" cruises.

World War Two was not an isolated evil incident. Given the kind of societies that existed, it was inevitable that World War Two would occur. World War One had been "inevitable" before that and so have the numerous upheavals and depressions between the wars and the many terrible wars that have occurred since in Korea and Vietnam and Lebanon and San Salvador. Wars are inevitable as long as this oppressive society in its aggressive and moribund stages dominates the world. Someone here has said that the Third World War is already going on and the firing of the missiles will mark the end of the war, not its beginning. If we take that view, then World War Three as it is at present has been inevitable from the nature of the society in which we live.

Appeared in **Present Time** No. 51.

The events for which the German RCers began to take responsibility and discharge on last night were not the kind of events that could only occur with one evil individual like Hitler and one population corrupted by complacency and terror, such as the parts of Germany were that supported him. (Repeat requested.)

The role which Hitler and the German people played was not the result of policies which occurred only with Hitler and only within this country (Germany). I would in no way excuse the German people from examining these events and taking responsibility for the future; but for the rest of us to think that this alone deals with what happened in World War Two would be a terrible mistake. There is no national group of people in the world that does not have to do this kind of examination.

Within every country there were and are individuals and groups of individuals whose policies are made up of the same kind of patterns that motivated Hitler. Such kinds of individuals and groups of individuals are prominent and powerful in the ruling classes of every country. They were present in the ruling classes of all these nations before World War Two and they continue to the present. In every country these powerful groups seek to promote racism, genocide, war, and destruction. They do this, not because they were not good human beings to start with; they were conceived and born just as good and dear and human as the rest of us; but because the conditioning of the oppressive society converted them into this monstrous role.

Hitler was of little importance until money from American and English financiers had supported him for many years and allowed him to present himself impressively to the most reactionary German rulers as a possible agent for them. The financiers behind the Ku Klux Klan in the United States and the ones behind the National Front in England are functionally just as evil and just as inhuman as Hitler and his supporters. They operate under different national and cultural banners but their content is equivalent.

Without a class analysis of our societies World War Two and the threat of World War Three cannot really be understood. The oppressive society converts young people who are destined to be rulers into conditioned automatons able to be concerned only about profits. If profits, or bigger profits, or faster profits, require war, slaughter, and genocide, then the machine grinds on heedless of human values. Intelligence is constrained only to excusing, justifying, or "glorifying" the madness, not to interrupting it.

The atrocities committed by the Third Reich are inexcusable, inhuman, and horrifying and will forever remain a warning to all people, but my own proud country, the U.S.A., tried to wipe out the Native peoples ruthlessly. Only the courage and vigor of the Native peoples of the U.S. and Canada have kept them from being wiped out completely.

The atrocities committed by the British Empire are beyond belief. The rubber workers working in the Congo on Belgian King Leopold's estates had their hands cut off if they did not gather sufficient rubber. And all this is only recent history which is much less vicious than the history of all countries a few hundred years ago.

The ruling classes of all societies are at continual war *with their own populations*. Prisons, armies, police, courts, and laws are used to legitimize the robbery that is carried on daily. Wars, when they occur, are always eagerly sought by the ruling class of a country as a pretext for robbing the population *of its own country* more deeply than usual. There are big profits to be made and big power to be seized by having a war. Of course the ruling classes always hope they will be able to rob even more deeply the people of the opposing country if they can conquer them.

War brings no real advantage to the humans underneath the patterns of the ruling classes which push for war. As human beings they suffer deeply too. Their humanness is destroyed, their sons are killed, and their lives are disrupted. But the patterned roles into which they have been conditioned by the society allow them no choice; they must act this way, they must defeat or be defeated in the endless competition which is the theme of their patterned lives. The occasional individual who rebels is labeled a traitor and severely punished. Many people from the ruling classes of all countries have given their lives in trying to oppose the policies of the class. Their small numbers have joined the thousands of working-class, farmers, and middle-class people whose lives also were given in struggling against war and for humanness.

The destruction committed by the Third Reich armies was terrible, but in the same war American and British bombers senselessly destroyed whole populations of German cities, deliberately creating fire storms which could sweep all the populations to death. It was businessman President Truman who launched the atomic bombs that wiped out Hiroshima and Nagasaki. The record of all the powers in Korea, and the role of the United States in Vietnam, is one long succession of atrocities. In each country the ruling class uses war as a tool for the deep exploitation of their own nation's people first, and then, if they are successful in the war, of the people of the other countries.

I welcomed the marvelous discharge and communication of Christine last night. She faced up to all the issues which every German must face, but if we do not get beyond "We Germans" in this respect, we will not get far. We must look beyond "We United Statesers" or "We British" or "We Netherlanders." There is a class structure in all these countries. Though the ruling-class individual's *humanness* is ruined by that society, that individual's *role* is very different than the role of the working-class person or the young person.

The German working class fought against Nazism. They did not always fight skillfully or wisely; they made serious tactical and strategical blunders; but as a class they fought for a long time and many of their leaders gave their lives in the struggle. This has been true in every country. If we do not understand that war is never a war primarily against other nations but primarily against the common people in the home country, we cannot effectively put a stop to it.

War impoverishes everyone except a small ruling clique in each country. The common people have the strength to stop a war any time. Only instilled confusion to keep us thinking that we are a *national* body instead of the highly oppressive class structure that is the reality, only this and the patterns of powerlessness have kept us from stopping wars that firmly. We, the working-class, farmers, intellectuals, middle-class, and the owning-class individuals who have transcended their class position to join us, must come to understand the class nature of war, or we can once again be led by the nose, in the name of patriotism, to our own destruction.

The Second World War arose as an almost purely imperialist war. A series of events made it eventually necessary for ordinary people to support one side against the other but only because many opportunities to prevent the conflict had been missed repeatedly up to that point. The Nazi movement could have been wiped out easily almost any time in the previous years.

I do not think it likely that any *future* war *between great powers* can possibly be a peoples' war on either side. I think we must take a firm decision that we, the common people, will be at war with our own warmakers to deprive them of their powers, or all our fine slogans and our big demonstrations will amount to very little.

Wars mean profit. I think that we must put at the heart of our programs to end profiteering through arms, to end the armaments race, to end war. We may have to change the society completely to bring this about, but that may occur anyway. It is becoming increasingly clear that our societies are in such disorder, so close to final collapse, that we cannot even have clean streets without a basic change in society. We cannot have schools where it is safe for teachers to teach without a basic change in society. We cannot have clean air or water without a change in society. The smallest problems are rapidly becoming insoluble except through a complete change in society. I would like to suggest to all Co-Counselors that once in a while they have a session on what a really decent, rational society would be like and what is one small step that each could take toward bringing it about.I think you will find this in very close accord with our goal for the elimination of nuclear weapons.

Also, we will not become or remain discouraged or confused by the great number of tasks that we must perform. The truth is that we have only one task, and that's to live well and intelligently, whatever that takes. We will eliminate nuclear arms while we eat our breakfast. It will be all one job.

Thank you for listening so attentively.

Organize the Unorganized

A New Trade Union Movement in the United States

The time has come for rapid, large-scale organization of unorganized U.S. workers along the lines of the Solidarity Union movement in Poland.

The organization of unorganized workers has long been a crucial need for the long-term interests of the U.S. population, and for the U.S. working class and the trade union movement at a short range. It is, however, an issue that has been faced only sporadically. The great organizing drives among the steel workers in 1919, among the packinghouse workers earlier, and the drives of the C.I.O. in the 1930's achieved good results, but never led to a consistently-pursued plan of having *all* workers organized in trade unions, nor to the unity of *all* working people.

What intruded each time to prevent general organization was the bribery and recruitment of important sections of the leadership of the trade unions by the employers and their agents. Union memberships were also won over to a *de facto* policy of settling for special benefits for the minority of organized workers, allowing capitalism to exploit the unorganized workers as the price for certain gains in the wages and conditions of the organized minority. This, of course, is internalized oppression. Some trade unions have been notorious for this, but it has also affected the union movement as a whole.

After World War II the anti-union offensives of the Cold War and Korean War periods were discouraging to union organization. When the struggle to end the Vietnam War finally

Presented to Wide World Changing III Workshop.

changed the political climate, most activists' attention was largely on middle-class organizing and issues such as nuclear power and protection of the environment, important issues, but not so immediately vital to the basic interests of the working class.

CONTINUING NEED

A few voices in labor have continued to raise the central importance of the organization of all the unorganized workers. Failure of this movement to make much headway must be due to lack of clear policies, to poor communication, and to timid leadership. Another factor is the disillusionment of unorganized workers with what they hear about union leadership and activities—its corruption and do-nothingness. The propaganda of the regular media and of the employers takes advantage of this confusion and misinformation.

It has been difficult for the unorganized workers to see any clear prospect as to *how* they could *organize themselves*, since few of the existing unions have seemed to be interested. Many of the AF of L-CIO unions have seemed to be initiation-fee grabbers and dictatorial cliques. Workers seeking to organize often have met an attitude of condescension from the "elite" organized group toward the "lower" unorganized workers, making them fight for the chance to win entrance into the established unions.

Under the labor laws which still remain on the books, every group of workers has a legal right to a union of their own choosing. With proper initiative, strong, democratic unions could have been organized during this past period of time. The lack of correct policy or the lack of committed leadership with correct policies has undoubtedly been the key factor in this not happening. The ability of unorganized workers to "get by" on welfare and unemployment compensation has also had a passivizing effect. These "scraps," paid for by the super-profits siphoned off workers abroad by the super-exploitation of the United States multi-national corporations, has served to keep down the motivation for organization.

A NEW BALL GAME

In the current period, all this is changing. The economic crisis is bringing real hardship to bear on all sections of the working class, including those with the most powerful unions. The very high unemployment in steel, auto, rubber, and transportation, and the spreading general unemployment (combined this time with a very high inflation rate, which did not occur in the Great Depression of the 30's) has forced U.S. working people to a high pitch of awareness of the need to act on solutions to their problems. The election of the Republican Senate and the Reagan administration and their obvious determination to scoop off an even higher rate of profits for the wealthy at the cost of abandonment of all supportive social programs for the poor, working class, and middle class has made the situation even more urgent.

SOMETHING NEW

In this objective situation there is a new subjective factor. The brilliant victories of the Polish working class in creating new, independent unions under the most difficult conditions and in securing widespread unity and great effectiveness in the face of disastrous economic conditions and the threat of armed intervention from abroad, has opened up exciting new perspectives. These undoubtedly are stirring the imagination of almost every U.S. worker even if the excitement has not yet taken any organizational form. Television and newspapers continually remind everyone of the reality of what workers can do, in the daily news from Poland.

TIME TO ACT

This situation calls for the formation of an independent organizing center with very clear policies for organizing all unorganized workers. A brochure should be issued and distributed nation-wide, calling on workers everywhere to form unions, to affiliate with this center if they wish, giving the actual facts on what is necessary to secure union recognition and bargaining rights, a summary of the labor legislation that workers need to be aware of, and an offer of help from the center. The center's program should call for labor unity and the organization of the unorganized. It should offer all new unions a place to pool their strengths, but call for eventual achievement of *one* U.S. labor federation. It should recommend that the newly formed unions eventually affiliate to an existing union (the AF of L-CIO, the Longshoremen-Warehousemen's Union, Teamsters, Machinists, or whatever unions exist) whenever that union meets the following conditions:

1. That it is democratic. That the membership has the control of the locals and through their conventions, of the international officials.

2. That there is no recent history of violence being used to dictate the policy of the union. That no union officials are associated with organized crime. That no union officials on the local or international scene are owners of businesses in which other workers are employed. That the newly formed union enters into its affiliation with all the rights of existing union members, and is not given any kind of second-class citizenship, or charged special fees.

3. That the union (to which they propose affiliation) itself is pledged to organize the unorganized and to secure the unity of all workers, in the U.S. and abroad.

The center's program should reject sexism and racism and clearly seek and welcome all women and Third World workers.

The first center would, of course, quickly lead to branch centers everywhere in the country. Great initiative and enthusiasm would be unleashed throughout the nation.

What could be the results of this? My conjecture is that a clear brochure, widely distributed through existing contacts, a small (to begin with) competent organizing staff, a battery of toll-free long-distance telephones, two or three good labor lawyers, and a computer could, in a very short time, using the name of *U.S. Solidarity*, begin a process that would work at least as rapidly as it has in Poland. It would lead to a trade union federation, eventually re-united with the AF of L-CIO and the other major, existing unions, of from 60 to 80 million workers.

Such a trade union federation under responsible leadership and good policies would be in a position to dramatically improve the living standards of all the U.S. people. It would be able to change completely the character of the Congress and the Administration. It would be able to act to protect the environment, stop the extermination of species, effectively do something about crime and pollution, the collapse-of-the-education-system, and all the other presently "unsolvable" plagues of U.S. life.

Why not?

(Permission granted to duplicate and distribute as widely as you wish. —H.)

Can Distress About the Holocaust Be Discharged?

Harvey was asked how heavy distress about the Holocaust could be contradicted enough for Jewish Co-Counselors to allow it to be discharged. The following is what transpired.

Harvey: Discussion of the Holocaust started at the First Jewish Liberation Workshop, and it became so heavy that everyone was reinforcing everyone else's distress and sinking slowly out of sight. As I remember it, at that point about three people were saying, "You can't contradict *that* (the Holocaust), it's a fact, it's a fact, it's a fact," and the only realistic thing I could think of at the moment was to say cheerfully and fearlessly, "By now most of them would have been dead anyway."

No one here thinks that's funny, huh? They didn't either easily, but they were so desperate for something to contradict it, that quite a number of people laughed and shook. We began to discharge and got out of the deep freeze.

In effect we encountered this heaviness in various drafts of the Jewish Liberation Policy. The cultural patterns came to address this question of policy with the assumption that no people has ever been persecuted as badly as the Jews. That is simply *not* true. All the people that lived around the Jews were attacked in pretty much the same way the Jews were. It was the way the old societies worked. What was distinctive about the Jews was that they survived while their neighbors were all wiped out. The Jewish culture with its particular strengths was so sturdy that it survived the persecution that destroyed the surrounding cultures over and over and over again. So the

From a demonstration at the Achziv Yad L Yad International Workshop in Israel, April 1981. Appeared in **Ruah Hadashah** No. 5.

reality is not greater persecution but *greater strength!* But because the Jews survived as a culture to tell the story, the stories of the persecution piled up enormously. The Meads, and the Assyrians, the Phoenicians, and the twenty or thirty other peoples who surrounded them in ancient times disappeared. The Hebrew Culture popped up to the top like a cork. Other peoples without the Jewish literary tradition who were conquered and sent into slavery, vanished. The Jews sent into slavery kept reading books to each other, and kept thinking together of some way to buy one Jew's freedom. That person would then set up shop and buy the freedom of a couple of other Jews, and pretty quickly there was a colony of Jews in a new city. This is the reality. The great strength of the Jewish culture allows the persecutions to be remembered; it is not that the persecutions were worse.

When I meet with a Jewish Support Group, say, in a United States' city, and they're faced with this "Alarm, alarm," I say fascism cannot happen again. And often someone hysterically responds, "How can you say that?" I say, "It's easy, I just open up my mouth and say it. But it's also true." Fascism was a particular historical phenomenon and could only arise in particular circumstances. Fascism is only one of many attempts to turn back the clock of social progress. It was one of the most threatening and one of the most nearly successful of all attempts, but it did its worst and it was defeated. We will have other difficult things to contend with, but we will not again have fascism. We might have something called Reaganism—or something—but it will not be fascism. If we think it's fascism, we will not deal with it well.

Okay, that's background. Now, who's got some distress on living through the Holocaust? (M volunteers.)

Harvey *(to M)*: Okay. I have a lot of respect for you, especially after hearing your poem. I'm going to endeavor to have no respect for your patterns, no matter how sacred they seem, and no matter if everybody here thinks that I'm a cruel person because I refuse to extend sympathy to your pattern. That warning may be for them and not for you. You'll do fine.

Tell me your thoughts about the Holocaust.

M: My thoughts are that those were terrible years, that somehow six years have been taken out of my life; it was six years that I could not live a normal life. I had to hide and run and feel fear of dying. Fear. I feared that I might die at almost any minute in those six years. That's it.

H: How did you survive?

M: By hiding. Primarily, by hiding.

H: Did you have any help?

M: Help from others? Yes.

H: Talk about that.

M: I had great help from my parents, particularly my father, a very strong man. He saved himself, his wife, and my brothers and me. He saved a lot of people through the war.

H: How did he do it?

M: I don't know. I don't know where he found the courage to do it, the determination—I don't know how he did it, but he did it.

H: Were there allies who came to his assistance?

M: Yes, there were some good people. There were some who were entirely kindness and charity. Perhaps there were others I didn't know about, but I'm grateful for the ones who did contribute to our survival. I know they did contribute.

H: They risked their lives to do it.

What about this period still bothers you?

M: As I get older it seems that I'm becoming more aware of the Holocaust instead of forgetting it. I find it almost incredible that things like these could have happened. I'm particularly sensitive to any denials of the Holocaust. It seems just impossible that someone thirty years later would in any way try to deny that it happened. It is part of history. It makes me terribly, terribly angry when I hear about that.

H: It's one of the plots of the political New Right to write books "explaining" that the Holocaust never happened.

Do you often think of the ones who perished in the Holocaust instead of surviving?

M: Yes, but I look at them as a whole. I don't remember or think of them as individual people.

H: I would like for you to say to those people, "I honor you by the meaningful life that I live!"

What are you thinking?

M: I did not expect to face this issue in RC. I came here to work on other burdens but somehow the past intruded on me, like a great wind.

H: Would you keep speaking to those people with your eyes closed, as if you're shouting to them over a distance of one hundred yards or so. Shout to them: "Good news! The Jewish people survived!"

M: Good news.

H: Keep your eyes closed. I want you to keep up the fantasy of the group of people standing waiting for your words, "Good news! The Jewish people survived!"

M: Good news! The Jewish people survived!

H: "In a sunlit room in a beautiful land."

M: *(repeats)*

H: "They meet together with their friends and allies to honor you."

M: *(repeats)*

H: "I who shared your terror..."

M: *(repeats)*

H: "...will speak to the others of your greatness..."

M: *(repeats, crying)*

H: "...to better honor you I will feel my fear and discharge it."

M: "To better honor you I will...*(cries). (Group discharge, crying abounds.)*

H: "There's never before in history been such widespread recognition and honor for the Jewish people."

M: *(repeats, crying; Group crying)*

H: "We mourned you but we will honor you..."

M: *(repeats)*

H: "...and not just in talk, in words, but also in good deeds. The Jewish people will never again be threatened."

M: *(repeats)*

H: "They have a land of their own now."

M: *(repeats)*

H: "Their sons and daughters reach out and forge good lives everywhere. Isolation is outdated."

M: *(repeats, crying. All crying)*

H: *(recites poem)* Sleep softly, eagle forgotten, under the stone
Time has its way with you there, and the grave has its own.
Sleep on, oh stout-hearted, oh brave ones who kindled the flame
To live in humankind is far more than to live a name,
To live in humankind far, far more than to live a name.*

Tell them, your ancestors and loved ones, "You can be proud of me...!"

M: *(Crying, repeats)*

H: "My life honors you."

M: *(repeats)*

H: What are you thinking? Would you say your goodbye to these people—"You may go to your rest now..."

M: *(crying)*

H: "We will look after things. You may rest in peace."

Part of the propaganda that attempts to divide the peoples of the world not only does, as we mentioned, deny that the

*"The Eagle Forgotten" by Vachel Lindsay

Holocaust happened, but it also—and sometimes we participate in this without meaning to—defames the memory of the role of these people. History is distorted to say that the Jews were alone, that no one stood up for them. This is repeated and repeated and repeated. This is not true! Thousands of Germans, thousands of people in the other countries in Europe gave their lives in the attempt to prevent the Holocaust. To preserve the isolation, history is distorted as "the Jews were completely isolated, no one raised a hand to defend them."

Our RC leader in Warsaw is a survivor. At the first workshop she ever attended people kept asking her to speak louder. Her attempt to speak louder forced into awareness, for the first time in years, the memory that for three years she was not allowed to make any sound. She said, "Do not say bad words about the Ukrainians to me. The Ukrainian peasants, numbers of them, risked their lives time and time again to keep me and my family alive."

The lies are told that the Jews went willingly, that they simply didn't fight. This is not true. Under conditions of extreme terror many people become paralyzed and immobile. This is distress. I know a survivor of Aufschwitz. She's a person of great integrity. When the gas ovens failed to kill her, the Nazis saved her and used her as an experimental animal. Everything brutal and degrading that could possibly be thought of was done to her, and yet her integrity shines out and is realized by everyone who meets her. It's a puzzle why she was not degraded. Slowly as the memories come out of occlusion, in the safety of counseling, the picture becomes clearer. The little girl, all alone and tortured by the people in whose charge she was, made a decision that she would love her torturers. She figured it out all alone in the midst of pain and terror that they didn't really want to act that way, that something was making them. So instead of being destroyed, she came through with a diamond-like integrity. Is there any higher achievement in human history than to make that decision for reality in such a position?

(To M) Did the Holocaust happen?

M: Yes.

H: Is it over?

M: Yes.

H: Can the effects of it be discharged?

M: Yes.

H: Do you know how to do it well yet?

M: No.

H: I suspect it would help if we had a large number of effective Gentile counselors, who understood the reality of Jewish oppression but refused to buy the despair. Did we make a little bit of a start?

M: Yes. *(Others: "Yes," agreeing.)*

H: I think so, and this was without preparation.

If we remember that distress can be discharged once it is contradicted, we can find ways to do it. Anything that contradicts it is useful. "Ghengis Khan piled up ten times as many bodies in Central Asia as there were Jews destroyed in the Holocaust." "Any one of one hundred major famines in China destroyed more people." "Some current events in Africa are leading to much greater destruction." That may not sound very positive but it can give us just a little perspective there. "Humanity has always survived." "It happened a long time ago." "There are more Jews now than ever."

(Someone tells Harvey that it is not true, that there are not more Jews now than before the Holocaust; others insist it is true.)

I think once we put our minds to it we can find enough things to contradict even the Holocaust—even that distress.

(To M) I think you should say a few words here. I'm talking all around you and you're the one doing the work.

M: I'd like to say that every once in a while I feel at peace despite everything that happened. I can't hate and I don't hate and I don't like the sound of the word hate. In my home, hate is never heard or preached. I cannot forget, I'm not sure I can forgive, but I cannot hate.

H: That's a big step.

I would like to say something before we move to another topic. As a Gentile and the head of the International Co-Counseling Community, I tell you that the Co-Counseling Community is officially and to an amazing and growing extent *actually* committed to the ending of the oppression of Jews and the ending of the isolation of Jews. At the Midwest workshop two years ago—you'll read the story in *Wide World Changing III*—the Neo-Nazis planned a march in Skokie, Illinois, and four of the Jews at the workshop announced they were leaving the workshop early because they felt they had a duty to be there and do whatever they could. Six times as many Gentiles rose and said, "In that case, we're going with them." When they got there the Nazis had called off the march. But you'll read in *Wide World Changing III* what happened later when the Nazis did stage a demonstration: some of the things that happened between Gentile and Jewish Co-Counselors going into this big battle—together.

(Applause)

Act Against Oppression of Jews

A Call to All RCers for Re-emphasis of the RC Unity Seder

For the past six year many RC Communities have sponsored Passover Seders (feasts) to inform ourselves on, and as an expression of, an RC commitment to Jewish liberation. Also, many individual RCers have initiated successful Unity Seders (reaching altogether thousands of people) in their own churches and community groups. The Seder is a re-enactment of the deliverance of the Hebrew people from bondage in Egypt, and it has come to represent for peoples everywhere a symbol of liberation from all forms of oppression.

We are calling on all RC Areas and unorganized areas to rededicate themselves to Jewish liberation through the sponsoring of RC Seders this upcoming Passover. We are particularly encouraging every Area to do the following:

1. Hold Passover Seders for RCers and their relatives and friends as a unique way to introduce non-RCers to RC and to the RC program for Jewish liberation.

2. *Actively* encourage and support Jewish and Gentile RCers to initiate Unity Seders (Seders conducted under Jewish guidance but to which Gentiles are actively invited) in their churches, synagogues, universities, unions, workplaces, YWCAs, and women's centers.

3. A resource packet with a sample Hagadda (guidelines and ritual for conducting a Passover feast) and a bibliography of standard Hagaddas for various constituencies will be available.

Appeared in **Present Time** No. 50.

We propose the initiation *by Gentiles* of *organizations of Gentiles* for ending anti-Jewish oppression (and anti-Semitic attitudes) everywhere, *in the interests of all Gentiles*. Such Gentile organizations speaking for Gentiles against the oppression of Jews can be very effective.

Let's welcome *every* Gentile to take on the ending of anti-Semitism as their own struggle. We have the strength to make a substantial contribution on a world-wide basis to the ending of anti-Jewish oppression. Let's make this Passover a time to express the actual power and resources we now have in our hands.

Chazak V'amatz! (Be powerful and brave!)

Cherie Brown
International Jewish Liberation
Reference Person

Harvey Jackins
International Reference Person

The "Belief" System of Re-evaluation Counseling

The "beliefs" of a religion are very similar, in some respects, to the "assumptions" or "axioms" or "postulates" of a system of deductive logic. In such a system, a mathematical structure for example, a certain small number of statements are assumed to be true to begin with, without any attempt to "prove" them, and then other useful statements are logically deduced from them which must be true if the original statements are true.

In practice, the assumptions made depend on "hunches" springing out of observation or example but derive no validity from these sources and clearly remain assumptions only. The only requirements are that they are consistent with one another and, if a model be shown to exist which reflects them, that they are adequate but not superfluous to a full description of the model being derived from them. Elegance and clarity of statement are desirable, of course.

In 1964, when a deductively logical description of Re-evaluation Counseling was attempted, the following twenty-four statements were proposed as "The Postulates of Re-evaluation Counseling." How do they compare and contrast to the "beliefs" of your religion? Can you re-state your religious beliefs in the form of a set of assumptions? Do you see any revision as necessary in the Re-evaluation Counseling postulates?

THE POSTULATES OF RE-EVALUATION COUNSELING

1. Rational human behavior is qualitatively different from the behavior of other forms of life. (It is not *just* more complicated.)

2. The essence of rational human behavior consists of responding to each instant of living with a *new* response,

Appeared in **Transcendence** No. 1.

created afresh at that moment to precisely fit and handle the situation of that moment as that situation is defined by the information received through the senses of the person. (All other living creatures respond with pre-set, inherited response patterns—"instincts.")

3. This ability to create new, exact responses may be defined as *human* intelligence. It operates by comparing *and contrasting* new information with that already on file from past experiences and constructing a response based on similarities to past situations but modified to allow for the differences.

4. Each human with a physically undamaged brain has a large inherent capacity for this rational kind of behavior, very large as compared to the best functioning of presently observable adult humans.

5. The natural emotional tone of a human being is zestful enjoyment of life. The natural relationship between any two human beings is loving affection, communication, and cooperation.

6. The special human capacity for rational response is interrupted or suspended by an experience of physical or emotional distress. Information input through the senses then stores as an unevaluated and rigid accumulation, exhibiting the characteristics of a very complete, literal recording of all aspects of the incident.

7. Immediately after the distress experience is concluded or at the first opportunity thereafter, the distressed human spontaneously seeks to claim the aware attention of another human. If the human is successful in claiming and keeping this aware attention of the other person, a process of what has been called *discharge* ensues.

8. *Discharge* is signalized externally by one or more of a precise set of physical processes. These are: crying or sobbing (with tears), trembling with cold perspiration, laughter, loud noises and vigorous movement with warm perspiration (tantrum), live, interested talking; and in a slightly different way, yawning, often with scratching and stretching. Discharge requires considerable time for completion.

9. During discharge, the residue of the distress experience or experiences are being recalled and reviewed. (Not necessarily with awareness.)

10. Rational evaluation and understanding of the information received during the distress experience occurs automatically following discharge and *only* following discharge. It occurs only to the degree that discharge is completed. On completion, the negative and anti-rational effects of the experience are completely eliminated.

11. As a result of long-term conditioning of the entire population, the spontaneous attempt to claim the aware attention of another person and proceed to discharge and evaluation is almost always rebuffed. (Don't cry. Be a big boy. Get a grip on yourself. Don't be afraid. Watch your temper.) Applied to small children, these rebuffs begin and perpetuate the conditioning of the population which prevents discharge.

12. Undischarged and unevaluated recordings of distress experiences become compulsive patterns of behavior, feeling, and verbalizing when restimulated by later experiences which resemble them strongly enough. Under such conditions of restimulation the rational faculty of the human is again suspended and the new information of the current experience is added to the rigid distress pattern, making it more far-reaching in its effect and more easily restimulated in the future.

13. This effect of an undischarged distress experience recording in "playing" the bearer through a compulsive, repetitive re-enactment of distress experiences is an adequate explanation for all observable irrational behavior in human beings, of whatever kind or degree.

14. Any human being, and human beings in general, can become free of the restrictions, inhibitions, and aberrations of the accumulated distress experience recordings by reinstating a relationship with some other person's or persons' aware attention and allowing the discharge and re-evaluation processes to proceed to completion.

15. Any infant can be allowed to remain free of aberration by protection from distress experiences and by allowing full discharge and re-evaluation on the ones that do occur.

16. Though a greater degree of awareness, rationality, understanding, and skill on the part of the person whose aware attention is used ("The second person," "the counselor") provides for more rapid and more complete discharge and re-evaluation, the process is workable if even a small degree of awareness is available and if even a roughly correct attitude is maintained by the second person.

17. By "taking turns," i.e., by exchanging the two roles periodically ("Co-Counseling"), two people can become increasingly effective with each other and can help free each other from accumulated distress patterns to a profound degree.

18. Distress patterns which have become too reinforced by repeated restimulation can become chronic, i.e., surround and envelop all behavior and activity. To discharge these requires initiative, skill, and resource on the part of the second person and considerable time for

handling, but they are not different in origin or effect from lighter distresses, and can also be completely discharged and evaluated.

19. Distress experiences result from any unfavorable aspect of the environment. In our present state of civilization, the bulk of early distress experiences of any child results exactly from the dramatized distress recordings of adults which the adults received from earlier generations when they were children. We have a sort of transmission of aberration by contagion here — well meaning adults unawarely but systematically infecting each new, healthy-to-begin-with child with their burdened distress patterns.

20. The irrationalities of society (enforcements, punishments, exploitations, oppressions, prejudices, group conflicts, wars) are reflections of the individual human distress patterns which have become fossilized in the society and often enforced by the rigidities of the society itself.

21. No individual human has an actual rational conflict of interest with another human. Given rationality, the actual desires of each can best be served by mutual cooperation.

22. Nothing prevents communication, agreement, and cooperation between any humans except distress patterns. Given knowledge of their nature, these distress patterns can be coped with, handled, and removed.

23. Any individual or group can act rationally first without waiting for rational action on the part of someone else, and can take control of the situation by so doing.

24. It is always safe to be rational. Knowledge of the above information can be applied to all aspects of living and to all relationships with real profit and success.

Letters and Replies

RC and Social Action: Conflicting or Complementary?

Dear Harvey,

I'm a graduate student in the school of social work at San Diego State University. I'm only in my first semester, but I'm already very impressed. The faculty is top-notch, and thought-provoking, challenging discussions are commonplace. A particularly stimulating course is "social work policy." It is exciting mainly because of my professor. He is fifty-nine years old, and until the age of forty, he was in the construction trade in New York (where I am also from). At forty he decided to become involved in social work. Since then he has had a private therapy practice, worked in hospitals, worked in a variety of agencies and on a variety of projects, and is now teacher at SDSU. He has an incredible amount of political savvy and insight. He looks at the population that we, as social workers, will be helping, and he describes their situation in political and economic terms.

We've had several long conversations and there is much that we agree on. We talk about the effects of the capitalist system as practiced in the U.S. We talk about the punitive aspect of welfare, how it makes people feel as if they aren't *entitled* to a decent standard of living. We agree that rich and poor alike are part of the same system that oppresses all of us. His main contention, however, is that in order to really be of any service to anyone we must *provide what they need.* All the therapy in the world, he constantly reminds the class, is useless if a person is hungry. All the support in the world (emotional, empathetic support) is for nothing if a person cannot pay the rent. If you

Appeared in **Present Time** No. 51.

want to reduce chronic absenteeism and alcoholism in a factory, for example, you have to give the workers more than they have in terms of wages, benefits. You can't approach the situation from a psychological viewpoint. Basically he tells us that if, as social workers, we can't help clients see specific ways in which they can improve their own situation and meet their own physical needs more easily, then we are ineffective.

My professor thinks that people are basically competitive, that they only abandon competitiveness when they don't *need* to be competitive. For example, I may not fight with another student for a parking place or a place in a food line in the cafeteria, but will I fight for the only social work job in a tight marketplace? If there are six of us and one piece of meat, what will become of each of our humanistic intentions?

Now, why am I saying all this? Probably because my talks with my teacher are pretty restimulating and they bring up questions that are always lurking in the back of my mind. Granted, RC is not meant to be an instrument of political and economic change, but sometimes I feel lost in seeing where RC *does* belong. (My faith in it is a result of differences that I have seen in my own life, after a year and a half of classes and workshops.) Sometimes it seems like RC is, for the most part, a white, middle-class phenomenon, engaged in by people who have the "slack," in terms of their material comfort, social status and privilege, to do so. Will RC ever be relevant to a person who is unemployed and worried about security? When we spend our time discharging those early hurts are we merely indulging in a luxury that is totally inaccessible to most of the world? I realize that a mistake I sometimes make (and I'm in the midst of it in this letter) is acting as if RC is supposed to save the world, when really it is a tool for personal re-emergence from distress patterns that will help us think and act better. This much I know and remind myself of. We all have work and commitments that are outside the realm of RC. And yet, Harvey, there is a nagging suspicion, possibly rooted in hopelessness, that I can't validate a connection between 1) working for my re-emergence and the re-emergence of others around me, and 2) effective social change.

I'm drawn back to the pivotal point that my professor and I disagree on: are humans inherently cooperative and loving or are they competitive and driven by survival impulses? If distress was completely eliminated, would you and I see that our interests are not in conflict with one another, or would there always be some level at which you or I would feel threatened, forcing us to deny the other? As a social worker, I can be "liberal" about the thought of 10,000 Haitian refugees coming to San Diego, for example, but if there were 10,000 European social workers migrating here, what would my reaction be?

Have I expressed myself clearly at all? I don't have any specific questions for you, but I would appreciate some feedback if you have the time. I think I'm writing because I respect your thinking, and because from what I know of you I know that you understand the realities of labor and economics. I imagine that somehow you have to some extent bridged the gap between a political understanding of the world and an optimistic view of what human beings are really like. (I don't want to ask for more of a response than you are prepared to give me, but a little more than "I appreciate your thinking, good luck" would be really nice!)

By the way, things are going well down here. My work and school schedule has prevented me from joining any classes, but I hear glowing reports from friends who are teaching RC classes. Also, the men's support group is going very well. Jim Lin is leading it and giving all of us the pushes that we need. We're doing a good job with him, too. I've just started a non-RC group for "expectant fathers" and it's off to a great start.

Thanks for reading this and I hope to hear from you. Take care of yourself.

Love,
Richard Lappin
San Diego, California, USA

Dear Richard,

Thank you for your letter and the questions which your professor raises with you and you raise with me. He sounds like a good man. I would like to meet him.

When your professor says that the real world has to change and that struggles to have a decent existence and be free from exploitation and oppression must be won and that all the "therapy" in the world can not make oppression palatable, he is correct. People who pit improving oneself against *social change are speaking within the patterns of oppression. ("Our goal in your analysis is to help you adjust to the world you live in.") In effect they are blaming the oppressed for the oppression. That is a familiar feature of all oppressions. "If you were only different or 'better' you wouldn't be oppressed." "If you weren't black you wouldn't suffer from racism." "You should have been born a male if you don't like sexist oppression." In the words of the Jewish folk song* Dona, Dona, *"You should have decided to be a swallow instead of a calf. It's your own fault that you are lying in a farmer's wagon, bound for slaughter."*

You say at one point in your letter, "Are humans inherently cooperative and loving or are they competitive and driven by survival impulses?" The answer, of course, is both. They are inherently *cooperative and loving, but as conditioned by the distress and the oppression they often are functionally competitive and driven as they have had to be.*

People will always strive for survival, but I'm quite sure that as they become free from distress, their survival tactics will become increasingly benign and cooperative rather than competitive and destructive to those around them.

I agree with your professor that, if *one had to choose between individual re-emergence and social struggle, then one should choose social struggle, but I think the real answer is that* one must choose both. *The most altruistic, self-sacrificing, heroic, and devoted social struggle is frequently defeated not by the powers of the oppressors but by the patterned timidities, rigidities, and uncooperative distresses of the people who are struggling. I see RC as a powerful, universal tool for survival and excellent living in the* broadest *sense. This includes making the environment supportive. This inevitably requires eliminating oppression and oppressive relationships from society. RC is not only completely* compatible *with effective social change, it is probably* necessary *(in view of the record so far of the best social change movements without it) for liberating social change to succeed decisively, universally, and permanently.*

It is true that as long as the tools of RC reach mainly white middle-class people in countries like the United States, the movement of RC will always be pulled in the direction of a distorted kind of self-centered individual self-improvement. Until RC is based solidly in the working class and the other oppressed sections of the people, it will be frustrated in its potential for preparing people to act with intelligence and power in social struggle. It is also true that such struggle, in its active form at present limited to a small minority of the population, will certainly engage almost all the population as the collapse of the society continues.

I don't think your professor would insist that people are "basically" competitive if he had access to RC theory. In terms of their conditioned superficial behavior at present, he is, of course, right. They have been forced to act out the roles assigned by the oppressive society which seems to offer only a choice of being a loser, submitting and going down, or competing to the best of one's ability in order to survive.

It is easy to become confused by the immensity of the superstructure of social patterns, patterned cultures, and individual distresses which have tangled us all up within it and which dominates the surface functioning of the world. This is not an indication of the basic nature of the human being, however. On that question I think RC is not only accurate but profoundly inspiring. Your use of RC will, I expect, lead you not only to being "liberal and tolerant" toward the plight of refugees, but rather, toward becoming an effective, aggressive "tiger" in fighting for equality and opportunity for all *human beings regardless of what existing structures or shibboleths have to be demolished in the process.*

Have you read the **Wide World Changing** *journals of RC? They haven't had a wide circulation yet, but I think that they would be very much to the point for you and your professor.*

Thanks for writing. This is not a complete answer to the questions you raise. They are complex and increasingly so as this society totters towards its collapse. Our interaction is, though, at least the kind of dialogue I think all of us need to participate in these days. I hope that our discussion will encourage others to speak up and write in about these questions.

Harvey

Intuition, Logic and Women

Dear Harvey,

These are questions I've always wanted to ask you. They have to do with thinking. I will ask them in a personal way because I can't abstract them yet, although I know the issues have wider implications.

I remember being in college and being expected to critique Kierkegaard or Niebuhr and finding myself at a loss about how to do it, despite years of being a brilliant student and writing "good" papers. It wasn't until I had my first course in ethics that I felt tremendously excited—at last a method for how to analyze problems. I remember the teacher doing a presentation and some male student challenging him and I could hardly follow what they were doing. BUT, I knew I wanted to think like that. I also knew, to some degree, their skills were learned, probably in courses in logic or in philosophy. I remember telling people of my excitement about that course but also that "my mind just doesn't work that way."

Simultaneously, while I wanted to acquire this mode of logical debate these men engaged in, I also knew that a lot of it was done just to be argumentative, to compete, to challenge just for the sake of seeing if you could catch the other person. That is, the goal wasn't for true understanding or penetration to some truth or agreement, but to attack on any front you can and if you say it well, pompously, and articulately, people will think you are doing something important.

Appeared in **Present Time** No. 50.

I cannot tell you the number of times I have ventured forth on that very unfamiliar terrain of logical attack and counterattack, trying to really communicate, only to have some male come along and point out a misuse of grammar or of a word and ignore the thrust of what I was saying. Sexism. Okay.

In **The Benign Reality** you speak very highly of rational thinking as logic. As a woman I can state that my mind does not work that way. I almost never sit down and think through a problem analytically, directly, logically, systematically. Do you want to know how my mind works? (Even if you don't, I want you to know.) I think about issues (abortion, war, how to counsel someone, what to teach in class) only very indirectly, on-the-side, and between the lines. I do most of my thinking while reading about something else. For example, when I read a book by Kierkegaard, I do my best thinking about another issue. I've learned to keep two pages of notes: one on Kierkegaard and one on all the other thoughts that I have. It takes me a long time to think through issues. The end result is a very logical analysis—certainly my M.A. thesis and other things I've written are cogent.

I remember once—exactly once—forcing myself to think through something logically—sitting myself down and *forcing* my brain to do it. I succeeded and got an A+ —but it was unnatural.

Questions? Is this some distress that I have? Is it a myth that logic is *really* the way people think? The effects of sexism on women make this tremendously difficult to evaluate. As Mary Daly points out over and over again, *of course* it is difficult for women to think in a language that excludes us and in categories that exclude female experience, and from a perspective very different than mine.

I am *not* saying that women think differently from men inherently. But, the women who make it are the ones who learn to think like men.

Harvey, would you help me with this? If it *is* distress that keeps my thinking in the back of my mind and indirect, I have never touched it in seven years of counseling. There's a lot of grief and rage surfacing as I write all this. About the most vulnerable thing I can do is tell a male that my mind works differently than his. I can trust you to be thoughtful and really *think* about this.

To end with an example. When you first introduced the Golden Ring I was terrified. It assumed that people think in the same ways (e.g., like you). I almost never sit down and logically say, "Here is the material, here is the contradiction, here is the direction." I counsel well and have given great directions, but I certainly arrive at them by some other means.

Now either I'm hot on the trail of something important *or* it's amazing that I've done what I have done given this handicap.

If you think you can help with this, please do.

There is no love like respect of one mind for another.

Judy Kay
Berkeley, California, USA

Dear Judy,

Farther down in the pile I find your letter of January 6th. I am delighted.

I think you have a genius for asking the right questions, or important questions, and I think you are on an important one here. Many other people struggle to ask the question, but you have put it the best that I know and in a way that I think I can hear. I will try to answer it, and both of us should keep in mind that I am of necessity answering it from my framework, from "the way my *mind thinks." However, I am quite sure that our minds work exactly the same basically, and that the differences are differences in how our functioning has been occluded by the oppressions and distresses that we have endured.*

I think when people speak of "women's intuition," that the phrase has great meaning in the sense that we use "intuition" in Re-evaluation Counseling discussions to mean the very swift, untrammeled, unchecked-out operation of human intelligence. I don't think it is a different process that takes place; it's just that the intuition or the intuitive leap is where we allow the mind to operate flexibly and freely without being suspicious of each step and checking on it so carefully. In the article, "Thinking About Thinking," I tried to hold this out as a necessary way of thinking but to be substantiated by the careful checking out to be done later. I think this is basically a good way, even though women have been so invalidated that they are afraid to try it, because the sexism sneers at them or laughs at them, or finds tiny faults in order to shut them up all the way through the process. In the actual operation of society, women's "unchecked" (in the usual sense of no laborious step-by-step demonstration) thinking is often much more accurate than the laborious but distorted-by-patterned-intrusions operation of men's "logic."

I think when you say that you use Kierkegaard to help you think about other things, you are putting your mind on a very important process. I have to work with my hands to think freely and well about a difficult process. To go on vacation, see a movie, read a good book of fiction, or do anything else is almost universally reported to be the way to solve a knotty problem. I think that anything that distracts us from our anxieties which operate in the name of "carefulness" allows our mind to function well enough and gives us enough confidence that we can fill in the missing parts even when we are once again being critical and self-conscious.

There's an old joke about a small boy replying "I don't know" to a bewildered traveler's repeated requests for directions in a country district. Finally, the exasperated traveler yelled, "You don't know much, do you?" To this the small boy replied, "No, but I ain't lost, either." It's like this with "women's intuition" vs. "men's logic." Many men give very "logical" demonstrations of "why war is necessary," and most women are quite clear that it isn't and that it must be stopped. This has something to do with why women are taking much more leadership in the present important drive to eliminate nuclear weapons.

This is all I'll say for now. I'll keep a copy of my letter and a copy of yours and try to work it out a little more clearly, and perhaps we have the foundation for another one of our famous collaboration articles.

Please call me if you would like to talk about it.

With much love,
Harvey

More

As this discussion progresses, I note a tendency to assume intuition and logic are different and opposite.

I would like to save the holistic nature of intelligence and logic, by talking of intuition as "fast logic" and deductive reasoning as "carefully checked-out logic" and treasure and respect both as complementary processes. They might be thought of as analagous to "writing a first draft" and "proofreading the final copy."

Appeared in **Present Time** No. 51.

Pacifism and Non-Violence

Dear Harvey,

Before going into my reason for writing, thank you for all that you have done for me and the wide world. I took a fundamentals course up in Cambridge last Spring and have joined a continuing course since moving here to Albany. I had gradually taken charge of my life in a variety of ways, but have been astonished at the "rightness" of RC theory on so many points and pleased at the value of my regular counseling session. Frankly, I get more out of the theory as a guide to living than I do out of counseling (at least that's my perception), but I continue to push at counseling.

I believe that RC was there for the finding (for example, much of what I wrote as a college professor built on the insights of Douglas McGregor, whose humanism you may have encountered). Nonetheless, you grasped it and have provided leadership which created the Community which in turn benefited me. Thanks.

On to the point. I am a pacifist. I got to pacifism in a roundabout way. I served thirteen months with the Marine Corps in combat in Vietnam. This culminated twenty-some-odd years of violent pastimes including eight years of football. I now work full-time for the Nuclear Weapons Freeze Campaign, so I have reached clarity on the wrongness of force and violence in human life.

At several points in the literature, I felt sure I had detected a

Appeared in **Present Time** No. 51.

similar rejection of all violence, at least between human beings. However, I made that assertion to my teacher and she reported hearing you speak in ways that stopped short of rejecting violence as a flexible, human response to any situation. Now, I accept my limitations and cannot predict how I would respond were, say, my child threatened. I do feel clear about the principle.

Where do you stand on pacifism and the use of violence? Feel free to refer me to the literature or to respond privately since I don't have a great need to generate some great debate in RC on the issue until I've counseled more on it myself.

Respectfully,
Jim Driscoll
Albany, New York, USA

Dear Jim,

Thank you for your letter of March 8, for your appreciation of RC, for your kind words for me, and for the careful way in which you raise the questions of attitudes toward violence and pacifism.

First, about some of your other comments:

I think many of us, at times, find the theory as a guide to living more dependably rewarding then our Co-Counseling sessions, but I think this is because of the way the level of counseling practice available still lags behind the level of the theoretical understandings we have reached. To close this gap is certainly one of our current preoccupations.

I appreciate your being "astonished" at discovering how many points of the theory fit your own conceptions of "rightness." This is, I think, in part due to one of our basic commitments, which is to regard all our theoretical conclusions as "permanently tentative," to be always open to improvement and correction, and periodically reviewed with that in mind.

I do not know of your mentor, Douglas McGregor. We made a deliberate decision at the beginnings of RC not to adopt any ideas or conclusions except from our own work and experience, from logic, and from rigorous work on the physical and biological levels of science. My own thinking may have been biased by my Biblical beginnings, but I have tried very hard to guard against this and am fairly sure that the compatibility of my conclusions with much of humanism is simply the result of the underlying consistency of reality.

It seems clear from your letter that you have made a commitment not to use violence under any circumstances at all. Though you indicate that you cannot yet flatly guarantee that you can keep that commitment under all provocations, you indicate that you think it would be correct to do so and ask where I stand on the question of pacifism and the use of violence.

First, I am quite sure that violence is not *an inherent characteristic of human natures, but, rather, has had to be conditioned into any individual in which it appears, by that individual having first undergone distressed participation in, or witnessing of, acts of violence. This, of course, takes place systematically in the U.S. culture and in many others. Dorothy Stoneman, in* **Present Time** *No. 50, says that the typical U.S. child of fourteen years has already seen 12,000 murders on television.*

Second, I am also sure that almost all *resorts to violence that do take place, that are rationalized as "justified decisions," are nothing of the sort, but are simply the compulsive "acting out" of old distress recordings, and all the tools of Co-Counseling, including commitments against yielding to the compulsions, can well be turned against this perpetuation of violence.*

Third, I would agree that non-violence should always be considered as a possible tactic in any social struggle of any kind, even where "traditions" are of the inescapability of violence. In many conflicts between nations, classes, and other groups the scenarios of violent struggle are pre-set to guarantee the victory of reaction, and for the people's side to be provoked into the use of violence is to play the enemy's game. The use of provocateurs and appeals to patriotism and prejudice are standard tools for oppressors to move the struggle into the arenas of violence on terms favorable to themselves. The successes of Gandhi and Martin Luther

King, in my opinion, were from correct use of non-violence in particular tactical situations.

Fourth, in a world of rational, unpatterned people, in a society which does the bidding of the intelligences that comprise it instead of one which rigidly dictates to and enforces its members, I am sure that violence will disappear. When one intelligence is dealing with another intelligence, there can be absolutely no use for or recourse to, violence. I think that this changeover will come, not automatically with the transfer to a classless, non-oppressive society, but with countless persistent sessions to discharge the innumerable patterns of violence which presently encrust the population, and which, until discharged, represent the principle reserve for reaction and counter-revolution.

We are not yet, however, in this state of freedom from violence patterns in the people around us, and this is why I think a rigid *commitment to pacifism is incorrect and will be unsuccessful. I think such a rigid commitment will itself be based on fear, even if it is a fear of the consequences of being violent, and so will substitute for the flexible thinking that I tend to think is the only acceptable mode for a human to operate in. To be committed to avoid violence whenever possible, to regard all life as sacred, and more sacred the closer it comes to intelligent life, is, in my opinion, correct. I don't think one can stop thinking at that point, however.*

For your child to die from someone else's violence because you felt bound by a rigid commitment to avoid using violence at the aggressor and so stayed passive too long, would be incorrect, it seems to me.

To have a goal of eventually eliminating all violence from human affairs, to be on watch at all times for better tactics of struggle than the use of violence, but to reserve freedom to act flexibly in any particular situation, including meeting violence with faster and more skillful violence, seems to me to be a more workable, and, at base, a more moral position than rigid, inflexible pacifism.

This question comes close to the question of "people's wars." Can there, any more, be a "people's war," in which all humans can support one side of the conflict? I would say probably not between "great" powers, but what of the liberation struggles of the Salvadorean peasants?

Mao, in his lectures on military strategy, used to say, "We must learn to wage war well in order to end all war." Superficially this can sound like the jingoistic recruiting slogan of the U.S. government in World War I—"The War to End War," but given the context of a liberation war and the general policies which Mao persisted with, I tend to view his position with respect.

There is a remote philosophical connection also, I think, to the morality of vegetarianism. Is it practical and moral to decline to eat the dead animal, but nourish oneself on the egg that would have otherwise become a chicken, or if one eschews the egg, to consume thousands of little alfalfa plants or thousands of wheat plant embryos, which are as surely related to us as the chicken, even if the relationship is more distant?

I hope we can continue to discuss these issues, and that others will join us in the discussion.

With respect,
Harvey

Racism Masquerading as RC

Dear R—,

I would like to call your attention to a major problem with RC, namely the potential of clients in RC to have a false sense of having taken care of their problems. For example, I will relate an experience I have had. I am a black male who recently met a white male Texan at work. Shortly after leaving the South five years ago, he began a three-year weekly experience with RC. Over the past year we made an unsuccessful try at friendship only to find ourselves yelling at each other every time we talk recently. He states that in RC he dealt with his racism, yet it is only now that he has bothered to make friends with a non-white person, although most of the effort has been on my part. My contention is that the problems between us are racial, due to his lack of experience with and tolerance for other cultures. He states that, having eliminated his racism in RC, all problems between us must be due to my need for counseling. He further states that if all black people were counseled they would be accepted by whites and experience little bigotry from even the most racist whites (i.e., racial unrest in this country is largely due to the emotional problems of blacks which turn whites off!). He makes other statements which I have recently shared with other black people, who recoiled in shock that someone so well-educated could be so backward in these times. I cannot even get him to agree to re-evaluate his racial feelings. He recently has admitted that he has a lot of work to do in this area but that this would only be worthwhile if he were in a romantic relationship with a black. (And obviously since he has not dealt with his racism he would never be inter-

Appeared in **Present Time** No. 50.

ested in forming such a relationship, and therefore will never have to deal with his racism. A vicious cycle.) He feels that there are more important issues such as nuclear war, or the problems of Native Americans or Lebanese or Poland or Jews or Gays (he was on KPFA recently where he expressed concern for all these oppressed groups, with the blatant omission of blacks).

Given this background, my questions are:

(1) Do you agree that the sorry state of race relations in this country is due to blacks, and that it is up to them to get themselves together so whites can like them more? Is this a general belief of Co-Counselors?

(2) After people do either RC or Eliminating Racism Workshops, are they encouraged by you to seek out friendships with other races? People often fantasize that they have gotten rid of their racism; by avoiding friendships with other races they conveniently perpetuate the fantasy.

(3) If you meet someone who has gone through RC and notice the person making racist or anti-Semitic remarks, how do you convince them that working on this distress should be a major priority, not just something when they have absolutely nothing else to do?

(4) Is there a mechanism for self-evaluation in RC? How could someone with so much racism go for three years in RC thinking he was one of the country's more progressive people? There should have been some mechanism to get him to direct more attention to racism, even though he felt the problem was taken care of.

(5) The more I try to reach this person, the more hostile he becomes. Can black people do anything to reach this type of person without their feeling threatened and running away (the present case), or do they have to hear it from a white? He states

that he has nothing more to learn from Eliminating Racism Workshops.

(6) This person states he has cried over the way blacks were treated in the South. These crocodile tears were obviously shed simply because he enjoys discharging. He most certainly never shed a tear over his present attitude toward me or blacks in general. Do people in RC get so caught up in the process of discharging (crying) that this becomes simply entertainment, an *end* in itself, and not a *means* of reaching the goal of correcting social attitudes?

Your thoughts on these questions would be appreciated. It might be useful to share them with readers of **Present Time**.

Sincerely,
T—

Dear T—,

R— has sent me a copy of your letter to her and a copy of her reply, with the word from you that we could publish your letter in **Present Time** *if we wish.*

I appreciate very much your boldly stating what's actually going on with this person who's had all this exposure to RC and yet obviously operates on chronic patterns of bigotry and racism. All his attitudes are as nonsensical to me as they are to you, and we're obviously dealing here, not with a considered, principled position, but with a pattern which has never been effectively challenged in his counseling and which is so chronic that he defends it and tries to represent it as theory or policy rather than work against it. Unfortunately, he's not an isolated example in RC and not only on the issue of racism.

Building a Community of effective Co-Counselors sometimes gets to seem very complicated since chronic patterns in their very nature try con-

tinually to camouflage themselves and take over rather than be discharged. The responsibility of the counselor to the client must actually extend to the firm interruption of these chronic patterns, rather than settling for permissive counseling, or progress is quite limited.

On your questions:

Of course the "sorry state of race relations" and the racism in this country came not from the blacks, but from the whites' patterns and their oppressive society. To the extent that any Co-Counselor still believes otherwise, it is simply a conditioning which they've had from the oppressive culture which is persisting in spite of their exposure to RC.

On your second question: Yes, people in RC are continually encouraged to seek friendships outside of their group and with people that they fear because their own group acts as an oppressor group in relation to them. In general, this encouragement has had good but not profound results in spite of some good modeling, simply because people are *terrified and they don't know where to get good enough counseling to get rid of this terror. Instead, they often pay lip service to eliminating racism, but go on acting on their fears, which in practice, of course, function as racism.*

Your third question was: "How do you convince a white person that he or she should get busy working on these fears?" I become very firm if the person doesn't respond to my gentle suggestions. The most effective way, of course, is to counsel them using the three-step technique, but sometimes you have to "get their attention first," as in the famous story about the reluctant mule.

On question 4: "Is there a mechanism for self-evaluation in RC?" Yes, there is, but using it is pretty well left up to individuals, and the only people who have some "official" obligation to do it are people who are holding leadership roles. Even these tend to forget to use it, and since enforcement is not a characteristic of RC relationships, it's only the use of aware pushing, skillful counseling, and persistence that seems to increase its use.

Your question 5 asks, "Can black people do anything to reach the committed and self-deceiving racist white person?" I would say not without interrupting the pattern, and this probably involves some risks. I like to use ridicule of the pattern in places like this, and at the same time be kindly to the person.

Your last question was, "Do people in RC get so caught up with the process of discharging that this becomes an end in itself and not a means of reaching the goal of correct social attitudes?" Yes, sometimes. Not always, not often, but sometimes.

This whole gamut of problems that you've raised so clearly is part of the body of unsolved questions with which our Communities are continually grappling and on which we're slowly achieving some progress. I appreciate very much your setting these out in such bold relief. The primary responsibility for change lies with us whites, but it's going to help to have a black Co-Counselor speak up so clearly. Thanks again for writing.

Harvey

"Spiritual" Needs

A Letter and A Reply

September 6, 1981

Dear Harvey,

I recently received, from a friend, a copy of the questionnaire about RC and religion. What I have to say about the topic doesn't quite fit into the questions, but perhaps I will end up answering some along the way.

I left the RC Community in Boston about four years ago, after having counseled regularly for three years. I left for reasons very related to this topic of "RC and religion." At the time (and I can only speak about then—I have had virtually no contact with the RC Community since then) it seemed to me that more and more people in the RC Community had begun to regard RC itself as a religion. That is to say, RC took on for them the aspect of a system which said the final word about reality, it held the ultimate truth. I found a great deal of value in some of the techniques I learned in RC (about which I will say more later), but it never seemed to me to contain the ultimate truth about life. What finally precipitated my decision to leave RC was when I tried to discuss some of the assumptions underlying the theory, but couldn't so do because the response I got was, "Would you like to counsel about that?" There was not an openness to discussion. I found that to be disturbing.

But that aside, let me share with you something of my spiritual journey. I hope it can shed some helpful light on your thinking in this area.

Appeared in **Transcendence** No. 1.

I purposely say "spiritual" rather than "religious," because I perceive an important distinction. Religion I take to refer to the tradition through which spirituality is handed down. Spirituality, for me, is the nurturing of the life of the spirit—the spark of life, the core, of each one of us. I believe the spirit to be personal, (in the sense of *person* rather than individual), eternal, given as gift (not created by ourselves), and universal (connected with all other spirits, or souls). My spiritual journey is a search for a connection, a union, an at-one-ness (or atonement) with that spirit or Self.

I was raised in Protestant churches which all had a decidedly intellectual bent (they *talked about* things in a rather moral way, rather than feeling them). When I became "intellectually mature," in college, I naturally became an atheist, which was the only "respectable" position to take given the intellectual approach. I also went to a Quaker college, which was a fine atmosphere, but which I regarded from almost an exclusively moral (rather than spiritual) point of view. I maintained an intellectual/moral stance with regard to the universe and its meaning, and with regard to myself, until a crisis in my life (a divorce) in which I was forced to seek a different kind of meaning. That was the beginning of a more spiritual search for me.

The meditation which I had learned in Quakerism took on a new meaning for me, and I also began to read and study about Buddhism and other Eastern religions. During this time I became conscious in an explicit way of realms of experience beyond the ordinary—realms of wonder and mystery.

Also, during this time, I began to co-counsel and was part of an RC class. That experience was very valuable because it allowed me to explore my inner spaces without fear. It was a great relief to feel no stigma about crying and therefore to be able to look at parts of myself which I had previously left alone because I was hesitant to arouse feelings—(that was also true, of course, about laughing, shaking, etc.). This openness to my feelings was a great gift that I received from counseling and for which I am very grateful.

I did not experience, however, the phenomenon of finally getting rid of a pattern. I found that there were some things (including the suffering of others) on which I could discharge deeply and interminably without it seeming to make the slightest bit of difference. (I am a very sensitive person—it was never even slightly difficult for me to discharge given a safe place.) I often felt physical relief after crying or laughing or shaking, often great release of tension. Sometimes I had new insight. Sometimes I was able to relate more openly because I was more aware of my feelings. But I sensed something missing.

As I would describe it now, I would say that what was missing was a transcendent element, the element of the spirit. God, if you will. The source and goal of my being.

This spirit took on a living reality for me when I met some people who lived within it. They happened to be Catholic monks. (I suppose they might just as well have happened to be Buddhist nuns or Hindu yogis.) Since I have been in touch with and conscious of this transcendent reality (which I now conceive of as the Christ spirit), my life has opened up in ways I would never have thought possible. Old patterns have fallen away as I have spent time sitting quietly in the presence of a loving God, seemingly without any effort. And really fallen away, in ways that have changed my life and relationships radically.

I want to share with you one such experience because of its relevance to RC.

I was sitting in quiet meditation a while ago when I suddenly remembered (for no apparent reason) a moment that happened to me some years ago, something I spent some time counseling about. It was the moment when I opened a letter from a friend telling me of a new direction in his life. I began to cry at the memory. Then I was immediately aware of how different I am now than I was then. So I asked Christ (the universal spirit of growth and love) to be with me back in that moment. And I knew immediately that I had made a *choice* in that moment, that I had chosen to react in a particular way, out of personal hurt. Crying all the while, using the skills I learned in RC of staying with the feelings, I relived the moment and changed my choice. Instead of choosing to be hurt, I chose to react in faith, to see that the situation had a sense to it even if I couldn't see it then. The moment was healed, redeemed. And it seemed to me that what allowed that deep healing to happen was the combination of my willingness to feel the pain (which is what I learned in RC) and my openness to the presence of transcendent spirit (Christ, I call it).

Since that happened, and since my spiritual life has become deeper and richer, I have thought occasionally about RC and have some things I would like to share with you. I hope you find them helpful. They come out of my experience and are therefore limited, but are the best I have to offer now.

From where I am now I see RC as very limited because of the fact that its theory has no metaphysical transcendent basis. For spirits like mine, who yearn deeply to relate to the stars, the mysteries of life and death, the way the light falls through the trees in a pine forest, the RC theory doesn't satisfy.

I feel, too, that there is a kind of a pride in the total newness of RC that is both limiting and dangerous. Dangerous because of the dogmatic aspect I have seen it take. And limiting because of what it leaves out of history. What incredible richness and truth in our human history! I am awed and grateful in the face of even the tiny fraction of it of which I am aware. And from what I know of RC it seems so cut off from history, like it has created the world anew. Without roots.

Perhaps, in this respect, a cross-fertilization of RC and religion could be very valuable. I think I mean that some RC techniques could be helpful on people's spiritual journeys, as they have been on mine. And perhaps the RC Community could explore the ancient religious myths (*myth* in the sense of deep truth expressible only in poetic terms). They offer such richness in exactly the areas which RC touches: sadness, fear, joy. And they have lived for thousands of years and continue to touch human hearts deeply. (My contact with the Christian myth as handed down by the Catholic Church has touched me deeply and has transformed my spirit in ways I cannot imagine having happened had I stayed in the RC Community as my primary source of strength and change.)

I hope these thoughts are valuable. I have given attention to them fairly frequently over the past few years and am glad of a forum (in the form of that questionnaire) in which to express them. It has been helpful to me to write them down.

Barbara Miles
Middletown Springs, Vermont, USA

September 28, 1981

Dear Barbara,

Thank you very much for your letter. I am perhaps slow in replying because I have been out of town doing workshops.

What you say has great meaning for me, and I certainly hope to use at least part of your letter in the RC journal on religion when we get it started. What I am sorry about is that you had such a limited view of RC, and I certainly agree with your feeling unsatisfied with it, and even parting company with it, in the view that you had.

What seems to have happened is that people have taken the view of RC that they got from their teachers in their particular Community, which is often shrouded in patterns and limitations and should's and should-not's, as the essence of the theory or practice, and have had difficulty in pushing that stuff aside to the continually open, continually growing content. We have been trying to cope with this a little bit recently in order to solve the problem of "naturalizing" RC for new groups of people by saying, "The way that you were taught RC is not the way RC should be taught," encouraging people to take the essence of it, and communicate it to working-class people, Third Worlders, religious people, and so on.

A great deal has happened in the last four years. I will enclose a catalogue of literature, and you can see some of the many journals that have been started to give a wider expression to people's concerns. I'll also enclose a copy of **Present Time**, *which is quite a different magazine now than I imagine that you last read.*

I would appeciate a continuing dialogue with you.

With love,
Harvey

Do We Need "Forgiveness"?

Dear Harvey,

Thank you very much for all your hard work and thinking. I know you have given a lot to make this workshop possible, and even more to make it work; and it has worked for me. I have come a long way in the past four days toward accomplishing the goal I came here with: to figure out what place God wants RC to have in my life as a Christian.

I appreciated your quick call for hands when I asked if there was anyone else here who believed in God and that Jesus died on the cross. I was taken by surprise by the number of hands and by yours in particular. Sometime I would like to trade interpretations of those beliefs with you.

One other thing I want to thank you for is the way you almost never put anything in front of your desire and your determination to help us get out of our ruts, and the real love that shines through your efforts. I particularly like the fact that you aren't too worried about being perfect; that you don't let hero worship get in people's way. You don't let them set you up as their salvation if there's anything you can do to prevent it.

There is a question I would like to ask you, which, for various reasons (mainly apprehension about your reaction to criticism of some of your basic assumptions at a time when you are trying to help people improve their counseling—in short, mainly fear) I decided not to ask during the open question periods.

Appeared in **Transcendence** No. 1.

Here it is: If reality is truly benign, and our perception of it as threatening, malicious, dangerous, etc. is just a distorted interpretation resulting from our patterns, and if human beings really are immensely intelligent, loving, creative, resourceful, courageous, and inherently committed to truth, beauty, and goodness, and if all distress, or all lasting distress, comes from other people's patterns and not from the universe, as is implied by "benign reality," why did those wonderful human beings ever let themselves be conquered and dominated by distress, and *where did the original distress come from?*

I have heard the explanation that it came from the environment at a time when humans had insufficient control over it, but this doesn't make sense to me in light of the idea of benign reality. I also can't see how there could not have been enough time to discharge distress as it came up, since we seem to be finding time in a very dangerous world to discharge current distress *and* a huge backlog.

I have also heard the idea that we evolved into human beings already run largely by distress patterns, or even that distress patterns are a sort of vestigial set of instinctive behaviors, or a remnant of our earlier way of "learning" and adapting to the environment. Aside from the fact that I haven't yet seen any good conclusive evidence for the theory of evolution (as opposed to natural selection *within* species), the idea of a function or an ability evolving under conditions in which it cannot be effectively used does not make even *evolutionary* sense. The idea that a part of an organism's adaptive repertoire becoming a disadvantage because it has improved that repertoire with a new kind of response doesn't make any sense to me at all.

So in keeping with the tradition of proposing an alternative, I would like to suggest that you re-examine another one of your assumptions: that everyone has always done the best they can at every moment in the past, or to put it another way, that nobody ever does anything wrong on purpose.

I understand what a great contradiction this is to people's tendency to blame one another, but I think there is a better way to do this. If you are willing to entertain the possibility of an external, objective, perfect, and absolute standard of goodness, of truth, of right and wrong in the universe, then you will see that we all stand in the same position with regard to that standard—we fall short. Then there can be no point in any one of us claiming to be better or worse than any other one of us. No need to point the finger if it's already pointing at all of us.

If you further admit the possibility that this standard of perfection belongs to a being to whom love is more valuable than anything else, then you will be able to see that the *forgiveness* given (at great cost) by this being is the perfect basis for our unconditional love for one another and ourselves.

One last related thought, or question, is this: how can one and the same action made by a human being be a matter of choice *before* it is made, and yet not the *result* of a choice *after* it is made? And yet this seems to me to be an inevitable consequence of the distinction you make between guilt and responsibility. I think the far more valuable distinction is between *feeling* guilty (and not *doing* anything about it—wallowing in self-loathing and self-pity) and *being* guilty, *admitting* your guilt, and *repenting* (which doesn't mean feeling sorry so much as deciding not to go on doing wrong on the basis of having admitted that you never *had* to).

In conclusion, if we say that we can be *forced* to accept a distress pattern, we are saying that, in spite of our best efforts, we may go back under everything we have emerged from already. We may have all gains taken away (all it takes is enough brute force, right?). We may be defeated.

I don't think you want to say that. I don't.

Once again, Harvey, thank you for everything you have done and are doing. I am going to be teaching a non-RC class in Co-Counseling for my sisters and brothers in the church soon, so your thinking on what I have been talking about here would be greatly appreciated. You can publish this letter if you'd like to. You could even answer me in **Present Time**; I would be able to handle the blow to my humility, I think.

John Hamilton
Drexel Hill, Pennsylvania, USA

Dear John,

I think the original distress came (and comes) from the vulnerability of this new, delicate, human intelligence to the as yet unmastered and un-understood environment.

It isn't that reality was prepared to "take care" of us in a parental way, but rather that we evolved in harmony with this reality and are capable of learning from it and coping with it elegantly.

I think you miss the vast power of precisely the distinction between past determinism and future free will, a distinction that has never been clearly made before, and which eliminates the need for guilt or its supposed cancelling by forgiveness. One can insist on going back to those concepts, but how much better to be free of them.

Harvey

Original Sin?

I've been wondering whether I was born a "sinner" or whether I was born perfect and then became spoilt by the "sin" in the world.

I have recently read reports that babies in the womb are affected in their development by how their parents feel towards them, and in some extreme cases will "give in" and die in the womb because they pick up feelings of rejection and resentment. Also, I've heard RCers claiming to have discharged on pre-birth distress during sessions. If this is true, then it follows that as none of us had "perfect" parents we all picked up, in varying degrees, distress while in the womb and were born already "infected" with this "original sin" which has been passed down generation to generation all the way from "Adam."

I would like to add that, as a Christian RCer, I believe in the underlying re-claimable *goodness* of us all.

Dave Sudbury
Derby, England

Dear Dave,

Katie has given me your piece on original sin. I am quite sure you were not *born a sinner. You probably had some distress recordings installed by the time you were born, because it is everyone's experience that as they work through distress they find some from prenatal. (That doesn't mean I*

Appeared in **Transcendence** No. 1.

think it's necessary. I think that we could organize pre-birth time for our babies so that it would all be good, but we haven't got things in that good shape yet.)

You have a wrong impression that babies pick up the feelings of rejection from their parents in the womb. What they do is pick up physical distress or, in the later months, some fear. This is from the discomfort caused by the hormone imbalance in their mothers when their mothers are upset and don't discharge, or from illnesses of the mother, or poisonings by mother's bad food or addictions, or injuries from violent intrusions on them, such as prenatal intercourse. I've never seen any indication of material before birth that needed to be discharged by anything but shaking and yawning.

This of course is not *"original sin." The notion of sin as it's used almost universally implies blame or reproach or failure on the part of the individual. Since we don't blame individuals for ever, in the past, doing any less well than they could handle, we certainly wouldn't blame a small child for what had happened to her or him before birth.*

Harvey

Teaching with a Disability

Dear Harvey,

...I'm a woman, twenty-nine years old, and I'm sitting in a wheelchair. I've got a muscular disease. I have been Co-Counseling for one year, and it has been good for me to do it. But during this time something has been bothering me.

The counseling of a client mostly takes place with the two people standing up. The client can lean on his or her counselor when closeness is needed, and when anger and violence come out, the counselor can receive it. I cannot stand on my feet. I must sit down, and it is hard to get really close to my clients. My client depends on me and has to adapt his/her way of wanting to be counseled to my limited capacities. I have the feeling that this is at the cost of the possibility of good discharging for my clients. So I'm withdrawing with the thought that I will never be a good leader.

The structure of Co-Counseling is that one becomes a teacher, but what about me? I just don't know how to deal with how to be a good counselor in a wheelchair.

I hope that you can help me with this question. And if not, maybe you know someone who has more experience on this subject.

Tineke v. Rooÿen
Nÿmegen, The Netherlands

Appeared in **Complete Elegance** No. 8.

Dear Tineke,

Thank you for your letter of April 6th. I'm very pleased to know of your existence and know that you are active in counseling. Your feelings that being in a wheelchair will interfere with your effectiveness as the counselor or client are not justified at all. People counsel in all kinds of ways—lying down, standing on their heads, over the phone, and so on. I think your negative feelings are just the invalidation that you've received in the past, and there are many excellent teachers of RC who are in wheelchairs and otherwise have to deal with many kinds of disabilities. The experience of having to deal with a disability seems on the average to have prepared people to be good leaders and teachers, so that they have already worked through some of the little difficulties and petty invalidations that able-bodied people often have to spend a lot of time on. So I welcome you into preparing for leadership in all ways in RC, and whatever assistance you need is something you should just ask for.

...It was good to hear from you.

With love,
Harvey

More Thoughtfulness Needed

Dear Harvey,

I would like you to make a statement on an issue of concern to physically different RCers. Able-bodied RCers often tell us that our handicap or illness has been caused by emotional distress and that counseling can cure it. This is even told to people who were born with their handicap or illness.

When we are told by able-bodied RCers that our physical difference is "just distress," we begin to believe that we are perhaps somehow at fault for having this difference and that it is our responsibilty to keep counseling until we remove this difference.

Other physically different RCers have told me that they also believe this attitude on the part of able-bodied RCers to be oppressive and hurtful to them. I don't think it is good theory to expect physically different people to be working on "curing" their physical difference through counseling.

Perhaps you could write something about this issue in the next **Present Time**?

—S

Dear S,

I completely agree. There **are** *physical malfunctions that are caused by distress, but they, in general, are not the ones that physically different persons have to contend with. For anyone else to push such an opinion on a physically different RCers is thoughtless, rude and* **very** *unhelpful, not to say uninformed and unintelligent.*

Harvey

Appeared in **Present Time** No. 49.

Workshops and Journals

A Salute to Powerful People

The International Disabled Persons' Workshop

The Disabled Persons' International Workshop on November 12-14 was, in my opinion, an outstanding event. I have never been at a workshop where people related better to each other as human beings to human beings and less as human beings to patterns or patterns to patterns. I would guess that this would be due, in a small amount, to luck, and more to some of the outstanding people there, but I also suspect that severely disabled RCers have had to recover some of the in-charge-ness and responsibility that we temporarily-able-bodied or concealed-disability RCers have not yet faced reclaiming.

There were about forty-five of us at Hemlock Center in Connecticut, USA, with about thirty different principal disabilities. The site was very supportive, the organizing was superb (Laurie Summers and Jean Baierlein), the Co-Counseling was excellent, and there was much initiative and creativity.

Three demonstrations stand out in my mind: solving competition patterns and internalized oppression between two leaders of disabled persons; becoming able to relaxedly face a possible future of rapid physical deterioration and death; and discharging accumulated despair, frustration, and hopelessness accumulated while trying to lead the general Community without support as a disabled person.

I made many new friends and lovers and renewed old friendships and loves. I expect much new thinking and new leaders to emerge from the people there in the months to come. (For an example, see the report of the Disabled Men's Caucus on page 49 of **Present Time** No. 50.)

Appeared in **Present Time** No. 50.

Young Leaders

The Young Leaders' Workshop, held in Devon, England at the end of last year, was a real breakthrough in young people's work. There were two young leaders from Sweden, two from Denmark, three from The Netherlands, two from Germany, one from Ireland, one from Canada, one from Italy, twenty-four from the U.S., and twenty from England.

The young leaders were models for all RCers in the ways in which they related to each other. The site conditions were a little rugged and not always perfectly comfortable, but the young people adjusted with great good humor. Language and cultural differences, age differences, home-sickness, and cold were all faced and solved with caring and affection. It was a period of intense growth for everyone. Many deep, permanent relationships were begun.

The building of young people's support groups and young leaders' groups were recommended as key moves to be taken on return home to each person's base and insistence on help from the leaders of the general Community was encouraged.

When an attempted demonstration of "stepping completely out of paying attention to any distress" was successful but not complete, a seventeen-year-old followed it, the last night of the workshop, by a spontaneous forty-minute expression of "discharge from zest" that carried most of the audience with her.

Gillian Turner and Adrianne Dworsky did self-estimation before the workshop as Young People's International Libera-

Appeared in **Present Time** No. 51.

tion Reference Person and as Editor of **Young and Powerful**, respectively. They were enthusiastically re-confirmed in their jobs after a magnificent and moving estimation of their functioning by a large number of the people there.

An important decision from the Young Leaders' Workshop was to begin organizing young people in groups roughly corresponding to age, and to furnish support and leadership help from each age group to the next younger group.

This will mean getting together the young adults (roughly 18 to 26 years) in RC and establishing occasional meetings of groups of leaders, regular support groups, classes, workshops, gather-ins, etc. This group of young adults will work out their own policies and programs and leadership but *as part of their program* will take responsibility for assisting, advising, and helping lead the group of young people in the 15 to 21 years age program.

This "late teens" group will also plan and lead their own activities but also, as part of their program, give help and leadership support to the 11 to 16 age group of RCers.

These, in turn, will play this role of "experienced friends" and leaders to the 8 to 12 age young people, who will help out with the 5 to 9ers, who will give a hand to the 2 to 6ers.

To accomplish this, and to learn what counseling activities will meet the real needs of each age level, will require much leadership and support from the general Community and its leaders. We have much to learn. I think, however, that we will be on the right track.

Young people have always looked eagerly to the next older individuals they know for information, modeling, and leadership. Young people have always enjoyed this trust and admiration from those younger. Unfortunately, much of the social conditioning has almost restricted the older ones' roles to passing on patterns and misinformation in the past.

The isolation and overwork which characterize the oppression of parents will require thorough-going social change to eliminate completely. If, however, we, as parents, can assist the young people to take charge of each other for much of their re-emergent and learning activities, part of our unreasonable burden will be lifted. The young people who have this experience of thoughtfully and successfully leading those younger will also come to their role as parents with far more confidence and skill than most of us possessed.

I ask parents everywhere in our Communities to give thought and assistance to the young people in carrying out those decisions.

We have a great treasure for our Communities in the Young Leaders who have already come forward to be active. Many thousands more are waiting only to be asked and to be welcomed. I heartily recommend that our Communities place a high priority on stepping out of our distresses from our childhoods and youths, which now function to oppress young people, and give top-notch leadership and support to young leaders' groups in offering RC to thousands of young people in the wide world and in bringing and welcoming thousands of young people into our Communities.

Young people and RC go well together!

A New Journal

At last! Here is **Creativity** No. 1, the first Re-evaluation Counseling journal for artists. It has taken a great deal of thinking, a great deal of writing and questionnaire-answering, much creating, communicating, and editing to prepare it.

I think it is a splendid issue. We will plan the next issue to be even better, but this issue is a truly significant achievement for all artists and for Re-evaluation Counseling. Heartfelt thanks to all the artists who thought, wrote, drew, and photographed to prepare it.

This journal is for *all* artists. It contains thinking and information that is not available anywhere else in the world that is needed by every artist. We count on the artists in Re-evaluation Counseling (and other Co-Counselors) to see that it is offered to and purchased by large numbers of artists in the wide world.

This issue is being subsidized from Community funds, but subsequent isses will have to be financed by the sales of this one.

It has been a satisfying challenge to put this issue together, but we would like a special editor and an editorial board, to do much of the preliminary work on the next issue. Qualifications include being an artist and possessed of writing and editorial skills. The jobs are unpaid.

The thinking in this issue needs to be responded to. We will expect and welcome responses from every artist who reads it.

Appeared in **Creativity** No. 1.

The shortage of visual art contributions, which has been a problem with all the other Re-evaluation Counseling journals, remained a problem (to our surprise) with this one, as well. We are delighted with the way we were able to "piece out" to such a fine, final result, but "our cupboards are bare," our portfolios are empty. We need (please, please) every scrap of visual art you can furnish that can be reproduced in black and white.

A Maturing Publication

In preparing this issue of **Ruah Hadashah**, I want first of all to express my deep appreciation and gratitude to Sheila Katz, the journal's first and, until now, only editor, on the occasion of her retirement from the job. Sheila is appreciated by all RCers for her pioneering work in establishing the RC Community in Israel, for her determinedly correct policies in insisting on an alliance with Palestinians from the very beginning, and for her effective work in training tough Co-Counselors. She has also contributed greatly to the development of the journal itself. Thanks from the Community, and my personal thanks, to Sheila Katz. May she and her husband and new baby thoroughly enjoy family life and the resurgence of her activity as an artist.

As editor-in-chief of the Re-evaluation Counseling publications, I am acting editor for this issue and take responsibility for the overall production. Much work had been done and much material already collected by Sheila. Cherie Brown has written and referred a great deal of material from her correspondence. Patsy Kempthorne has been responsible for detailed editing. Katie Kauffman has loaned her talents and her skill at makeup for the final touches. A great many people, including Cherie, Donny Perlstein, Patsy, and myself have participated in the revision and editing of the draft policy.

The draft policy, now in its fourth revision, continues to be an amazing document. Successive drafts of the policy have spurred fresh thinking in many corners of the world. I think the present draft will continue to do so.

Appeared in **Ruah Hadashah** No. 5.

It is plain by now that we need a separate draft policy for Israeli liberation. Work has begun on such a draft but it is not ready for publication at this time.

Warm congratulations to Jaap Sanders and the other European Jewish RCers for launching **Lechaim**, a European RC Jewish journal. You will notice many reprints from it in this issue.

Work on internalized Jewish oppression continues to be very fruitful. (This is the case with all oppressions that we have challenged in Re-evaluation Counseling.)

The active and informed participation of non-Jewish RCers in combatting Jewish oppression in the wide world as well as in RC is extremely heartening. The lagging in commitment against Jewish oppression which was noticeable a year ago has been reversed. The turn around in this matter was signalized by the letter in **Present Time** No. 41 from Cherie and myself and by Joan Karp's letter. The Communities everywhere are combatting Jewish oppression as an integral part of their programs for re-emergence.

We will need a new editor for **Ruah Hadashah**. I welcome suggestions or nominations for the post from readers.

Welcome to a feast of ideas, achievements, news, and warmth in the pages of your journal, **Ruah Hadashah** No. 5.

Progress and Opportunity

I congratulate Ginny Jacobs and all the elders who have contributed to and worked on this issue of **The Elders Speak**.

Elders' affairs in Re-evaluation Counseling are moving ahead in general, and we can all be very pleased if we look back at what significant gains we have made. Support groups are meeting, elders are speaking out at workshops, individual elders are assuming proud leadership in a number of places.

I don't think we can be completely satisfied, however, with our rate of progress. There are getting to be a lot of us elders as time goes by, and we certainly need the tools of RC spread widely in the population to defend ourselves against the oppressions and hardships which the society and the economic situation impose upon us. At the same time, our experience, our viewpoints, and sometimes our spare time make us able to make more of a contribution to the general work of the Communities than many of us are doing.

I have the impression that many of us elders, even those already in RC, are still waiting to be "included," and that we do this waiting over and over again as if the Community "belonged" to someone else.

I think it's important to realize that RC belongs to us. The Community is ours. If some classes and meetings have backward attitudes toward us that make us uncomfortable, we can speak up. In particular, I think that more of us can take the initiative to organize meetings and support groups and classes

Appeared as the introduction to **The Elders Speak** No. 4.

that other elders will be comfortable in. It's time for those of us with experience in RC to get our act together and act powerfully.

Elders spoke out well and were a much stronger influence at the 1981 World Conference of the Communities than they have done or been previously. It was good to see their initiative and their purposefulness. The proposal for a Council of Elders that was adopted in 1979 was re-adopted this time, and notice was taken of the fact that it has not been tried in most places (probably because of overt or internalized ageist oppression), but that where it has been tried, it has been helpful.

The argument that we should only ask elders who have already been powerfully active in RC to be on such an Advisory Council misses the point, I think. Everyone's opinion is worthy of respect, and to provide such a platform for elders to begin to speak out within RC is a valuable contradiction to the patterned lack of respect for elders in the wide world and also to the passivity of elders caused by internalized oppression.

I think all pulls toward retreat, retirement, passivity, or "being on the periphery" are our enemies. We should continue to advance and expand our influence as long as we are alive, and if we achieve greatly extended lives or even immortality, so much the better. Certainly, physical difficulties sometimes require inventing a new way to function fully, but our physically different RCers have already modeled fully and boldly for us there.

I sometimes receive messages from other elders in RC that I, in particular, should "participate more fully" in the elders' activities in RC. I do enjoy very much the times I can attend elders' meetings. It's nice to be with such sensible people. All the time, however, I am doing what I think is the proper job for an RC elder—participating fully and sharing leadership in *everything* that goes on in RC.

My heartfelt thanks and congratulations to Clemmie Barry as she retires from the demanding activity of being International Liberation Reference Person for Elders. Health difficulties, not age, is what is forcing Clemmie to take a somewhat less active role, although she continues to act powerfully in wide world elders' activities and her advice and influence will continue to be sought. Clemmie's was the insistent voice that forced elders' liberation into open activity in RC, and her contribution will never be forgotten.

Congratulations to Elsie Darling, the new International Liberation Reference Person for Elders. Elsie, as Clemmie's assistant, has been doing most of the work in the days of Clemmie's ill health. She is a delightful person, a whole-hearted and skilled Co-Counselor, a vigorous advocate of elders taking the initiative in their own behalf, and an ally of all people. She will do a good job.

I invite all elders to enter into written dialogues with me about our policies, as well as writing letters to our journals.

Regional Leadership

Our Regional leaders are making great and obvious strides these days. When I meet with a group of them after a few months' separation, it is a pleasure to observe how much they have changed in the interim, how much closer and easier their relations with each other have become, how well they Co-Counsel, how confident they are, and how they are developing support around themselves. They are bringing other people into confident leadership at a much greater rate and in much greater numbers than used to happen.

The people who have succeeded in handling this level of responsibility are being very remarkable models to us all. With these people we're seeing in a clear way the advantages of becoming a leader. To function on the level of a Regional Reference Person is apparently to release a great deal of previously inhibited initiative and confidence and to stimulate thinking in dozens of channels that would not otherwise be explored.

Regional Reference Persons currently seem to enjoy a growing sense of power, a pleasant (rather than a desperate) sense of responsibility, fine relations with each other and with me, and a feeling of being in charge of the world. They all have plans available to carry out and achieve the goals which they and all of us in the Community have set together.

Apparently at this level as well as at previous levels, assuming leadership can accelerate re-emergence.

Our Communities are flourishing almost everywhere and in

Appeared in **Reference Point** No. 21.

almost all respects. The central importance of our concepts to human survival, the workability of our skills, and the consistent rewards of organized Co-Counseling (which includes having organized Communities) are ever more deeply and widely appreciated. Every new activity which we participate in on a local or international scale brings enthusiastic responses from new populations. There are many indications that a very large proportion of the people who have been through our classes are still using the knowledge they gained and continue to use and spread RC ideas in their relations with people around them.

The theory continues to progress. New Communities continue to develop. Language barriers continue to (slowly) crumble with more and more translations of at least our basic works.

In this issue I discuss a phenomenon that all leaders will have to deal with at some time or other. Many already struggle with this, but not all our leaders have recognized it for what it is. This is the phenomenon of attacks on RC *and on leaders.* As the struggle to keep the world from atomic destruction intensifies and as this society reels closer to total collapse, dealing with this phenomenon will have to become a skill that we master and use in our everyday lives.

What Has Re-evaluation Counseling To Do With Religion?

This first issue of **Transcendence** begins a new stage of interaction between Re-evaluation Counseling the *process*, Re-evaluation Counseling the *movement*, and the ideas and practices and organizations of religion in the world. We are finding many new viewpoints for examining ancient topics and dilemmas.

Re-evaluation Counseling has, in the past, proclaimed itself as "determinedly non-religious." It has insisted on a completely scientific and logical approach to human behavior and thought. Yet profoundly religious people have embraced it enthusiastically.

ECUMENISM IN RC

Many "founding" RC classes were held in Quaker Meeting Houses as Re-evaluation Counseling spread across the United States. Roman Catholic priests and nuns furnished hard work and leadership in establishing RC in many localities, particularly in the United States and Ireland. Church of England, Church of Ireland, Methodist, Presbyterian, Muslim, Hindu, Buddhist, Baha'i, Native Spiritualist, and many other kinds of religious people have eagerly grasped RC, often with the comment that RC is the tool they have been seeking to make their religion "workable." All seem to have found co-existence within the RC Community with their diverse fellow religionists both comfortable and rewarding.

At the same time, materialist philosophers, Marxists, agnostics, atheists, and logicians have been comfortable in the Com-

Appeared in **Transcendence** No. 1.

munity, seeing RC as "determinedly non-religious," but quarreling not at all with their fellow religious Co-Counselors.

Can ecumenism, eagerly sought by enlightened individuals of all faiths over long periods of history, become a reality within the safety of the Co-Counseling "oases" with the tools of discharge and re-evaluation at hand?

WHAT IS RELIGION?

What is religion all about? It is certainly a persistent and pervasive phenomenon in human affairs over all the Earth's surface and over long periods of time. As human beings have created religions, what have they been seeking? What needs have they been attempting to fill? What use do they originally intuit for their faiths? How do original intentions get lost in the development of ritual and structure?

Certainly much will be learned of the nature of the universe and of our own human natures while examining these questions. We can expect a great variety of answers.

WELCOME, NEW WRITERS

Many active Co-Counselors who have not written for our journals before found their pens and voices in response to the questionnaire in **Present Time** that preceded this issue. The essay, "Where Did God Come From?", reprinted in this journal from **The Benign Reality**, has elicited much interest when it has been given as a lecture at RC workshops. Now we have **Transcendence** No. 1. What can we do next?

PLEASE WRITE

We are reprinting the **Present Time** questionnaire for those of you whose religion is not described in the present issue. We do not need additional descriptions of the religions told about in this issue; but there are other religious beliefs among RCers which are not yet represented, and we would like to hear about them. Will all such please write to us, using the questionnaire as a framework, and tell us for future issues "what I would like you to know about my religion."

We have some reports on work for re-emergence done *within* religious activities and institutions. We know that a great deal more of this goes on and we would like to have many additional reports for the next issue. What are you doing in your church or mosque or synagogue or temple or sweat lodge or chapel or mission?

EDITOR NEEDED

The editorial work on **Transcendence** No. 1 has been the responsibility of Katie Kauffman and myself, since we take overall responsibility for all RC publications. We would like to find a special editor for **Transcendence**, however, as soon as possible. Ideal qualifications would include profound knowledge of RC theory, great Co-Counseling skill, being deeply religious but not sectarian, theological training, a pleasing personality, writing and editing ability, commitment to the highest standards, and a willingness to work hard.

Anyone fitting the above description completely is urged to telephone immediately. Anyone who has *some* of the above characteristics and is interested in the job, please write. The job is unpaid.

A NEW QUESTIONNAIRE

On the inside back cover is a new questionnaire. We would appreciate a response from every reader. The questions are intended to push our thinking decisively forward.

This first issue of **Transcendence** is a very good one, I think. It is possible because of much hard work by a few individuals and an initial subsidy from the general Outreach Funds of the Communities. For later issues to be published, it will be necessary that this issue be sold and distributed. The income from sale of this issue will have to finance the next issue. So, you are invited to become a "literature agent," helping see that it is widely purchased and read.

Harvey Jackins
International Reference Person
The Re-evaluation Counseling Communities

A Landmark Event

The period since the last issue of **Recovery and Re-emergence** has seen many very rapid developments among RCers associated with the "mental health" establishment.

There has been increasing awareness of the actual roles that "mental health" professionals play on their jobs and in the society. There has been increasing awareness of the oppression and internalized oppression which they have to endure. There has been growing awareness of the actual functioning, the misfunctioning, and the oppressive role of the "mental health system" itself.

Previous issues of **Recovery and Re-emergence** met a warm response from people in the field. Realization of the need for Co-Counseling for such professionals and for support-group type of relationships between them on the job has spread far beyond the people actually involved in RC. Excellent initiatives have been taken by many RCers to set up support groups for the staffs of the institutions in which they work. These have been successful in relieving strain and burn-out and have also led to considerable curiosity about the theory behind them.

Questioning our roles as workers in the "mental health" field has gone beyond skepticism about the use of drugs, to fundamental questioning of the roles we play.

The first Mental Health Professionals' Workshop, held last year in Minnesota, brought a large group of people together. These included three invited guests who were what they called

Appeared in **Recovery and Re-emergence** No. 3.

"mental health system survivors." They were very impressive in their understanding of RC theory and in their clarity as to their experiences as "patients" in the system.

A movement within RC of such "mental health system survivors" has gained great momentum in the last few months. After a few courageous people dared to appear publicly in this role and spoke out against the oppression and for the liberation of the victims of the oppression, large numbers of active RCers have "come out of the closet." They had concealed their history of "mental health" oppression because of fears that they would be discriminated against within RC if their history as "patients" was known. There are still many such concealed victims within the RC Community, but large numbers of them have declared their identity and are working together in support groups, classes, and workshops. A number of local workshops on this topic have been held.

This is having a very salutary and challenging effect upon the "mental health" workers within RC. It is impossible to argue with the clarity about the system expressed by the people who have seen it on the seamy side. An alliance is in the process of being forged between the "survivors" and the "professionals." The realization is growing rapidly that the oppression is against both groups and that the antagonisms between the two groups are fabricated and manipulated by the system itself.

Differences between the various levels of the hierarchy of "mental health" workers are also being explored. There are, for example, many psychiatrists who participate in Co-Counseling and use it for their own benefit, but only two attempted to come to the Mental Health Professionals' Workshop and (because of weather) only one actually arrived and participated. Clinical psychologists are active in larger numbers and more challenging of their own roles. Psychiatric nurses, social workers, and counselors of various sorts, of course, are more easily aware of their oppression and more fearless in questioning the oppression and participating in the development of policies against it.

The whole term and concept itself of "mental health" is being called into question, as you will see in much of the material within this journal.

The "mental health system survivors" have contributed a great deal to this issue. To begin with, they requested a journal of their own, but dialogue is continuing as to whether their participation in **Recovery and Re-emergence** is not the healthiest possible expression of the growing unity between all of the people caught within the system. Whether you are "general public," "survivor," or "professional," you will, as you read this issue, receive much clarity and understanding from the contributions of the people who have "been through the mill."

A substantial number of individuals have been in both roles. They have been "survivors" and then fought to become "professionals" in an effort to reform the system with their knowledge. These people are to be especially treasured because of their insights.

I appreciate Joan Vigushin for her persistence in developing the journal, for sharing editorship with Denny for a long time and for now continuing solo, for her insistence on the Mental Health Professionals' Workshop, and for her determined communication with people throughout the field. Special appreciation also for the trio of Janet Foner, Dewey Bandy, and Jamie Alexander, who have so brilliantly developed the beginning policy for the survivors.

It is becoming plain that this particular oppression is the sword of Damocles over every other group of the oppressed. "Mental health" oppression in our current society replaces the slave master's whip or the knight's spear of previous societies in enforcing conformity and repressing dissent.

I encourage all RCers to become expert and informed in combatting this oppression as part of being successful against all the others.